本书是广东海洋大学博士启动项目"英汉句式中的领属关系研究"（项目编号：102002/R20084）的阶段性成果；并得到2019校级教改项目"基于思维导图的英语词汇学教学模式研究"（项目编号：102001/570219106）的资助

现代汉语领属关系的
形式语义分析

A Study of Possessive Relations in
Mandarin Chinese:
A Formal Semantic Perspective

安胜昔　著

中国社会科学出版社

图书在版编目（CIP）数据

现代汉语领属关系的形式语义分析：英文 / 安胜昔
著. —北京：中国社会科学出版社，2022.8
ISBN 978-7-5227-0312-1

Ⅰ.①现… Ⅱ.①安… Ⅲ.①现代汉语 – 形式语义学
– 研究 – 英文 Ⅳ.①H109.4

中国版本图书馆CIP数据核字（2022）第099008号

出　版　人　赵剑英
责任编辑　张冰洁　李　沫
责任校对　董宇姗　张　友
责任印制　王　超

出　　版　中国社会科学出版社
社　　址　北京鼓楼西大街甲 158 号
邮　　编　100720
网　　址　http://www.csspw.cn
发 行 部　010 – 84083685
门 市 部　010 – 84029450
经　　销　新华书店及其他书店

印　　刷　北京明恒达印务有限公司
装　　订　廊坊市广阳区广增装订厂
版　　次　2022 年 8 月第 1 版
印　　次　2022 年 8 月第 1 次印刷

开　　本　710 × 1000　1/16
印　　张　15
字　　数　258千字
定　　价　79.00 元

摘　要

本文在形式语义理论框架下，对现代汉语中领属关系进行分析。领属关系在汉语中主要表现为"NP$_1$+ 的 +NP$_2$"短语结构形式。"的"作为领属关系的标记体现领有者与被领有者的领属结构关系。

除了"NP$_1$ 的 NP$_2$"领属关系的基本形式之外，汉语中还有大量的存在于句式中的领属结构形式。典型的汉语式话题句中话题与述题中的成分，表消失义的存现句中消失主体与地点名词，领主属宾句中的主语和宾语，抢夺类双宾语中的直接宾语和间接宾语之间都存在领属关系，领属关系同时还与"把"字句和"被"字句中的保留宾语被动句这一小类有联系。

以往的研究主要是从意义的角度对领属进行分类，本文首先从形式化角度对领属关系进行重新的界定和分类。对领属关系的形式刻画存在于词法到句法的各个层面。本文认为，领有者的出现是为了满足语义饱和的需要，领属关系在语言中体现在三个层面上。

第一，词汇语义层面。作为两个名词之间的语义关系，领属关系可以是关系名词的词库信息的一部分，由关系名词直接带入句中并获得解读。关系名词体现的是最典型的领属关系，是领属关系最为紧密的类型。在汉语中体现为不可让渡领属关系类型，即亲属关系以及整体与部分的关系。这类词汇性的领属关系普遍存在于各类语言当中。

除了关系名词的词库信息中含有领属关系信息以外，某些动词的论元结构中也包含着领属关系信息。双宾句式中"抢夺"类动词的论元结构中包含有"来源"这一语义信息，伴随来源出现的是直接宾语与间接宾语之间的领属关系。领有者在论元结构中体现为来源，这一部分信息可隐可现。当"来源"不出现时，论元结构中也相应地不包含领属关系。

第二，结构层面。关系名词以及动词论元结构中所包含的领属关系都属于词汇语义层面的领属意义。领属关系作为一种语义关系同时也是汉语部分句式本身句式语义的一部分。汉语中典型的原位话题句毫无例外地包含有领属关系。领属关系的语义是话题句本身所具有的意义。这种领属关系纯粹是句式语义的要求，句式中的除了领属关系以外，还包括一类特殊的上下义关系的语义类型。名词之间的上下位关系也被认为是一种领属关系。话题句是汉语中常见的句式，话题句包含领属关系。因此领属关系也广泛地存在于汉语当中。

第三，接口层面。除了语义层面以及句式层面产生的领属关系以外，还有一类领属关系是产生在两者之间的接口层面。接口层面的领属关系是句式与动词的词汇意义共同作用的结果。消失义动词出现在存现句的句式，抢夺类动词的被动形式构成话题句都会触发领属关系。此外，领属关系的语义解读还应该包括语用因素，说话者的主观性在句式的选择中起到决定性作用。

本文将领属关系界定为词汇语义标记"的"，话题句以及某一类句式中动词的词条信息所带来的领属关系。三种不同机制触发的领属关系分别属于不同层面的语义类型。关系名词的词汇意义，动词词义与句式相互作用所带来的领属关系属于语义 - 语用界面的意义，而由句式带来的领属关系则属于语用层面的领属关系。不同层面的领属关系以不同的方式出现，在语义推衍过程中，产生领属关系的节点也不尽相同。

本文所采用的形式化的分析手段使得领属的分类更具有操作性。形式化手段所分出来的领属关系分类边界清晰，能够覆盖更多的语言事实，并具有一定的可预测性。通过对事件结构的分析，揭示不同类型领属关系的呈现方式和理解差异。事件结构的分析，使得领属关系的方向性以及领属关系的产生，相互依赖及互动能够呈现得更为清晰。句法层面的领属关系是能够通过事件结构来进行呈现并进行相应形式化的描写。结合类型论，λ 算子等形式语义学手段对领属结构进行逻辑语义的刻画以及句法语义同步的推导。本文对领属关系所做的形式化分析概括性更强，分类也更加合理清晰，事件结构的分析方法使我们对结构中的领属关系具有了一定的解释力。

关键词：汉语；领属关系；词汇领属；句式领属；结构领属；

Abstract

This book elaborates on a study investigating the possessive relations in Mandarin Chinese in the framework of formal semantics. Possessive relation in Mandarin Chinese is mainly presented in the form of "NP$_1$+de+ NP$_2$" phrase (*wo de shu*). *De* is considered to be the possessive marker denoting possessive relation between possessor nominal and possessum nominal and Zhu (1961) illustrates three functions of *de*.

In addition to "NP$_1$+de+NP$_2$" phrase as the basic form for possessive relation, possessive relation is widely embodied between discontinuous constituents in constructions in Mandarin Chinese: between the entity denoted by the topic NP and the entity denoted by a certain NP in comment part of topic sentences; between the disappearing entity and the locative nominal in Existential Constructions; between the entities denoted by the indirect object and direct object in Double Object Constructions; between the entities denoted by the retained objects in some *Ba* Constructions and *Bei* Constructions. All of these are included in Discontinuous Possession Constructions, which are marked forms expressing possessive relations.

The relevant research is mainly done in the classifications of "NP$_1$+de+NP$_2$" phrase from the perspective of the meaning between two nouns contained in attributive phrase. In this book, we try to re-classify possessive relations, employing form standard. The description of possessive relations in formal way refers to each layer from lexicon to syntax. We hold that the establishment of possessive relation is to satisfy unsaturated meaning. Possessive relation is manifested at three different layers.

First, possessive relation can be derived at lexical layer. The compulsory appearance of the possessor mainly results from the requirement of semantic saturation. The information of possessive relation can be stored in the lexicon of relational nouns. In this case, relational nouns introduce possessive relation into constructions to create prototype possession, which is the most solid possession. In Mandarin Chinese, such kind of relation is presented as inalienable possession, which is redefined as referring to kinship relation and part/whole relation. Possessive relation introduced by lexical items is universal in almost all languages.

In addition to relational nouns, possessive information can also be stored in the argument structure of verbs. The verbs in *Depriving-type* Double Object Constructions include possessive relation information in its argument structure,which is represented in the form of thematic role of source of the indirect object. With the information of source appearing in the construction, the possessive relation between the indirect object and direct object is triggered. What is more, source information can be either overt or covert in the construction. If the source is covert, the possessive relation will not be triggered accordingly.

Second, Topic Construction involves possessive relation. It is generated at structure layer. In typical canonical Topic Constructions in Mandarin Chinese, the possessive meaning is indispensable, which serves as the "topic chain", combining the topic with the comment. The motivation to include possessive relation is to compose Topic Construction. Occasionally, the possessive relation is represented as the hy ponymy between the topic and certain element in the comment part. Such kind of possessive relation is triggered at syntactic layer. Mandarin Chinese is prominent in its Topic Constructions and Topic Constructions are common and widely exist in Mandarin Chinese. Owing to the relationship between Topic Construction and possessive relation, possessive relation is widely found in Mandarin Chinese as well.

Third, Possessive relation can be derived at syntactic/semantic interface, as the result of the interaction between lexical information of the verb and the semantic meaning of the construction. When verbs denoting the meaning of disappearance occur in Existential Constructions or *Depriving-type* Double Object Construction verbs co-occur with *Bei* in Topic Construction, the possessive relation will be triggered.

Therefore, we define three types of possessive relations in Mandarin Chinese:

(i) possessive relation generated at lexical layer.

(ii) possessive relation brought at semantic and syntax interface.

(iii) possessive relation triggered by Topic Construction.

The meanings derived at different levels are of different types.

Possessive meaning brought by relational nouns and possessive meaning information brought by verbs belong to the meaning at semantics level. The possession brought by the construction is out of pragmatic motivation. The possessive relations at different levels are derived via different modes.

The form standard we propose makes it easy and feasible to classify possessive relations in Mandarin Chinese. The classifications we draw have a clear border and can cover more language phenomenon. What is more, possessive relation becomes predictable in constructions. The book employs eventuality analysis, since the eventuality analysis can give a clear description and account for the generation of the possessive relation. Through the eventuality analysis, the generation, the interdependence and the interaction of the possessor and pessessum, as well as the direction of the possession transfer can be illustrated more clearly. We may identify the modes in which the possessive relation enters the constructions. With the aid of event semantic theory, combining with Type Theory and λ operator, we attempt to represent formally the derivation process of the possessive relations in eventuality analysis.

The analysis on possessive relations in formal semantic way is more general and the classifications are much clearer. The eventuality analysis enables us to better account for possessive relation.

Keywords: Mandarin Chinese; possessive constructions; lexical possession; structure possession; construction possession;

Abbreviations

AFF	Affectedness
Ba	marker of *Ba* construction in Chinese（把）
Bei	passive marker in Chinese（被）
CL	classifier
de	genitive marker in Chinese-*de*（的）
DAT	dative case
Disappearing-type EC	disappearing-type Existential Construction
DOC	Double Object Construction
DPC	Discontinuous Possessive Construction
EPC	External Possessive Construction
GB	Government and Binding
GEN	genitive case
IPC	Internal Possession Construction
Perf.	perfective marker in Chinese-*le*（了）
PR	possessor
PM	possessum
Pm	Possessum in Logical form
PSPO	Possessor as Subject and Possessee as Object
p.n	proper name
TC	Topic Construction
NOM	Nominal case

Contents

Chapter One

Introduction

1.1 Research objectives

Possessive relation is one of the most fundamental relationships between human beings and the entities. It is a universal domain, that is, almost all languages have conventional expressions to represent possessive relation. The most common strategy is to use a special morphological marker to indicate the relation between the possessor (PR) and the possessum (PM). Nichols (1988) calls this type dependent-marked, which is familiar to us as the name of genitive case. This can be exemplified by means of the genitive constructions in English, which represents dependent marking through use of the suffix "-s". Mandarin Chinese can be classified as possessing a dependent-marked genitive construction, using the suffix-like particle *de* to mark the dependent noun. The construction in (1) is used to express ordinary possession in English and Mandarin Chinese.

    (1) Genitive construction: NP1 de NP2
        那个先生的房子
        nage xiansheng de fangzi
        that-CL gentleman GEN-de house
        the gentleman GEN-'s house
        "That gentleman's house"

The first NP slot can be filled by a pronoun. Possessive pronouns in Mandarin Chinese are typically formed by suffixing *de* to the basic pronoun as *wode, tamende*.

Possessive relations and its corresponding structures in any language system have the distinctive features of their own and exert great influence on other grammatical structures as well. Possession is a very important semantic concept between two entities. It is an abstract "relation". In Mandarin Chinese, the following construction, including possessive relation, has long been the focus of research:

(2) a. 王冕死了父亲。
  Wangmian si-le fuqin.
  Wangmian die-Perf father
  "Wangmian's father died on him".

The construction is firstly thought to be unique in Chinese, but in fact it can be studied from the perspective of typology as well. The construction in (3) is termed to be "split possession", which means that the possessor and possessum are separated by other grammatical elements. The sentence of this kind is termed as *Lingzhu Shubin* construction, in which the possessor occupies the position of the subject and the possessum is in the object position. It is a kind of semantic-syntax mismatch, for the possessor and possessum do not form a constituent, although they are semantically related.

Possession splitting sentences[1] is not rare in Mandarin Chinese. Shen (1995: 85) illustrates the structural restriction for splitting and movement of Noun Phrase[2]:

> *The component or potential component of an NP appears as an independent constituent in a sentence, which is the splitting of NP argument movement.*
>
>   Shen (1995: 85)

---

[1] Possession splitting or possessor raising analysis are based on the movement of the PR or PM. The original idea is that PR nominal and PM nominal belong to the same constituent to maintain the possessive relation.

[2] Shen (1995, 1996, 2001) talked about argument properties separately appeared NP, which is the initial topic nominal.

Specifically speaking, any element with reference in an NP can occupy the initial position of the sentence by means of movement. The "possession splitting" refers to the phenomenon that the syntactic status of the original PR and PM in a possessive phrase has been alternated as independent elements in a sentence. The syntactic relation between PR and PM in such kind of possessive constructions is different from that of normal possessive phrase. On the one hand, PR and PM don not form a possessive constituent and they become an independent constituent respectively; on the other hand, they remain to be PM and PR in the semantic interpretation. Besides the above-mentioned (2) example, we may find possessive relation in other constructions. For example, we find possession in both examples in (3):

> (3) a. 小明的一本书
>   Xiaoming   de   yi   ben   shu.
>   p.n   de   one   CL   book
>   "Xiaoming's book"
>   b. 小明被偷了一本书。
>   <u>Xiaoming</u>   bei   tou-le   yi   ben   shu.
>   p.n   bei   steal-Perf one   CL   book
>   "One of Xiaoming's book has been stolen."

The relation between *Xiaoming* and *yibenshu* in (3a) and (3b) is not the same syntacticly: in (3a), *Xiao Ming* is to modify *yi ben shu*, while in (3b), *Xiao Ming* occupies the initial position and *yi ben shu* occupies post-verbal position. Although the possessive relation between *Xiaoming* and *yibenshu* in (3b) is not overt, the initial NP *Xiaoming* is naturally interpreted as the owner of *yibenshu*. (3a) is the passive construction with retained object, where the retained object acts like an incorporated noun, not permitting attributive modification (which will be referred to as the passives DPC). According to the explanation offered by generative studies, such a structure is named "possessor raising structure" or "possessor splitting structure". Deng (2014) names the structure Discontinuous Possession Construction (DPC). In this book, we follow the term Discontinuous Possession Construction since the PR and PM are in different constituents but remain the possessive relation in meaning. Such a phenomenon is commonly found in Mandarin Chinese:

(4) a. 口袋里少了二百块钱。
    Koudai li shao-le   er bai   kuai qian.
    pocket in less-Perf two hundred CL   money
    "Two hundred yuan in the pocket was lost."
  b. 口袋里的二百块钱少了。
    Koudai li de er bai   kuai qian   shao-le
    pocket in of two hundred CL money less-Perf
    "Two hundred yuan in the pocket was lost."
  c. 口袋里有二百块钱。
    Koudai li you er bai   kuai qian.
    pocket in have two hundred CL money
    "There was two hundred yuan in the pocket."

(4a) is a typical Existential Construction expressing the disappearance of a certain entity (we term it as *disappearing-type* EC). In the construction, *erbai-kuai qian* was in the pocket before it is missing.

(5) a. 李四断了一条腿。
    Lisi duan-le   yi tiao tui.
    p.n break-Perf one CL leg
    "One of Lisi's leg was broken."
  b. 李四的一条腿断了。
    Lisi de yi tiao tui duan-le
    p.n of one CL leg break-Perf
    "One of Lisi's leg was broken."
  c. 李四有一条腿。
    Lisi you yi tiao tui.
    p.n has one CL leg
    "Lisi has one leg."

(5a) is the so-called intransitive verb, taking retained object construction, also known as the "possessor as subject and possessum as object" construction (the PSPO construction). (5a) is of the same type with (2). The pre-verbal and post-verbal nominal elements denote possession.

(6) a. 老张把苹果削了皮。

Laozhang ba <u>pingguo</u> xiao le   pi.

p.n   Ba apple   peel-Perf skin

"Laozhang peeled the apple."

   b. 老张削了苹果的皮。

Laozhang xiao le   pingguo de pi.

p.n   peel-Perf apple   of skin

"Laozhang peeled the apple."

   c. 苹果有皮。

Pingguo you   pi.

apple   have peel

"The apple has peel."

(6a) is a typical *Ba* construction involving discontinuous possession. There is retained object after the predicate verb (which will be termed as the *Ba* DPC).

(7) a. 张三偷了李四一辆自行车。

Zhangsan tou-le   <u>Lisi</u> yi   liang zixingche.

p.n   steal-Perf Lisi one CL   bicycle.

"Zhangsan stole a bicycle from Lisi."

   b. 张三偷了李四的一辆自行车。

Zhangsan tou-le   Lisi de yi   liang zixingche.

p.n   steal-Perf p.n of one CL   bicycle.

"Zhangsan stole a bicycle from Lisi."

   c. 李四有一辆自行车。

Lisi you   yi   liang zixingche.

p.n have one CL   bicycle.

"Lisi had a bicycle."

(7a) is an example of *depriving-type* Double Object Construction (*depriving-type* DOC) and possession is found between indirect object and direct object.

(8) a. 水果，   小李   喜欢   吃   苹果。

<u>Shuiguo</u>, Xiaoli xihuan chi pingguo.

    fruit   p.n   like   eat apple.

    "As for fruit, Xiaoli likes eating apples".

b. 水果里，　　小李　喜欢　　苹果。

    Shuiguo li, Xiaoli xihuan pingguo.

    Fruits, p.n   like   apple.

    "As for fruit, Xiaoli likes eating apples".

c. 水果　　中　　有　苹果。

    Shuiguo zhong you pingguo.

    fruit   among have apple.

    "Apple is included in fruits."

(8a) is referred to as the construction with subject-predicate phrase as its predicate or the typical Topic Construction (which will be termed as TC).

From (3) to (8), all the sentences in group (a) can be paraphrased as sentences in group (b), and the most obvious difference between group (a) and group (b) is that the PR and PM in the possessive relation in group (b) are not split. They are not separated by other elements and, therefore, stay in the same constituent. Possession in group (b) is distinct with the possessive marker *de*. All the sentences in group (a) entail the ones in group (b).

Furthermore, all the sentences in group (a) presuppose the possession contained in group (c). They encode the existing possessive relation between PR and PM, where *you* "have" is employed to compose predicative possession construction.

To sum up, there is a spectrum of the constructions in Mandarin Chinese for which the claim of expressing the narrow-sensed possession, the part-whole relation or inalienable possession has been made. The underlined elements in the examples are unexpected if we consider the canonical valency properties of each verb and if we consider the thematic relations typically associated with eventualities encoded by these verbs.

The focus is the phenomenon, where a nominal is syntactically encoded as a verbal dependent but semantically understood as the possessor of one of its co-arguments. The phenomenon is very common cross-linguistically.

Examples from French and Japanese are given in (9) in order to illustrate the points.

> (9) a. Je   lui   ai   pris   la   main.
>   I 3SG. DAT have taken the hand.
>   "I took his hand."
>   b. Mary-ga   kami-ga   naga-i.
>   Mary-NOM hair-NOM long-be.
>   "Mary's hair is long."
>   (Ura 1996: 100)

The nominals, interpreted as possessors in these examples, bear markings which are typical of verbal dependents—the dative case in (9a) and the nominative case in (9b). We can compare these two sentences with their counterparts in (10). The possessor nominals are encoded syntactically as dependents of the possessum nouns.

> (10) a. J'ai   pris   sa   main.
>   I-have taken his hand.
>   "I took his hand."
>   b. Mary-no Kami-ga naga-i.
>   Mary-GEN hair-NOM long-be.
>   "Mary's hair is long."
>   (Immanuel Barshi 1996: 3)

Vergnaud and Zubizarreta (1992) introduce the term "Internal Possession"[①] to refer to the cases in (11). "Internal possession" is the most regular grammatical form employed by language system to indicate possession.

As for the cases like (9), the term "External Possession Construction" is introduced by Doris L. Payne (1996). In their paper, External Possession Construction in language is:

"We take core instances of external possession (EP) to be

---

① Internal Possession is a construction in which the PR is internal to the constituent containing the PM, as in Genitive-NP construction like: *wo de mao*.

constructions in which a semantic possessor-possessum relation is expressed by coding the possessor (PR) as a core grammatical relation of the verb and in a constituent separate from that which contains the possessum (PM). The PR may be expressed as subject, direct object, indirect object or dative, or as ergative or absolutive depending on the language type—but not, for example, as an oblique. That is, the PR is expressed like a direct, governed, argument of one of the three universally attested basic predicate types (intransitive, transitive, or ditransitive). In addition to being expressed as a core grammatical relation, in some languages, the PR can simultaneously be expressed by a pronoun or pronominal affix internal to the NP containing the PM; but this Genitive-NP-internal coding cannot be the only expression of the PR. Furthermore, the possessor-possessum relationship cannot reside in a possessive lexical predicate such as have, own or be located at and the lexical verb root does not in any other way have a PR within its core argument frame. Thus, despite being coded as a core argument, the PR is not licensed by the argument frame of the verb root itself."

Doris L. Payne (1999: 1)

The separated PR and PM are not in the form of modification but the two syntactic elements appear in a juxtaposed pattern, namely, subjects or objects. For example, PR occupies subject position and PM is a post-verbal nominal. PSPO construction, *disappearing-type* Existential construction and *Ba* DPC all belong to this type. Both PR and PM behave as if there are double subjects or double objects in the constructions.

Mandarin Chinese lacks of morphological marking, and there is no overt morphological markers such as applicative form to indicate possession in the discontinuous constructions. The only difference is that the PR and PM are separated from each other by certain elements and there is no *de* to go between them. According to the linear order of the sentence, Discontinuous Possession Constructions in Mandarin Chinese can be generalized in the following pattern:

(11) N_1+Vi+N_2

N_1 is the PR nominal and N_2 is the PM nominal. The verb is usually an unaccusative one which takes only one argument. We find *disappearing-type* Existential Construction, PSPO construction, *Ba* DPC and passives DPC fall into this pattern.

	N_3	N_1(PR)	Vi	N_2(PM)
DEC		*dongwuyuan*	*pao-le*	*yizhi gouxiong*
PSPO		*gongchang*	*dao-le*	*yidu qiang*
Passive DPC		*Zhangsan*	*bei-sha-le*	*fuqin*
Ba DPC	*Zhangsan*	*Ba Lisi*	*da-duan-le*	*yitiaotui*

(12) a. N_1+N_2+V
  b. $V+N_1+N_2$

The second pattern includes Topic Construction and Double Object Construction. In this type, the PR and PM are seemingly together, but they belong to different constituents. In *Ta piqi buhao*, *ta* is treated as the topic and *piqi buhao* serves as the predicate. In the Double Object Construction, PR is the indirect object and PM is the direct object. This paper mainly focuses on a sub-type of these constructions: the Possessive Topic Construction and *depriving-type* DOC.

	N3	N1	N2	V
Possessive TC		*ta*	*piqi*	*hao*
	shuiguo	*wo*	*xihuan*	*pingguo*
		V	**N1**	**N2**
Depriving DOC	*Zhangsan*	*daduan-le*	*Lisi*	*yitiaotui*

Wu (2011: 238) lists three types of EPCs in Mandarin Chinese, which are all included in our DPC study:

(13) a. Type A: PR+V1+PM
  b. Type B: PR+*Bei*+Agent+V_2+PM

c. Type C: Agent+V+PR+PM

Among three types, type A is considered to be the most typical External Possession Construction found in Mandarin Chinese. Type A and B in Wu (2011) abide with our first type and type C is included in our second type. We think that the range of Discontinuous Possession Constructions in Chinese is wider than EPCs in other languages, but the Discontinuous Possession Constructions in Mandarin Chinese concerned in this study are quite similar to the EPC in that they both involve the phenomenon of splitting between the PR and the PM. At present, the existent analyses of the Discontinuous Possession Construction are arguably unsystematic and they are seldom investigated under a unified framework from the perspective of possession.

1.2 Properties in Common

Although all the examples mentioned above, have properties of their own, they are common at least in the following aspects, which make it possible to analyze these constructions under a unified framework.

First, the nominal semantically understood as the possessor splits or separates from another nominal semantically understood as the possessum. This is the most distinctive feature existing in all the constructions listed above. In other words, other elements can be inserted between these two nominals. For example, we can add an adverb or preposition phrase between PR and PM without changing the possessive relation between them. We may find semantic entailment between DPCs and corresponding *de* phrase constructions.

Second, the nominal PR is not selected by predicate verbs in all these constructions. Taken the canonical valency properties and the thematic relations typically associated with eventualities encoded by these verbs into consideration, the PM nominals are unexpected. *Kou dai*, W*angmian*, *Zhang san*, *pingguo*, *Lisi* and *shuiguo* are so-called "extra arguments", compared with those core arguments licensed by the verb in the constructions. They are interesting because syntactic and semantic dependency relations mismatch. On the semantic grounds, they are possessor nominals which have possessive relation with another nominal in the construction. On the syntactic grounds, they are independent syntactic elements in the constructions.

Third, in these constructions, there exists a single nominal element that can be understood to bear two theta roles. In Locative construction and Topic Constructions, the "affectedness" is not so typical. For example, in (3), *Wangmian* is understood as both the possessor of *fuqin* and the affectee of the event that his father died. *Wo* in (4) plays the roles of both the possessor of *qianbao* and the affectee of the event that my wallet was stolen. Thematic roles of "experiencer" or "affectee" are likely to be attached with possessors.

DPCs bring together crucial questions in language processing and in syntax, including the intersection of verbal valence and event construal and voice. As noted, certain DPCs types appear to "break the rules" about how many arguments a verb of a given valence can carry, and challenge the notion that clause-level syntax depends directly on the argument structure and subcategorization frames of individual verbs or verb stems. Based on the observations, this paper aims at exploring following issues:

(1) How is the possessive relation introduced into the constructions?

(2) What function does possessive relation play in yielding these constructions?

(3) How is the PR licensed in its syntactic position? Are they really "extra arguments"?

(4) Compared with the attributive possession and predicative possession, what connections and defining features do DPC have?

(5) Is it possible to give a formal description to pin down the possessive relation in Mandarin Chinese?

1.3 Organization of the book

A natural language like Chinese can be considered as an abstract system analogous to formal language of logic or mathematics. Both natural and formal languages are compositional in the sense that the meaning of any syntactically well-formed expressions is uniquely determined by the meaning of its constituent parts and the pattern used to combine these constituents. In this dissertation, DPCs will be studied mainly from the perspective of formal semantics in order to find out the constraints that the possessive relation undergoes by investigating the semantic properties of the sentences with discontinuous possession. The semantic properties of DPCs, elucidated in this study, are expressed in an underlying event analysis (Parsons 1980, 1990) and argument introducing theory (Pylkkänen 1996, 2004). In addition, it is of great interest to study DPCs from a cross-linguistic perspective, since most analyses of EPC of other languages appeal largely to morphosyntactic patterns of agreement and finiteness, which are not overtly marked in Mandarin Chinese.

In order to accomplish the goals, a brief literature review of the researches relevant to possessive relation and DPCs will be first provided in chapter 2. The contents include the identification of the status of the possessive relation, the classifications of possessive relation and the characteristics of each subcategory of possession. Researches on each construction will be briefly introduced from syntactic, cognitive, and pragmatic perspectives. This chapter provides the empirical foundations for addressing the issue aforementioned, that is, to find out what mechanism yields to the possessive relation in Discontinuous Possession Constructions.

Chapter 3 provides the introduction of the theoretical framework that will be employed to analyze DPCs, as well as the motivations for choosing such theories. The relevant latest development of the theory will also be introduced. The classifications of eventuality, the shift between different eventuality types, as well as the way to employ the functional node are illustrated in details in this section to explain how the possessive relation can be accounted for and described in the framework of eventuality analysis. It provides the background and makes preparations to propose our assumptions in the next chapter.

In Chapter 4, the definition of inalienable possession is clarified and the inalienable possession in Mandarin Chinese is redefined as including two types: (i) kin terms denoting the kinship relation like *baba*, *mama*; (ii) part-whole relation (including body-parts) like *shou, zhitiao*. The concepts of the "part" and "whole" are confined to the noun with physical forms, that is, they denote physical objects in the real world. In my definition, the entity serving as the whole can not be an abstract or psychology concept. "Belonging_to" as the logic predicate is used to denote the concept. Type raising proposal is applied to the verb to ensure the semantic derivation of the construction. This kind of possession gets introduced at lexical level.

Chapter 5 is about possessive relation existing in Double Object Construction. There are two sub-types of DOC in Mandarin Chinese. In *depriving-type* DOC, we find the possessive relation between the indirect object and direct object. What is more, the information about the possessive relation is contained in argument structure of the verbs in form of the "source". The "source" element is optional in the construction. Generally speaking, the possessive relation, existing in *depriving-type* DOC, is alienable possession, which is represented by "Having" in this dissertation.

Chapter 6 illustrates the process in which possessive relation is triggered by the initial topic. Topic Construction is base-generated by having an additional topic at the initial position of the sentence. Since there should be "aboutness" condition which is to link the topic nominal with the comment clause, the canonical position Topic Construction in Mandarin Chinese is licensed by semantic condition. It is the appearance of the initial topic that triggers the possessive relation between the topic and the element contained in comment part. There is a "Topic Chain", of which one side is the possessor topic and the other side is the possessum in comment proposition. Besides the inalienable possession in Topic Construction, there is set-subset relation in the construction, which is also a kind of possessive relation. We employ "Included-in" as the predicate to denote the relation, which means that one entity is included in the other. Besides canonical position Topic Construction, the *disappearing-type* Existential Construction and *Bei* DPC all share the same eventuality with the Topic Construction and can be treated as the Topic Construction. The difference lies in that the topics function differently and the ways to trigger the possessive relation. In *disappearing-type* Existential Construction, Existential Construction by itself does not bring in possession and only when verbs with disappearing meaning enter the construction, can the possessive relation be generated. Possessive relation is generated either at syntactic layer or at syntactic and semantic interfaces.

Chapter 7 covers the complex possessive relation constructions. Since relational nouns, argument structure of verbs and Topic Construction can all introduce the possessive relation into the constructions, when thcy work individually, they generate singular possessive relation type. That is there is only one element that brings in one kind of possessive relation. We may find the sentences which contain more than one element, which is of complex type. The final interpretation of the possession is always with the inalienable type.

Chapter 8 concentrates on the semantic and pragmatic interpretation of the possessive relation. The DPCs are in nature still a kind of constructions denoting the possessive relation and share similarities with common possessive construction. What is more, the DPCs are more informative marked constructions with speaker's subjective perspective and empathy with the possessor.

The conclusion of the research and the direction of further researches on DPCs will be presented in Chapter 9.

In sum, It is hoped that the research, conducted in this book, will shed light on understanding of the possessive relation in DPCs in Mandarin, of the generating mechanism of the possessive relation and of the dynamic and incremental process of the interpretation.

Chapter Two

Literature Review

DPCs in Mandarin have long been one of the focuses of research due to the abnormal performances of such constituents. Study on DPCs has produced a wealth of empirical generalizations as well as some theoretical insights. In this chapter, the existing researches on possessive relation, DPCs in Mandarin Chinese will be sketched and the organization of this chapter is as follows. Section 2.1 focuses on the identification of the status of the possessive relation. From the section 2.2 to section 2.6, researches on the DPCs in Mandarin Chinese will be illustrated in details. Section 2.2 is mainly about *disappearing-type* Existential Construction. The focus is on unaccusative verbs in the construction. Section 2.3 sums up the studies on PSPO, which is a hot issue in recent years. Section 2.4 is the research on Passive DPC. The three constructions share some similarities. Section 2.5 is about the Double Object Construction in Mandarin Chinese and the focus is on the status of the *depriving-type* DOC. Section 2.6 is about the Topic Construction. The role of possession as well as pragmatic researches on possessive relation in Topic Construction is the focus of this section. In each section, the connection between the constructions in DPCs will be the main point that we will cover. A summary of this chapter is given in section 2.7.

2.1 Possessive Relation in Mandarin Chinese

A wide range of expressions have been found in Mandarin Chinese which are related with manifestations of possession. Besides the attributive possession with *de* phrase, Mandarin Chinese is rich in possessive constructions, which are to demonstrate clausal rather than phrasal possession.

2.1.1 Definition and Classifications

Lu & Shen (2003) state that possession, in linguistic sense, is a very important semantic category. It usually refers to an attributive noun phrase where one nominal indicating "possessor" (PR) is used to modify the other nominal of "possessum"(PM). This is the core conception of possession and is generally agreed in grammatical field. Usually, there is *de* to go between two nominals to serve as the possessive marker of possessive relation. For example, in *"wo de qianbi", wo* is the PR and *qianbi* is the PM. *De* is employed in Mandarin Chinese to indicate the possessive relation and the modification relation, where PM is the head nominal and PR is the modifier to form a possessive phrase.

Taylor (1989: 202-3) views possession as an experiential gestalt and defines it as a prototypical notion involving a constellation of properties such as the ones listed in (1):

(1) a. The possessor is a specific human being.
   b. The possessum is a specific concrete thing (usually inanimate), not an abstract concept.
   c. The relation between the two is an exclusive one, that is, for each PM there is only one PR.
   d. The PR has the right to make use of the PM; other people can make use of the PM only with the permission of the PR.
   e. The relationship of possession is a long-term one, measured in month or year rather than in minute or hour.
   f. In linguistic discourse, the PR is presented as a referential entity.

This does not conclude the lists of all the properties that are associated with prototypical instances of possession. Taylor (1989: 202) proposes the following properties in addition: the possessor's rights over the PM are invested in him/her in virtue of transaction, through purchase, donation, or inheritance, the PR is responsible for the PM, and the two are in close spatial proximity. Not all of possession should exhibit the entire range of these properties. Nevertheless, the more of the properties are presented, the more the expression concerned correspond to the prototypical notion of possession.

Heine (1997) also defines the possession from semantic perspective. Possession, as a semantic concept, refers to a kind of relation. It is obvious that this relation involves in two entities: one is the PR and the other is the PM. This kind of relation is asymmetric and there is "Belonging_to" concept in it. That is to say, PM nominal belongs to PR nominal.

Heine (1997: 38-9) gives two parameters to determine the possessive relation: "contact" and "control". That is to say, the PR and the PM have "contact" for shared space. The second parameter illustrates different status: PR has a kind of "power" over PM. For example, PR is entitled to decide where PM is put, how to deal with PM and whether remains or stops the possessive relation. Based on these two parameters, Heine (1997;40-41) gives the definition of the possessive relation as follows:

A prototypical case of possession is characterized by the presence of two entities(the possessor and possessee) such that the possessor and the possessee are in some relatively enduring locational relation and the possessor exerts control over the possessee (and is therefore typically human).

From the definition above, the possessive relation is considered as a kind of semantic relation. Two points should be taken into the consideration: there must be two entities involved and the two must form an abstract relation. It is a semantic relation but should be represented with syntactic means.

Heine (1997) divides the possessive constructions into two kinds: attributive possession and predicative possession:

The possessive structures		
Types of possessive structure	structure	Examples in MC
1.Attributive possession	X+possessive marker *De* +Y	*Wo DE shu*
2.Predicative possession	Eight forms	*Wo YOU yibenshu*

All languages we are familiar with have a morphosyntatic distinction between what is variously called attributive, nominal possession on the one hand, (the form of *Zhangsan de diannao*) and predicative or verbal possession on the other (*Zhangsan yongyou diannao*). Both kinds of possession typically concern a relation between two niminals or between two thing-like items and both can be described with reference to a set of prototypical properties as proposed by Taylor. It may be suffice to note that the two kinds of morphosyntactic structures represent different encoding patterns and that this difference is likely to be reflected in some way or another in their respective meanings.

2.1.2 Attributive Possession

The typical possessive construction in Chinese is "N_1 *de* N_2". Zhu (1982) classifies the possession according to semantic function N_1 has on N_2: to indicate ownership *women de xuexiao, haizi de yifu*; to indicate the material *mutou fangzi, shuliaodai*; to indicate the time *zuotian de baozhi*; to indicate the location *Beijing de tianqi*; to indicate the quality *huangtoufa de haizi*; to indicate apposition *wo de ke*. In addition, there are three kinds of "quasi-attributive":

(A) *Zhangsan de yuangao*: "Zhangsan is the prosecutor";
(B) *Ta de lanqiu dade hao*: "he plays basketball well";
(C) *Wo lai bang ni de mang*: "I will come to help you".

The account Zhu (1980) gives is that these attributives are composed of the noun referring persons or personal pronoun, which can be used to show possessive relation, but *wode, nide and tade* in (A)(B)(C) do not indicate possession. Zhu (1980) also points out that "*wo-de, ni-de, ta-de*" should indicate possessive relation, but in (A)(B)(C), they do not denote possessive relation. Zhu (1980) further holds that constructions as *xiongmao de beizi* "panda's cup", *Luxun de shu* "Luxun's book" *dizhu de fuqin* "landlord's father" are ambiguous: they can be interpreted as possessive construction or may have other interpretation rather than the possession.

Lv (1976) gave a more general classifications and tries to transfer different semantic types into different syntactic forms. He also sums up the transformation variants for different semantic types of possession.

> 1. Possessive construction: *Zhongguo renming de xiongxin* "Chinese people's ambition", the corresponding sentence is the one with "*you*": *zhongguo renming you xiongxin* "Chinese people have the ambition".
> 2. Descriptive construction: *shier sui de haizi*, "twelve-year-old boy", the corresponding sentence is the one with the noun to be the predicate or the one with *shi* "be": the boy is twelve years old. The construction has the "*SHI-DE*".
> 3. Appositive construction: *Xuexi Leifeng de hao bangyang* "the good example to learn from Leifeng"; *renmingzhanshi de guangrong chenghao* "the honor to be called solider". The corresponding sentence is the *shi* construction: Leifeng is a good example.

The point here is that for the expression of the possessive relation between two entities, both the attributive possession and predicative possession can fulfill the task.

Shen (1995) proposes two types of possession: broad-sensed and narrow-sensed possession. Narrow-sensed possession includes two sub-types: there is a unique and definite relationship between two nouns. That is to say, when they go with particular verbs or adj, the mention of the PR is equal to the mention of the PM. The other is that the relationship is definite but is not the only possible relation. That is to say, if the "possessor" exists, there must be a "possessum", but when we mention the possessor, it does not necessarily refer to "possessum" simultaneously. Broad-sensed possession means that the PR and PM exist simultaneously, but they don't necessarily form possessive relation.

The possession they formed is a temporary possession. For example, *er lou de lao Wang*, "Lao Wang living at the second floor" *Gongchang de weiqiang*. As a conceptual category of relation, it is advisable to have a broad-sensed and narrow-sensed definition for possession and the idea is widely agreed.

Lu (2002) agrees with Guo's (2002) "Grammar Dynamic Theory" to further analyze possessive construction. Guo (2002) thinks that grammatical features of the words should be distinguished into two levels: "grammatical features at lexical level" and "grammatical features at syntactic level".

Grammatical features at lexical level are inherent natures of the words and can be included in the lexicon while the grammatical features at syntactic level are generated in the specific language environment, controlled by syntactic rules. Usually the features at these two levels are concordant. What Lu (2002) emphasized is the final state resulting from the combination of the lexical meaning in pragmatical sense with grammatical meaning. He also sets the standards to distinguish alienable and inalienable possession. In his classifications, there are 17 sub-types: addressing possession; ownership possession; organ possession; component possession; material possession; property possession; characteristic possession; conception possession; membership possession; transformation possession; achievement possession; product possession; condition possession; trauma possession; occupation possession; landscape possession and location possession.

Yuan (1995) holds that in nature, the construction of "NP_1 *de* NP_2" is an implying predicate construction, which means NP_1 and NP_2 can compose subject and predicate construction with omitted predicate verb, in which Np_1 behaves like the subject and NP_2 to be the object. According to the logic relationship existing between PR and PM and the semantic features of omitted verbs, possessive phrases are divided into 7 types:

> (1) inherent relation. There is a stable and logic possessive relationship, which is expressed as "NP_1 inherently has NP_2".
> a. *rongshu de yezi /daxiang de yanjing* —"whole-part"

b. *youqi de yanse/mangguo de weidao* —*"entity-property"*

(2) allocated possession. NP$_1$ does not have NP$_2$ at the very beginning, but after a kind of allocation, NP$_2$ is possessed by NP$_1$ which means: "NP$_1$ is allocated with NP$_2$."

   a. *kongtiao de zhaozi*   *xiongmao de mingzi*

   b. *jingli de baobiao*   *Lihong de dadang*

   c. *daxue de xiaozhang*   *gongsi de jingli*

   d. *qiangshang de nianhua* *mengwai de taijie*

   e. *Xiaowang de gongzi*   *shengchu de shiwu*

(3) presentation relation: NP$_2$ is what NP$_1$ presented though a kind of means. "NP$_1$ presents NP$_2$".

   a. *Laozhang de guandian*   *Xiaowang de jianyi* —"entity and idea"

   b. *Xiaozhang de lingqiao*   *guniang de chuanzhao* —"entity and feature"

   c. *wanjian de xinwen*   *wuhou de taiyang* —"time and entity"

(4) production: NP$_2$ is the final result of NP$_1$'s production. "NP$_1$ produce NP$_2$". NP$_2$ is the final result of the action initiated by NP$_1$. "NP$_1$ produced NP$_2$".

   a. *Maodun de zhuzuo*   *Guoxiaochuan de shi*

The two entities involved in this type are in the relation of agent and the theme. Sometimes, the omit predicate may lead to ambiguity. For example:

   b. *Laoli de mantou*   *Fangfang de caomao*

Group (b) can be the final production, where the PR made the PM; it can be allocated possession, which means that the PR get the PM by other means rather than producing by himself.

(5) selection: NP$_1$ delimits the scope, NP$_2$ is the selected part of NP$_1$. NP$_2$ is a subset in the set denoting NP$_1$.

   a. *gongren zhong de jiji fenzi jiaoshi zhong de shiren*

   b. *dongwuzhong de shizi*   *jiajuzhong de shugui*

   c. *sange zhong de liangge*   *gongrenzhong de dabufen*

(6) experience relation: NP$_2$ is what NP1 experienced. "NP$_1$ experience NP$_2$".

a. *huiyi de richeng*   *Xiaowang de jiaoling*
b. *Leifeng de gushi*   *zuguo de weilai*
(7) addressing: NP$_2$ is the title NP1 use to address NP$_2$. "NP$_1$ addresses sb with the title (NP$_2$)"
a. *Huangsong de yeye*   *Zhangxiu de laolao*
b. *Yufu de laopo*   *Xiaoming de laoshi*

Yuan (1995) also points out that there are two points that worth mentioning: first, all the possessive constructions mentioned above have the corresponding constructions with *you*, but the subtle semantic relationship may be shown by activating omitted predicate verb. Second, the semantic type of the omitted predicate verbs depends on the semantic types of both PR and PM. The multiple possibilities existing in semantic combination of the two entities lead to ambiguity.

Zhang (1994) studies possession from pragmatic perspective. He holds that referential and non-referential is pragmatic meaning and possession and affiliation are grammatical meanings. The grammatical meaning of possessive construction is possessive relation, no matter what is possessed is a concrete item or an abstract quality. Possessive meaning is inherent meaning of possessive construction as a static unit and the pragmatic meaning acquired once this unit is put into use is temporary. This kind of pragmatic meaning is decided by speaker's intention and the cognitive background shared by two sides. Pragmatic meaning is not always shown in the form of syntactic construction.

In the studies abroad, Langacker (1995) explores 18 types of possession and holds that ownership, kinship and part\whole relationship are the prototype of possession. Heine's (1997: 34-41) classifications are:

physical possession;
temporary possession;
permanent possession;
inalienable possession;
abstract possession;
inanimate inalienable possession;
inanimate alienable possession.

Among these 7 kinds of possession types, according to the typical features they share with prototype possession, permanent possession is considered to be the most typical possession and abstract possession, inanimate inalienable possession, inanimate alienable possession are at the margin. All the rest go in between.

"Contact" and "Control" are used in Heine (1997) to pin down the classifications of the possessive relation: alienable possession, inalienable possession, temporary possession and abstract possession.

Possession Types	Permanent Contact	Control
alienable	+	+
inlalienable	+	-
temporary	-	+
abstract	-	-

The difference in the study of the possessive construction "NP$_1$ *de* NP$_2$" lies in two aspect. One is the internal semantic relation between two entities. The internal semantic relations are in different forms. It can be the ownership or the relation in the spatial dimension or time dimension. There are various possible relations between two entities, which makes it difficult to offer the clear-cut definition for the possession. The second aspect is how to judge this semantic relation. Not all the nominal phrases are considered to be possessive constructions. The possession has its own defining features. Zhu and Lv's standard is the function NP$_2$ played on NP$_1$: "to be modified" is the possessive relation and "to be descriptive" is the quality relationship.

With different perspectives and theories, we get different understanding of possession and different classifications. From the studies of the definition and the classifications of the possession, the core conception of the possessive relation is agreed. The prototypes of possession are ownership, kinship and part/whole relation.

The traditional study on the possession is confined to possessive phrase and the classification is based on the specific semantic relation PR bears on PM. It is the study on the static situation without involving in other syntactic elements.

Attributive possession can be analyzed as containing an implying predicate verb. Yuan (1995) employs implying predicate to classify the possession, which is meaningful in that predicate verb can be involved in explaining the possessive relation. It is not just a static relation. The possessive relation is represented at the clausal level as well.

It indicates the possibility that PR and PM can be split or separated in the construction and maintain the inherent semantic relation between the two entities in the meanwhile. It is of particular quality for the possessive relation. Lv (1976) and Yuan (1995) focus on the similarity between the phrasal level possession and clausal level possession. As the semantic relation, the possessive interpretation can be achieved syntactically in the construction.

What is more, Zhang's study shows that pragmatic meaning should be taken into the consideration in order to get a whole picture. The possession has its pragmatic value in expressing the meaning, which enlarges our scope into pragmatic field. We see the necessity to study the possession in the dynamic situations. Possessive meaning becomes a property the constructions acquire since we do need the expressions to describe the process concerned with the possession: the establishment, the continuity and discontinuity of the possessive relation.

2.2 Existential Construction

In many languages, existential and possessive constructions are related to locatives or possession belongs to the same general category as location.

Lv (1942) suggests the definition of Existential Construction for the first time. When talking about "starting words" and "ending words", he notices two kinds of sentences *dong gebi dianli wuhou zou-le yibang ke* "a group of guests left the restaurant in the afternoon" and *mei ge xiaochuanshang dian-le yige xiaodenglong* "there is a small lantern hanging on each boat". He illustrates that the initial position is occupied by a locative word. The surface structures are "location nominal+verb+starting word" and "location nominal+verb+ending word". He argues that these two kinds of sentences are of the same kind. Existential Construction can be further divided into two kinds: the one denoting static existence and the other denoting the appearance or disappearance of the entity.

The key features of *disappearing-type* construction are: they are in the form of "locative word+verb +noun" and semantically they mean that someone or something appear or disappear from some place (Li 1986: 92; Song 1987: 192). *Disappearing-type* EC is named after its construction meaning. It can be further classified into: *appearing-type* Existential Construction and *disappearing-type* Existential Construction, which includes constructions denoting changes.

The predicate verbs in *appearing-type* Existential Construction denote the meaning of "appearance" or the verbs which mean the action towards the speaker. Such as *fasheng* "happen"; *chuxian, chu, xianchu, louchu, tuchu* "appear or emerge"; *lai, paolai, feilai* "come". While for the *disappearing-type* Existential Construction, the verbs either have the meaning of "disappearance" or denote the process of the action: *tao*, "flee"; *zou or pao*, "run away"; *shiqu* "fade away"; *shiqu or diao* "lose"; *si* "die". The verbs denoting changes also find their way to the construction: *bian* "change", *duo* "more", *shao* "less". The semantic constrain for the verbs in *disappearing-type* Existential Construction is that they denote change of state.

We can summarize the features of typical *disappearing-type* Existential Construction as follows: someone or something appears or disappears in someplace and this process is accomplished successfully on the spot. The defining features are:

(i) The initial position of the sentence is the locative word denoting space or location.
(ii) The predicate verbs should denote the change of state.
(iii) The aspect of the verb is usually the perfective aspect, the commonly used form is *le*, which indicates the completion of the event.

2.2.1 Syntactic analysis

The focuses of the book are mainly on the syntactic status of the initial locative element and the post-verbal noun as well as its case assignment. In fact, these two points are closely related with the syntactic features of the predicate verbs: they are unaccusative verbs.

As for the predicate verbs in Existential Construction, verbs in "there be" construction and those in locative existential construction all belong to unaccusative intransitive verbs, which has only one internal argument. This is called "Unaccusative Hypothesis" in the literature (Perhnutter 1978; Burzino 1986). For example:

> (8) a. There <u>is</u> a man in the room.
>   b. There <u>came</u> a guest.
>   c. There <u>appeared</u> a group of enemy.
>   d. In front of the building stands a high tree.
>   e. Above the horizon <u>arose</u> a bright morning star.

The predicate verbs in the examples are prototype unaccusative verbs with only one internal argument. Although scholars find that there are exceptions, they accept this hypothesis in general (Huang 1987; Pan1996; Gu 1997; Han 2001; Tang 2001, 2005)

Sui and Wang (2009) propose that according to Huang (1997), the event verb "Occur" is projected in Existential Construction and therefore under its influence, the predicate verbs in the construction show the features of unaccusative verbs. The information focus is not on the action denoted by the verb but on the description of the event or the state. As for the event type, it represents the event centering on the patient, and the function is to describe a state.

Pan (1996, 1997) uses Lexical Mapping Theory to explain the features of the verbs. He proposes that the transitive verbs in Existential Construction have undergone a process of reconstruction. This process changes the argument structure of the verb, which deletes the agent and just keeps the thematic roles of the theme and location. When the verb is projected to syntactic level, the noun with locative meaning is mapped to be the subject. Han (2001) thinks that the initial locative nominal phrase is not the subject but the adverbial topic.

Based on Bellett (1988) "Partitive Case's", Gu (1997) thinks that the unaccusative verbs in EC assign partitive case to its logic object.

Han (2001) thinks that partitive case theory weakens the universality of the "Unaccusative Hypothesis" and instead, he proposes "Case Chain Hypothesis". Logic affix and the trace made by the movement form a chain, through the chain, the subject can transfer the subjective case to pose-verb nominal phrase which is logic object in deep structure.

The syntactic analysis mainly centers on the features of unaccusative verbs in the construction. Since the unaccusative verb can offer just one argument position and cannot assign the case directly to the object after the verb, many proposals aim to solve these two problems.

2.2.2 *Disappearing-type* Existential Construction & PSPO

The relation between the *disappearing-type* Existential Construction and PSPO has its root in the study on the connection between the constructions from cognitive perspective.

Ren (2009) studies the similarities between two semantic concepts: "possession" and "existence". She points out the constructive relevance between PSPO and typical Existential Construction. She reaches the conclusion that two constructions share so many similarities that they can be brought into the same semantic category in cognitive framework.

Li (2009) argues there exists a light verb "OCCUR" in semantic construction of these two kinds, which plays the key role in understanding the complete meaning of the constructions. Her proposal is to combine *disappearing-type* Existential Construction with "PSPO" into "Occurrence construction". Her explanation is that the main verb has acquired extended meaning in the structures of PSPO. The extended meaning can build double categorization relation for Existential Construction with conventional meaning and the conceptual meaning of the construction. The initial locative nominal will get licensed so as to give a unified explanation to Existential Construction and PSPO construction.

Lv (2013) puts forward the idea that the structural meaning of *wan mian si-le fuqin* is the abstract meaning of "appearance" or "disappearance", but not "gain or loss" or "occurrence". He illustrates his points from the perspectives of the relations among three elements: metonymy of sentence initial animate words to location, verbs and constructive meaning.

Xuan's study (2011) is from cognitive perspective and the similarities he sums up are as follows:

First, they share more or less the same sentence structure, which is "NP$_1$+Vi+NP$_2$," structure.

Second, the transformation to make the possession overt is basically the same. There are differences in clausal meaning between typical *disappearing-type* Existent Construction and PSPO. *Disappearing-type* existent sentences means that someone or something appears or disappears in some place while PSPO means possessors obtains or loses the possessum. In the structural meaning, PSPO represents underlying possessive relation.

As far as the identity consistency, this kind of transformation is invalid. The meaning that *ta you yi wei keren* implied in *jiali lai-le yiwei keren* can not maintain in the sentence *ta de keren lai-le*. What is more, the guest in *lai keren le* is a non-referential element while in *keren lai-le*, the guest is a clear referential element. The definiteness in the construction of *keren lai-le* is lost if we transfer it to *lai-le keren*.

Disappearing-type Existent Construction denotes the process of "appearance, disappearance and change" of the entity while PSPO denotes "obtain, loss and change" of the possessum.

Thirdly, the predicate verbs in these two constructions are alike. The predicate verbs employed in the constructions tend to be mono-syllable verbs with the oral-speaking features.

Cui (1987) lists the verbs used in *disappearing-type* Existential Construction and his conclusion is "just as Existential Construction, mono-syllable verbs are dominated in *disappearing-type* Existential Construction and tend to be oral vocabulary, but verbs usually take some additional elements".

Guo (1990) does not mention this point but when he further studies the 52 verbs, he finds that only 9 of them are disyllabic. What is more, the verbs involved cannot be in its bare form. They are followed by aspect particles, among which, *le* is the most commonly used and sometimes it is *guo* but it can never be *zhe*.

Xuan (2011) further investigates 52 verbs mentioned by Guo (1990) and finds that most of them can be used in *disappearing-type* Existential Construction, as *si* "die", *diao* "fall", *duan* "break", *diu* "lose", *zou* "run away", The verbs in both *disappearing-type* Existential Construction and

PSPO construction are one-way verbs denoting one direction and the overwhelming majority are non-automous verbs.

Cui (1987) sums up the features of the verbs in *disappearing-type* Existential Construction:

> *From the point of the grammatical function, the verb should be one-way nominal-object verb. What is worth mentioning is that when a verb can be either one-way or two-way verb, it should function as one-way verb in the construction.*

From the perspective of the PSPO, the typical construction denoting disappearance is the least typical PSPO, since the pre-verbal nominal and pose-verbal nominal have a broad-sensed possessive relation, while from the perspective of Existential Construction, the typical PSPO is a typical construction denoting disappearance, since the initial nominal can be considered to be a subjective location.

The study of the Existential Construction is always considered to be hot issue in Mandarin Chinese in that it shows distinguishing features in its verbs. Unaccusative verbs and Definiteness Effect are the main concerns for syntactic and semantic research respectively. Nowadays, the focus is shifted from syntactic features to semantic and pragmatic features of the construction. The connections between constructions have been explored from the perspective of cognitive Grammar. Scholars begin to account for the derivation of the construction rather than just describe the elements contained in the construction.

There is not so much study on the relationship between the possession and existence. In fact, they are closely related concepts. Existential Construction in a sense is the basic construction for other forms of DPCs.

2.3 PSPO Construction

Possessor-subject and possessum-object construction (PSPO

Construction)① is unique in its syntax and semantics structure. Sentence-initial nominal and sentence-final nominal are in the relation of possession while the predicate verbs usually belong to unaccusative verbs, which take only one argument. The structure goes as follows: $NP_1+Vi+NP_2$. Actually, Np_2 is the theme of the action while NP_1 has no direct semantic relation with the action verb. For example, *Wangmian si le fuqin.* There is no semantic relation between *si* and *wangmian*. It is not *Wangmian* who died, but it is his father who died. As the possessor of *fuqin*, *Wangmian* experienced or was greatly affected by his father's death. We listed examples used in Guo (1990):

> (9) a. 王冕七岁上死了父亲。
>   Wangmian qisui shang si-le fuqin.
>   Wangmian 7 year at die-Perf father.
>   "Wangmian's father died on him when he was seven years old."
>   b. 他死了四棵桃树。
>   ta si-le sike taoshu.
>   he die-Perf four CL peach tree.
>   "He suffered from the fact that four of his peach trees died."
>   c. 他一下子来了精神。
>   ta yixiazi lai-le jingshen.
>   he immediately come-Perf spirit
>   "He was immediately high in spirit."
>   d. 他掉了两颗牙。
>   ta diao-le liang ke ya.
>   he fall-Perf two CL teeth.
>   "He suffered from the fact that two of his teeth fell."

Lv (2013) holds that the initial nominal is the animate word denoting the entity with life, which has no direct connection with the predicate. What is more, it's not the argument selected by the predicate verb. The

---

① The construction is also termed as Unaccusative Construction of Possessor-subject and Possessun-onject in Ma(2013, The intransitive verb taking retained object by Li(2002) and Double unaccusative construction by Chappel(1999). Most of the terms highlight the syntactic features.

middle part is the intransitive verbs which include both intransitive verbs and some adjectives with aspect marker *le*. Sentence-final position is usually occupied by the theme nominal. The parallel structure in each part of three elements is found in both the Existential Construction and PSPO construction.

2.3.1 Possession in PSPO

Guo (1990) is the first who proposes the name of the construction. He points out: "there is a stable "possessor-possessum" relation between the subject and the object". The subject is "possessor" and the object is "possessum". As for the possessive relation between these two elements, scholars may hold different opinions. Those who support "possessor raising" suggest that the initial nominal is moved out of a even bigger possessive NP constituent and definitely the two elements have possessive relation (Cheng 2007; An 2007; Chen&Xiao 2007; Ma 2008). Xu (2004) points out that the type of the possessive relation includes three kinds: broad-sensed "ownership" possessive relation; kinship relation and part-whole relation.

Ma (2009) tries to clarify the possessive relation employed in PSPO. He adopts Taylor' definition (1989), among which, two points are worth special attention: (i) The relation between the two is an exclusive one, that is, for each PM, there is only one PR. (ii) The PR has the right to make use of the PM; other people can make use of the PM only with the permission of the PR.

These two features are the "ownership" and "control" of the PR over the PM. Narrow-sensed possession refers to the typical possessive relation: a human-being owns the material wealth, including his properties and his body-parts. Broad-sensed possession refers to the one that is not so typical, which is either lack of "ownership" or "control". He lists the specific possessive relation in the chart:

Classification	Broad-sensed	Narrow-sensed
Ownership	+	+
Part-whole	+	+
Kinship	+	-

Ma Zhigang (2013: 67)

Some scholars think that the scope of the relationship between these two nominals is wider than possession. Zhang (2010) proposes referential point relationship in cognitive grammar. Cognitive subject builds cognitive connection by motivating one entity (referential point) with the other one. That is to say, referential point is the bridge to reach the goal. In PSPO, both the speaker and the hearer need to interpret *fu qin* by means of *Wang mian*. At the lexical level, the most typical form of referential point is the possessive relation. What is more, from the perspective of construction meaning, the referential point relation means that the two participants involved in the event have a concept relation. It is natural that what one participant experienced imposed influence on the other. It is not proper to summarize the characteristic of NP$_1$ as the possessor. There should be a more abstract idea to cover the point.

2.3.2 Syntactic Analysis

As early as 20th century, in the "Subject and Object discussion", many scholars show great interests in this construction. The focus was the relation and the classifications of the pre-verbal and post-verbal nominals. People argue about the subject and object status of the construction.

In the late 1980s, the construction became hot issue again. Li (1987) illustrates the syntactic properties and features of the PSPO construction and she first employs grammatical category of "transitive/intransitive". Guo's study (1990) is the most elaborated and systematic up to now. He focuses on each part of the construction: subject, object, verb and the functional verbs "*zhe/le/guo*". It is agreed that his study on the construction has achieved description adequacy.

With the linguistic shift from description to explanation, the construction attracts more concerns and scholars begin to explain how the construction is generated. The discussion on "PSPO" in the framework of Generative Grammar mainly involves two aspects: source of the possessor and the case of the possessum. On the basis of the answers to these questions, we find two kinds of analysis: one is the movement of the PR and the other is canonical analysis.

The main point of "Movement" is that the possessor nominal in the position of the subject is moved from a larger embedded noun phrase, the operation which is known as "possessor raising". The dispute lies in the former position of the possessor, how it acquires the case and the motivation for the movement.

2.3.2.1 Movement analysis

Based on Burzio's "Unaccusative Hypothesis" (1986) and Belletti's "Partitive Case" (1998), Xu (1999) proposes "Possessor Raising Hypothesis" to account for both PSPO and Passive DPC. He thinks that the possessor nominal moves from the position of the specifier of an embedded noun phrase in order to get nominative case; while the remained-in-situ possessum nominal gets a special case called partitive case.

Han (2000) agrees with Xu (1999) on that the possessor nominal moves to get the nominative case, but he thinks that "Partitive Case" theory is not good enough to explain the difference in the ability of case assignment between Mandarin Chinese and other languages. He adopts "Case Chain", where the possessor nominal moves to the position of the subject in surface structure in order to get the case and through the trace bounded by the initial nominal, the chain is formed and the whole deep logic objective can get its case.

Wen and Chen (2001) think that D_p has [+D][+Case] feature and [+D] is the strong feature while I_p has [+D][+Assign Nominative] feature. The movement for the possessor nominal is to check the strong [+D] feature carried by the possessor with the [+D] feature of I_p.

Liu (2008) proposes that the properties of the possessor in PSPO construction are rooted in its double objects construction in deep structure. In double objects construction, indirect object receives thematic role of the theme. Thematic role and the predicate verb assign two object cases. Restricted with unaccusative feature, indirect object loses the case and moves to the subject position.

These analyses, though differing in the Case assignment mechanism, have one point in common: the original position of the initial possessor is in a bigger noun phrase. Another common point shared by all the analysis is that they all involve some kind of movement. The scholars differ in the case assignment mechanism and the motivation of the movement.

On the other hand, there are some problems of the "movement" approach summarized against "possessor raising" analysis by some researchers. Shen (2006) and Pan (2005) give a detailed description.

The first problem often discussed is the disappearance of the genitive marker *de*. There should be a word-*de* in the sentence that contains both the surface sentential subject and object if the "movement" analysis is correct. And because *de* indicates possessive relation between two nominals, it may lead to the result that the possessor nominal may get two cases at the same time in the construction. This problem has been recognized in the literature, but no satisfactory answer is proposed. In fact, if the two arguments of the sentence are not analyzed within the same constitute, there will be no need of such a word.

The second problem is closely related with the first problem. The possessor raising analysis treats the constructions in the way that the possession splitting structure is derived from the construction which contains the bigger possessive phrase. The base for the analysis is that the two sentences are equivalent in meaning. In fact, we find that PSPO has different construction meaning with internal possession construction. The possessor in PSPO is adversely affected by the event involved in the PR. The affectedness meaning is missing in the corresponding possessive construction.

2.3.2.2 Canonical Position Analysis

Since the movement approach encounters so many problems, some other alternatives are proposed, such as the "base-generation" approach. Instead of the movement, the initial possessor is said to be base-generated in the lexicon. For the fact that there is an argument that needs to be introduced into the constructions, the existing investigations supporting canonical position analysis can be summarized as four approaches: (i) the approach of empty verb; (ii) the approach of light verb; (iii) the approach of applicative construction; (iv) the approach of dangling topic.

Sun and Wu (2003) hold that *Zhangsan si-le fuqin* and *Zhangsan de fuqin si-le* are two different constructions. They propose that in lexicon, there is an empty verb with [+Effect] feature. In the former construction, Zhangsan is the malefactive argument and is licensed by the empty verb. This construction is composed of two events, therefore, the derivation contains two steps: the first step is abide with normal sentence and in second step, the hypothesis is that there is an empty verb with [+Effect] feature but without phonetic feature.

In the light of Huang' light verb analysis (1997), Zhu (2005) argues that in PSPO construction, it is the light verb "EXPERIENCE" or "OCCUR" that assigns the possessor nominal case at external argument position and chooses a VP as its complement. He thinks that the light verb and intransitive verb work together to explain why an intransitive verb takes two argument nominals. Lin (2008), Li (2009) and Sui (2009) all suppose there to be the light verb "OCCUR" in the construction which helps to build the construction.

On the base of Cuervo's (2003) dative case theory, Wang (2006) thinks that PSPO is not unique in Chinese Mandarin but very common in language system. He holds that these two nominals are not in the same large phrase and they are not necessarily in the relation of possession. Possessor is first generated in the specifier position of the applicative head and then moves to the subject position. The applicative approach is more employed to explain Double Object Construction in both Mandarin Chinese and other languages.

Pan and Han (2005) treat the sentence-initial element as base-generated topics. In the construction with overt noun movement, the motivation for the nominal to move is to check the strong EPP feature, while in Mandarin Chinese, the EPP feature is weak and the motivation of the nominal is to generate an unmarked topic. Pan and Hu (2002) propose that the topic can be licensed either in syntax or at the semantic-pragmatic interface. There is no direct semantic relation between the topic and predicate verb, but there must be a semantic variable in the comment clause. It is not a syntactic gap or a resumptive pronoun, but a semantic gap, which can be used to license the topic. He defines this condition as "Set Intersection Analysis". Yang (2008) agrees with Pan in treating the sentence-initial nominal to be base-generated topic.

2.3.3 Meaning of PSPO

Shen (2006) puts forward a new explanation to PSPO construction. He proposes "blending" analysis. In his approach, *Wangmian si-le fuqin* is the blending of *Wangmian de fuqin si-le* and *Wangmian diu-le mouwu*. He maintains the theory of generation by analogical blending. Blending may generate emegergent meaning. The loss or gain of the possessor is the construction meaning as the result of the blending of the two constructions. Liu (2007) shares the same idea and adds three points: (i) *Wangmian si-le fuqin* is broad-sensed Existential Construction; (ii) *le* in the construction is important in completing the sentence; (iii) the causative usage of *si* doesn't exist in Mandarin Chinese now but the construction frame can be reserved to some degree.

People have different opinions on the construction meaning of PSPO. The representative idea is that PSPO belongs to Existential Construction, so basically it has the meaning of "existence". Liu (2007) and Ren (2005) are among the first to sum up the connection. Lv (2013) tries to illustrate the connection between "occurrence" and "existence". It is the occurrence of the events that leads to spatial existence of the objects. The appearance and disappearance of the objects are the results of the occurrence of some action. There is a natural connection between "occurrence" and "existence". The "occurrence" of the event is the precondition for the state of "appearance/disappearance".

Zhang (2012) holds that the construction meaning of PSPO is: NP_1 is the "experiencer", who goes through the event of "NP_2+V" and the emphasis is on the influence the event imposed on NP_1. The influence includes two kinds: "loss" or "gain". As for "loss", NP_1 should bear malefactive role[1]. This kind of meaning can not be obtained from the component parts but exists in the combination.

The negative influence on the possessor is inseparable part of the construction meaning for PSPO. Shen (2006; 2009) thinks that *lai* is a kind of "gain" and *si* is a kind of "loss". He further illustrates the point from the perspective of language subjectivity. The construction is not just to show a kind of "gain" or "loss", what is important is whether the speaker cares it or not. The construction meaning is "to mind gain and loss" rather than "to measure gain and loss".

From the discussion of the construction meaning, the connection between PSPO and Existential Construction becomes evident. In a sense, the existential meaning is to represent the objective world. In PSPO construction, the speaker may choose the construction intentionally to

---

[1] The effect may be beneficial as *ta lai le keren*, but usually even the verb means to get sth. When it happened, the possessor does not expecte the happening of the event.

express the appearance and disappearance of the PM.

The study on PSPO has undergone three important stages. The study shows to some degree the hot issues of different stages. In the 1950s, researchers began to notice the unique features of the construction. In the late 1980s, Li (1987) and Guo (1990) did influential work by describing the construction in details and try to give some explanation. In recent years, the studies are mainly done under the framework of Generative Grammar on the syntax of the construction. When we first introduce the theory and put the theory into practical use, we sometimes do not really understand and fully assimilate the theory. Once there is a new theory, we just use it to explain the phenomenon in Chinese, as can be shown by the fact that the study on PSPO matches more or less with the developing stages of Generative Grammar. In these ten years, there is a good turning, scholars begin to integrate foreign linguistic theory with the features of Mandarin Chinese. Huang (1996) focus on the Topic Construction. Pan (2008) further proposes "dangling topic" to explain both PSPO and passive DPC. Hu (2006) tries to use the abstract verb "HAVE" to explain a series of language constructions.

There are not many studies done on the construction from the perspective of possession. The relationship between the two nominals is involved but no further discussion is done in details. From the perspective of the possession, PSPO is the typical External Possession Construction form in other languages.

2.4 Passive DPC

2.4.1 Similarities between PSPO and Passive DPC

Xu (1999; 2001) is among the first to point out the similarities between PSPO and Passive DPC, which are seemingly different constructions. He also tries to give a unified account for these two constructions. Here are the examples he lists: example (10) to (3) are Passive DPC.

(10) 李四被打伤了一条腿。
     Lisi bei dashang-le yi-tiao tui.

Lisi Bei break-Perf. One-CL leg

"Lisi got one of his legs broken."

(11) 张三被杀了父亲。

Zhangsan bei sha-le fuqin.

Zhangsan Bei kill-Perf. Father

"Zhangsan got his father killed."

(12) 苹果被削了皮。

Pingguo bei xiao-le pi.

pingguo Bei peel-Perf. skin

"The apple was peeled off the skin."

(13) 他终于被免去了最后一个职务。

Ta zhongyu bei mianqu-le zuihou yige zhiwu.

he finally Bei take-away-Perf last one-CL title

"He was finally taken away of his last title."

(14)-(17) are PSPO.

(14) 王冕七岁上死了父亲。

Wangmian qisuishang si-le fuqin.

Wangmian seven year at die-Perf. Father

"Wangmian's father died on him when he was seven years old."

(15) 那个工厂塌了一堵墙。

Nage gongchang ta-le yi-du qiang.

that factory fall-down-Perf. One-CL wall

"One of the walls of that factory fell down."

(16) 那家公司沉了一条船。

najia gongsi chen-le yitiao chuan.

that conpany sink-Perf. one-CL ship

"One of the ships of that company sank."

(17) 张三烂了一筐梨。

Zhangsan lan-le yi-kuang li.

Zhangsan go-bad-Perf. one-CL pear

"One basket of Zhangsan's pears went bad."

When these two constructions are put together, we find they are different in that the predicate verbs, which decide the nature of the constructions, are of completely different proprieties. One contains transitive verbs in their passive forms; the other is intransitive verbs. According to Xu (1999), the similarities include:

Firstly, semantically, the pre-verbal nominal and post-verbal nominal in both constructions are in the relation of possession. The broad-sensed possessive relation can be "ownership", "part/whole" or "kinship" relation.

Secondly, the post-verbal nominals can be put either before or after the predicate verb. When the object is before the verb, *de* is used to join two nominals together. For example, we can say (18a) with *Zhangsan* and *fuqin* being separated by the predicate verb. But in (18b) *de* must be used to indicate the possessive relation.

> (18) a. 张三被杀了父亲。
> Zhangsan   bei sha-le fuqin.
> Zhangsan   Bei kill-Perf. Father
> "Zhangsan got his father killed."
> b. 张三的父亲被杀了。
> Zhangsan de fuqin bei sha-le.
> Zhangsan De father Bei kill-Perf.
> "Mr Zhang's father was killed."

Thirdly, the objects in these two constructions can not be preposed before the subjects as what we do in other ordinary "subject-verb-object" constructions.

> (19) a. 他吃了那个桔子。
> Ta chi-le nage juzi.
> he eat-Perf. that-CL orange
> "He ate the orange."
> b. 那个桔子他吃了。
> Nage juzi ta chi-le.
> that-CL orange he eat-Perf.
> "As for that orange, he ate it."

(20) a. 他断了一条腿。

　　　Ta duan-le　yi-tiao tui.

　　　he break-Perf. one-CL leg

　　　"he got one of the leg broken."

　 b. * 一条腿他断了。

　　　* yitiao tui ta duan-le.

　　　one leg he break-Perf.

(21) a. 他被绑了一条腿。

　　　ta bei bang-le yitiao tui.

　　　he Bei tie-Perf. One-CL leg

　　　"He got one of his legs tied."

　 b. * 一条腿他被绑了。

　　　* Yitiao tui ta bei bang-le

　　　one-CL leg he Bei tie-Perf.

(19a) is a normal SVO construction and we can move the object to the initial position of the sentence functions as the topic. Both (19a) and (19b) are acceptable sentences. Y*i tiao tui* in neither (20b) nor (21b) can be moved to serve as the topics for the construction although they occupy the syntactic position of the object position.

The last point is that the verbs in the constructions are not able to assign structure case to object nominal but there are nominal elements that need structure cases.

The account Xu (1999) offered is the "Possessor Raising Hypothesis". The predicate verbs happen to share the same defining features. They both have the object position which can be assigned a thematic role but can not receive objective case. What is more, they have the subject position which can be assigned nominal case but can not receive the theme/patient thematic role. The syntactic feature fits the syntactic condition for "possessor raising". It is feasible to move the possessor nominal, which occupies the attributive position of the object to the subject position. The syntactic features for unaccusitive verbs are from the lexicon while the syntactic features of passive verbs are the result of the passivation of the transitive verbs. The predicate verbs in Passive DPC behave just the same as the unaccusitive verbs in PSPO. The subject in surface structure occupies object position in the deep structure. They are constructions without subject in deep structure. For example:

(22) a. Lisi bei tou-le yige qianbao (surface structure)

b. bei tou-le Lisi de yi-ge qianbao (deep structure)

The possessor moves to the subject position in order to get nominal case and the possessum as retained part remained in the original object position. The case the retained part gets is the partitive case. The reason the object can get the partitive case is that "partitive case" is an inherent case. The transitive verb in its passive form loses the ability to assign "structure case" but it can still assign "inherent case" to its object.

Xu (2004) further restricts the partitive assignment constrains: when the partitive case is assigned to a certain noun phrase, it requires the possessor of the nominal to be at the subject position in the same construction. What is more, the possessor nominal must be a lexical NPs instead of an empty category.

Xu uses "Possessor Raising Analysis" to give a unified explanation to these constructions while Pan and Han (2008) treat them both as the initial topics.

To sum up, the passive DPC should obtain the defining features syntactically and semantically:

(i) The subject and the object should maintain narrowed-sensed possessive relation, rather than kinship relation;

(ii) The object which stands post-verbal position must in the form of "number+classifier+noun" construction;

(iii) The subject must be the affectee suffering from the misfortunate event.

2.4.2 Construction Meaning of Passive DPC

Fang and Wang (2008) focus on the verbs in these two constructions. They find they share some syntactic and semantic properties. At syntactic level, transitive verbs and di-transitive verbs may enter Passive DOC and intransitive verb can appear in PSPO. At semantic level, the meaning of verbs mainly denotes unwillingness. What's more, the event denoted by the predicate verb has great influence on the subject.

Ma (2013) holds that the Passive DPC in essence is the *Bei* construction which denotes the fact that someone suffers from loss of something. It is a construction to show the loss. The relationship between the subject and the object is narrow-sensed possessive relation: the object must be the entity that belongs to the possessor. Two kinds of possessive relations find their way to the constructions: the ownership possessive relation and body-part relation.

Since the Passive DPC is the sub-type of Passive Construction, the meaning of *Bei* may bring "suffering" or the "adversely affected" meaning to the whole construction.

2.5 Topic Construction

Topic Construction is the construction where the subject-predicate phrase serves as the predicate of the construction. It seems that in surface structure, two nominals are found in juxtaposition at the initial position of the sentence. Therefore, the construction is called "The double-subject construction" (Chao 1968; Li-Thompson 1976,1981). It is Chen (1921) who first proposes the term, which means "a clause serves as the comment". It is generally accepted that this kind of construction exists in Mandarin Chinese and is considered to be one of the characteristics of Mandarin Chinese. Chao (1968) thinks the construction includes the S-P clause to be the predicate.

2.5.1 The Scope of Topic Construction

If we just focus on the feature of two NPs juxtaposed in sentence-initial position, we may have a wider scope of the construction. Double subject sentences can be superficially analyzed as formed by a loose conjunction of NP+S. It is characterized by the fact that there is no necessity for an argument relation to hold between the topic NP and the main verb of the comment. What we are concerned with is the construction with the possessive relation, which is accepted to be typical "sentences with a subject-predicate predicate".[①]

---

① Lv thinks that the Topic Construction with possessive relation between the topic nominal and the element in proposition is the only type that Mandarin has for Topic Construction.

(23) a. 他身体健康。

　　　Ta shenti jiankang.

　　　he body   healthy

　　　"As for him, he is quite healthy."

　　b. 他一向态度和蔼。

　　　Ta yixiang taidu heai.

　　　he always attitude good

　　　"As for him, his attitude is always good."

　　c. 这马眼瞎了。

　　　Zhe ma yan xia-le.

　　　this horse eye blind

　　　"As for the horse, the eyes of the horse are blind."

The initial nominal and the nominal contained in the comment clause are in the inalienable possessive relation.

From the point of syntax, the S-P phrase has no direct syntactic relation with the sentence initial nominal. The S-P phrase by itself is an independent constitute, such as, *"shenti jiankang"* ; *"piqi hao."* They are phrases with "subject-predicate" construction. As a syntactic constitute, the phrase is comparatively self-supporting. For the examples in (23), the initial nominal is not the subject in a strict sense. If we observe the semantic relation between the elements, we find the small-subjects contained in the comment belong to the big-subjecst. The big-subjects denote the person or the entity and the small-subjects denote a certain part or a certain inherent property of the person. Usually, we can add *de* to make the possessive relation overt and the whole construction will become a normal SVO construction. The elements without *de* have possessive relation just in semantic sense and can't be treated as an independent constitute. A pause or adverbs like *"yixiang", "cai", "benlai"* can be inserted in between them. For example:

(24) 小林，心眼好，脾气也好。

　　　Xiaoling, xinyan hao, piqi ye hao.

　　　Xiaoling, heart good, nature good

　　　"As far as Xiaoling is concerned, she is good both in the heart and nature."

Sun (2010) proposes that the double subject construction is the one that is based on unaccusative construction. She sums up five syntactic and semantic features of the construction:

a. possessive relation exists between the big-subject and the small-subject

b. small-subject receives the thematic role from the predicate verb

c. what the S-P expressed involves the big-subject in

d. the verbs in S-P belong to unaccusative verbs

e. double subject construction is the one that contains an "extra" argument

As mentioned above, the initial nominal is not the real subject but should be treated as a initial topic. From the point of the pragmatics, the purpose of the initial topic is to set a particular point for the conversation. It is the information shared by both the speaker and the hearer involved in the conversation. The function of the topic is to introduce new information. Being an indispensable part of the sentence as the basic communicative unit, any sentence should refer to a person or an entity. For example, we have constructions as (25):

(25) a. 他身体健康。

Ta shenti jiankang.

ta body health

"As for him, he is in good condition."

b. 他的身体健康。

Ta de shenti jiankang.

his body healthy

"He is healthy."

(25a) and (25b) have different topics. The topic in (25a) is *ta*, and the sentence is to be followed by more information about *ta*. It can form a group of sentences in the form of "Topic chain". The topic in (25b) is *ta de shenti*, what is going to be illustrated all centers on "his health".

2.5.2 Relationship between Subject and Topic

The earliest writing on Topic Construction can be traced to Chao (1968). Chao denies the status of such grammatical terms as subject, object, and verb-predicate in the Chinese Grammar and proposes to replace them with topic and comment.

> *The grammatical meaning of subject and predicate in a Chinese sentence is topic and comment, rather than actor and action. The subject is literally the subject matter to talk about, and the predicate is what the speaker comments on when a subject is presented to be talked about—In poetry, [the topics] only set the scene and the actor is simply shifted somewhere else.*
>
> Chao (1968: 69)

As for the relationship between the subject and the topic, there are three representative opinions. The first is that the subject and the topic are the same element in the construction. Chao (1984) holds "it is proper to treat the subject and the predicate as the topic and the comment". As for the relationship between the topic and comment, he thinks that "the relation is so loose that this construction will be considered to be ungrammatical in other languages"(Chao 1968: 45). Li (1985) gives similar idea. He thinks

> *the subject is the initial noun functioning as the topic. The subject is somewhat general and not quite stable. The relation with the predicate is quite loose and the subject has few form features.*

The standard they use is from the syntactic position. The initial element is both the subject and the topic.

The subject and the topic are of different quality. Zhu (1982) and Lu (1985) distinguish the concept of the topic with the subject in that they belong to pragmatic layer and syntactic layer respectively. Zhu (1982) thinks that the topic is used from the perspective of expression. Lu (1986) clearly points out that the subject and the topic are two concepts at two different layers.

> *He thinks that the subject in Mandarin Chinese is not*
> *necessarily the topic. Correspondingly, the elements to be treated*
> *as the topic in Mandarin Chinese are not necessarily the subject.*

Hu and Fan (2003) stick to the idea that the subject is the concept at syntactic layer while the topic is the practical one. The topic should not be included in the syntactic analysis. Song (1987), Chen (2002) and Yuan (2003) further propose that the big subject is the result of topicalization. That is to say, the basic construction in Mandarin Chinese is SVO and Topic Construction is derived from the basic construction. The way to derive the Topic Construction is the topicalization of a certain element.

Li and Thompson (1976), Tsao (1977), Huang (1982), Xu & Liu (1998) support the idea that the topic occupies the syntactic position. They think that in Mandarin Chinese, at syntactic layer, there are both subject and topic elements. They are separated independent elements. The topic has its own syntactic position and is an independent syntactic element just as the subject, predicate and object. They are all paralleling elements. In Xu's (1998) study, the topic nominal occupies the specifier of the IP. The conclusion is drawn from the perspective of typology. Mandarin Chinese is considered to be TSVO as its basic structure. Under this frame work, the topic is the based-generated element in the construction and Topic Construction is the most common structure in Mandarin Chinese.

2.6 Double Object Construction

2.6.1 *Depriving-type* Double Object Construction

The internal structure of a sentence with two nominal elements following the predicate verb has been one of the controversies in grammar study. Some hold strict standard on the DOC and only consider *giving-type* DOC to be DOC and *depriving-type* DOC to be single object construction. (Shen 1994; Yang 1996; Li 1996).

Li (1984), Lu (1997), Xu (1999), Zhang (2000), Lin (2013) and Zhang (2001) insist that *deprivinging-type* DOC also belongs to DOC.

The focus is on the relationship of the two post-verbal elements: possessive relation or double objects relationship.

De is used to insert between direct object and indirect object to judge whether they are in the possessive relation. If there is no possessive relation after *de* is added, the construction is considered to be DOC; while if d*e* is used to build the possessive relation between the two elements, the construction is treated as single object construction.

Scholars have done a lot of study on the construction "*Zhangsan chi-le ta san-ge pingguo*". Chen (2009) thinks that this construction has syntactic ambiguity. When it is treated as single object construction, "NP$_1$+NP$_2$" after the verb is Top Construction. NP$_1$ is the topic of nominal phrase and NP$_2$ is the comment; when it is treated as DOC, NP$_1$ and NP$_2$ are two objects individually, the former is the "affectee" and the latter is the "theme". He further summarizes some evidence to support DOC.

Lu (2002) provides an investigation of this phenomenon through an analysis of the semantic orientation of adverbs such as *zonggong/yigong* "totally"[①]. When *zonggong/yigong* serves as an adverbial element, it orients to a numerical constituent as can be shown in the following examples:

> (26) a. 总共吃了他三个苹果。
>   zonggong chi-le ta san-ge pingguo.
>   totally   eat-Perf. ta three-CL apple
>   "Totally three of his apples are eaten."
>
>   b. 一共打碎了他四个杯子。
>   yigong dasui-le ta si-ge beizi.
>   totally break-Perf him four-CL cups
>   "Totelly four of his cups are broken."
>
>   c. 只浪费了他两个下午。
>   zhi langfei-le   ta liangge xiawu.
>   only waste-Perf him two-CL afternoon
>   "Only two-afternoon time is ruined."
>
>   d. 仅仅偷了他五百块钱。
>   jinjin tou-le ta wubai-kuai qian.

---

① Yigong orients to a numerical constituent, which in turn can not be preceded by definite attributive element.

only   steal-Perf him five hundred-CL money

"Only steal five hundred money from him."

When *de* is added, these sentences are not grammatical. Attributive element, including possessive attributive component can not precede the construction.

(27) * zonggong/yigong Lisi-de hong-de san-ge pingguo

The reason, according to Lu, is that there is no direct syntactic relation between *ta* and *san-ge pingguo*. It indicates that although *chi-le ta san-ge pingguo* appears to stand in a semantically possessive relation, they are not in direct relation and do not form the construction of a modification one.

Secondly, Xu (1999) is one of the representative studies of DOC under the framework of generative grammar. With the binding theory, he analyzes the properties of the construction *dasui le ta si-ge beizi*. He points out that *zhengzheng, manman, buduobushao* can be inserted between NP_1 and NP_2.

(28) a. 张三吃了他满满三筐苹果。

Zhangsan chi-le ta manman san-kuang pingguo.

Zhangsan consume-Perf him full three-CL apple

"Zhangsan ate someone's three full baskets of apples."

His argument is that these words occupy the initial position of the phrase and can not be preceded by other attributives, which shows that NP_1 is not an attributive element.

Thirdly, Xu (2004) compares the referential property of the pronoun in (29a) and (29b). He finds that in (29a), the pronoun can not be co-indexed with the subject while the pronoun in (29b) can, as (30) shows:

(29) a. 张三吃了他三个苹果。

Zhangsan chi-le ta san-ge pingguo.

Zhangsan chi-Perf him three-CL apple

"Zhangsan ate three of his apples."

b. 张三吃了他的三个苹果。

Zhangsan chile ta-de san-ge pingguo.

Zhangsan eat-up-Perf him-De three-CL apple

"Zhangsan ate-up three of Zhangsan/Lisi's apples."

(30) a. 张三 $_i$ 吃了他 $_{i/j}$ 三个苹果。

Zhangsan$_i$ chi-le ta$_{*i/j}$ san-ge pingguo.

Zhangsan eat-Perf ta three-CL apple

"Zhangsan$_i$ ate three of his$_{*i/j}$ apples."

b. 张三 $_i$ 吃了他 $_{i/j}$ 的三个苹果。

Zhangsan$_i$ chile ta$_{i/j}$-de san-ge pingguo.

Zhangsan eat-up-Perf him-De three-CL apple

"Zhangsan$_i$ ate-up three of his $_{i/j}$ apples."

Xu suggests that according to Principle B of Binding Theory, the scope of these two pronouns are different, the former is the whole sentence while the latter is just the possessive phrase.

Forthly, Xu (1999; 2004) notices that "NP$_1$+NP$_2$" construction is different semantically from the common possessive "NP$_1$ *de* NP$_2$". "NP$_1$ *de* NP$_2$" has maximal presupposition, that is, in a certain context, the number of X owned by NP$_1$ equals to the number in NP$_2$ phrase. For example, "his four cups" presupposes that in the context, he just has four cups. "NP$_1$+NP$_2$" does not require such presupposition. What is more, the construction indicates that the number of the cups is more than or at least four. It composes of the part-whole relation between the two nominals.

Fifthly, Zhang (1998; 2000) thinks that in Chinese, *de* in the inalienable possession in Mandarin Chinese can be omitted under certain condition but *de* can not be omitted in alienable possession. In DOC, the typical possession is alienable possession. Zhang (1998; 2000) also points that NP$_1$ in these two constructions behaves differently in passivization. NP$_1$ in "NP$_1$+NP$_2$" construction can be raised to the front to be the subject while NP$_1$ in "NP$_1$ *de* NP$_2$" can not be fronted.

(31) a. 他被张三吃了三个苹果。

Ta bei Zhangsan chi-le san-ge pingguo

he Bei Zhangsan eat-le three-CL apple

"He had his three apples eaten by Zhangsan."

b. * 他被张三吃了的三个苹果。

　 * Ta　bei　Zhangsan　chi-le　de san-ge pingguo.

　 he　Bei Zhangsan　eat-Perf De three-CL apple

There are some evidences to support single object construction. Firstly, different from typical DOC, NP₁ and NP₂ in *depriving-type* DOC are in possessive relation. The verb in *depriving-type* DOC precedes two nominal elements but its lexical meaning allows it to go with just one object. There is no direct semantic relation between the predicate verb and NP₁ (Liu 2001; Man 2004).

The most important point is that *depriving-type* DOC is different from the typical *giving-type* DOC when we transform the construction into *Ba* construction and *Bei* construction (Liu 2001; Man 2004; Shen 2003).

(32) * 张三把三个苹果吃了他。

　　 * Zhangsan　ba　san-ge　pingguo　chi-le　ta.

　　 Zhangsan　ba　san-ge　 pingguo　gei-le ta

(33) 张三把他三个苹果吃了。

　　 Zhangsan　ba　ta　san-ge　pingguo　chi-le.

　　 * Zhangsan　ba　ta　san-ge　pingguo　gei-le

(34) 他三个苹果被张三吃了。

　　 Ta san-ge　pingguo　bei　Zhangsan　chi-le.

　　 * ta san-ge　pingguo　bei　Zhangsan　gei-le.

2.6.2 Connection between Passive DPC and PSPO Construction

The connection between the Passive DPC and PSPO construction has been noticed since Xu'(1999) illustration. Liu (2008) puts forward the analysis that both PSPO construction and Passive DPC in Mandarin Chinese are related with Double Object Construction. The connection is that in deep structure, whether the structure contains single object or double objects makes the difference in the movement of the pose-verbal nouns. In the single-object construction, the object as the whole moves to generate the surface structure while in double object construction, it is the patient that moves. The reason for the move is for case assignment, since the unaccusative verbs can not offer case to both the patient and the theme. For the two types of unaccusative verbs to appear into double objection construction, he mentions semantic constrains on both the nouns and the verb: (i) there must be possessive relation between NP$_1$ and NP$_2$; (ii) the verb in its lexical meaning should contain [+transfer] feature.

Ma (2013) comes up with two proposals. The Passive Construction with retained objects is in essence the corresponding passive form of the *depriving-type* DOC. The semantic connection is the base for the syntactic similarities. Ma (2011, 2014) also holds that PSPO construction serves as the basic structure for Passive DPC as well was the *depriving-type* DOC. For the derivation of the Passive DPC, the morphological *Bei* is added above the light verb and for *depriving-type* DPC, the transitive light verb *DA* together with the agent as the causer is added to the construction. Then we have three semantic related constructions: *Lisi duan-le yi-tiao tui*; *Lisi bei daduan-le yi-tiao tui*; *Zhangsan daduan-le Lisi yitiao tui*. The light verbs in construction are complex ones: duan-le+empty light verb; *beida+duan-le*; *da+duan-le*.

For the study on the semantic relation in DOC, the possessive relation plays the key role. The status of the *depriving-type* DOC largely depends on whether the two objects are in the relation of possession. Double Object Construction involves the transfer of the possession. The three elements, namely, the subject, indirect object and direct object are related both syntactically and semantically. They are related with the verb and they are related with each other semantically. The feature of the three nouns in the event reminds us to include the possessive relation in the study of the double object construction.

2.7 Summary

We mainly commit ourselves to a detailed discussion of the DPCs. When we come to the study done to these constructions from the perspective of possessive relation, the connections between the constructions become more evident. Scholars have illustrated the connection between two or three constructions. For example, Ren (2009), Li (2004), Xuan (2009), Wu (2014) all explore the relation between *disappearing-type* Existential Construction and PSPO construction. Xu (1999), Pan (2008), Ma (2012), Liu (2009) illustrate the syntactic and semantic similarities among Passive DPC, PSPO construction and *depriving-type* DOC. The semantic constrains of possessive relation proposed in the study are just the base for our study.

The approaches to account for the problems in syntax are similar to each other. Possessor raising is taken to explain the derivation of PSPO, passive DPC as well as the Topic Construction. Without further debating these proposals and insights they offer, we propose that the primary explanation lies in the domain of voice and differing construals of an event or situation.

The studies establish the empirical foundations for my present study under the framework of the formal semantic approach, which will be discussed in the next chapter.

Chapter Three

Theoretical Framework and Relevant Notions

This chapter focuses on the theoretical framework that will be applied in analyzing DPCs. The analysis is crouched in the framework of event semantics. The one-to-many argument mismatch involves in both the predicate verbs as well as the arguments. It is the eventuality that may combine them together. With the introduction of the *e* element, the derivation process may help to explain the possession in the constructions, which are represented by the separate logic predicate in the logic form. The organization of this chapter is as follows. Section 3.1 mainly focuses on event semantics. Davidsonian and neo-Davidsonian approaches are sketched and compared briefly. The feature of the theory is to build complex predications from the conjunction of several smaller predications that all contribute to the characterization of a single event. In section 3.2, some tentative analyses of possession taken the event entity into consideration are overviewed. A summary is given in section 3.3 to highlight the theoretical advantages of event semantics in exploring the possessive relation of natural languages.

3.1 Event Semantics

The idea that a verb is related to an event came over a long time ago. Philosophers, such as Plato and Russell, proposed that verbs should be related to events or states in certain way. Both Ramsey (1924), and Hans Reichenbach (1947) once mentioned the concept of event in their works. An underlying event argument is introduced into the logical form of action sentences by Davidson (1967). From then on, this newly-added argument as an ontology has been taking on an important role in linguistic theorizing.

Without the underlying event argument, an intransitive verb, such as *to dance* in (1a) and a transitive one *to butter* in (2a) would be represented in first-order predicate logic as (1b) and (2b).

> (1) a. Mary dances.
>   b. Dance (Mary)
> (2) a. John buttered the toast.
>   b. Butter (John, the toast)

After introducing adverbial modifiers, the logic formula of sentences in (3) will be represented as those in (4) respectively:

> (3) a. John buttered the toast.
>   b. John buttered the toast in the bathroom.
>   c. John buttered the toast in the bathroom with a knife.
>   d. John buttered the toast in the bathroom with a knife at midnight.
> (4) a. Butter (J, the toast)
>   b. Butter (J, the toast, the bathroom)
>   c. Butter (J, the toast, the bathroom, a knife)
>   d. Butter (J, the toast, the bathroom, a knife, midnight)

Then some questions are waiting for answers. What is the lexical entry of BUTTER in lexicon? More exactly, how to determine the actual number of places for a given verb? If the "butter" in (4d) is set as its lexical entry in lexicon, all the other three would be the elliptical forms of it. However, it should be remembered that if necessary, the possible number of the arguments that a verb can take still can be increased further. As long as the NPs in adverbials are treated as arguments of the verb, it is impossible to decide the number of arguments that a verb can take, thus, the lexical entry for the verb in the lexicon is not possible to set. Furthermore, what is the relationship between these sentences in (3)?

3.1.1 Davidson's Analysis of Action Sentences

Davidson (1967) proposes that certain predicates take an implicit variable over event as an argument and these adverbial modifiers are treated as predicates of the hidden event variable, which provides a proper way to get out of the dilemma when facing adverbial modifiers such as *deliberately, slowly, in the bathroom, with a knife, at midnight*, In Davidson's original proposal, a predicate should have one more argument and this newly-added argument is an event variable which is existentially bounded. Based on such a proposal, the logical structures of sentences in (1a) and (2a) will be changed as (5) respectively:

(5) a. $\exists e$[Dance (Mary, e)]

b. $\exists e$ [Butter (John, the toast, e)]

A traditional intransitive verb is analyzed as expressing a two-place relation between an individual who dances, and a dancing event, while traditional transitive verb is expressed as a three-place relation between a buttering event, an individual who butters, and an entity what is buttered. With the increasing of the underlying event argument, some puzzles in traditional predicate logic are solved. The Davidsonian logical forms of the sentences in (3) are listed in (6):

(6) a. $\exists e$ [Butter (John, the toast, e)]

b. $\exists e$ [Butter (John, the toast, e) $\wedge$ In(the bathroom,e)]

c. $\exists e$ [Butter (John, the toast, e) $\wedge$ In(the bathroom,e)
$\wedge$ With(a knife, e)]

d. $\exists e$ [Butter (John, the toast, e) $\wedge$ In(the bathroom, e)
$\wedge$With(a knife, e) $\wedge$ At(midnight, e)]

According to (6d), the sentence (3d) expresses that there was an event of John buttering the toast, and this event took place in the bathroom, in addition, this event happened at midnight; and it was performed with a knife. With the introducing the underlying event variable, every adverbial gets its own target to modify.

Davidson's analysis is a refinement of the standard predicate logic, for an elegant intersective pattern of interpreting adverbials is provided, which is in analogous to the interpretation of adjectives. Firstly, the verb "butter" is consistently treated as a three-place predicate and adverbial modifiers are interpreted conjunctively. Secondly, it is indicated obviously that all the sentences (6b), (6c) and (6d) entail (6a). Davidson distinguishes indispensible places of the verbal predicate from those optional ones. All the indispensible ones are included in the parenthesis following the verb and all others are treated as independent conjuncts (Davidson 1969/1980: 167). Donald Davidson once claimed that:

> *"There is a lot of language we can make systematic sense of if we suppose events exist.", "Armed with the theory, we can always answer the question, "What are these familiar words doing here?" by saying how they contribute to the truth conditionals of the sentence".*
>
> Davison (1968: 94)

Besides enlarging the source of event variable, another concern of neo-Davidsonian paradigm is to extend the practice of treating the adverbial modifier as a separate conjunct to the regular argument of the predicate.

In order to get rid of such dilemma, neo-Davidsonian approach treats the participants of event analogously to the adverbial modifiers. In this pattern, verbs are uniformly treated as one-place predicates of eventualities, which means the event variable e is the only argument that the verb directly predicates of, while the other arguments such as, subject, direct object, are mapped respectively to the event variable e thorough their thematic roles. Each adjunct gives rise to its own clause in logical structure, and these are combined with the clause corresponding to the verb and its arguments by ordinary propositional conjunction. The existential binding of the event variable takes scope over the whole structure. Neo-Davidsonian logic forms of the sentences in (3) are given in (7) respectively:

(7) a. $\exists e$ [Butter (e) $\wedge$ Agt(John, e) $\wedge$ Th(the toast, e)]

    b. $\exists e$ [Butter(e) $\wedge$ Agt(John, e) $\wedge$ Th(the toast, e)

        $\wedge$ In(the bathroom, e)]

   c. ∃e [Butter(e) ∧ Agt(John, e) ∧ Th(the toast, e)
        ∧ In(the bathroom, e)∧ With(a knife, e)]
   d. ∃e [Butter(e) ∧Agt(John, e) ∧Th(the toast, e)
        ∧In(the bathroom, e) ∧With(a knife, e) ∧At(midnight, e)]

'Agt' is the abbreviation of 'agent' and 'Th' is abbreviated from 'theme'. Out of personal style, some semanticists (Chierchia & McConnell-Ginet 1990, Landman 2000, 2004, Rothestin 1998, 2001, 2004) express the logic forms in (7a, b) as (8a, b):

   (8) a. ∃e [Butter (e) ∧Agt(e)=j ∧Th(e)= t]
        b. ∃e [Butter (e)∧ Agt(e)=j∧ Th(e)= t ∧In(e)= b]

'j', 't', and 'b' means 'John', 'the toast', and 'the bathroom' respectively. Such logical forms appear different from those in (7). However, actually, there is no much difference. In our analysis, we will take the form in (8).

   In neo-Davidsonian paradigm, the distinction between arguments and modifiers is blurred, and it is impossible to tell arguments from adverbial modifiers apart from the logical form.

3.1.2 Parsons' Subatomic Semantics

   Vendler (1967) classifies situation types into four groups: states, activities, accomplishment and achievements. However, Davidson applies the underlying event variable to the action sentences only. So it is quite natural to explore the feasibility of extending the event variable to cover all the four groups in Vendler's classification. Higginbotham (1985, 2000), Parsons (1980, 1985, 1990) support that the source of event variable should not be confined to the action sentences, and they argue that any verbal predicate should include an underlying Davidsonian event argument.

   The position E corresponds to the "hidden" argument place
   for event, originally suggested by Donald Davidson (1967).
   There seem to be strong arguments in favor it, and little to be
   said against, extending Davidson's ideas to verbs other than

> *verbs of changes or action. Under this extension, statives will*
> *also have E-position*
>
>   Higginbotham (1985, 10)

Nowadays, scholars working in what has been called the neo-Davidsonian paradigm, following Higginbotham (1985, 2000) and Parsons (1990, 2000), assume that any predicate may introduce such a hidden event argument. That is, not only verbs, no matter eventive or stative, but also adjectives, nouns, and prepositions are capable of introducing Davidsonian eventuality arguments.[1] Motivation for this move comes from the observation that all kinds of predicates provide basically the same kind of empirical evidence that motivated Davison's proposal and thus call for a broader application of the Davisonian analysis. while some are against this trend (Krifka 1988, 1995, Maienborn 2005), some scholars (Higginbotham & Ramchand 1997)[2] advocate such extension.

Davidson's approach of introducing an underlying event variable and analyzing adverbial modifiers as separate propositions adjoining to the logic form through conjunctive operation is to maintain the entailment relationship in case of adjunct-dropping. While Davidson increases an event variable in the logical form, he keeps the consistency of the theta-grid of the verb and keeps the traditional arguments of the verb inside the parenthesis following it. When sentences in (3) are transformed into passive voice, Davidsonian approach will run into the same awkward situation just as traditional first-order logic facing in dealing with adjuncts.

---

[1] Parsons doesn't support that noun predicate also has an underlying event argument.

[2] Higginbotham & Ramchand (1997: 54) support the idea that all predicates introduce an event variable: *"Once we assume that predicates (or their verbal, etc. heads) have a position for events, taking the many consequences that stem therefrom, as outlined in publications originating with Donald Davidson (1967), and further applied in Higginbotham (1985, 1989), and Terence Parsons (1990), we are not in a position to deny an event-position for any predicate; for the evidence for, and applications of, the assumption are the same for all predicates."*

(9) a. The toast was buttered by John.

    b. ∃e [Butter (John, the toast, e)]

    c. ∃e [Butter (the toast, e) ∧ By(John, e)]

(10) a. The toast was buttered by John in the bathroom.

    b. ∃e [Butter (John, the toast, e) ∧ By(John, e)

        ∧ In(the bathroom, e)]

(9a) should be interpreted as (9b) or (9c)? If the logic structure of (9a) is (9b), what is the difference between an active form and a passive one? If the (9c) is the choice, the uniform of the lexical entry of "butter" cannot be maintained. Being confronted with such a challenge, it is quite natural to wonder whether it is practical to separate the arguments in the parenthesis after the verb in (6) in the same pattern in which modifiers are analyzed. Although Davidson himself rejects such extension, such extension both in the application categories of event variable and the separation of the argument is well-motivated and promising.

Terence Parsons, one of the leading figures of the neo-Davidsonian approach, subdivides formal logic formulas into two groups: atomic formulas and non-atomic formulas. Subatomic structures are the inputs of atomic formulas. Parsons (1990: 6) claims that "*Further, plenty of linguistic constructions in addition to adverbial modification can be well accounted for by positing underlying quantification over events.*" He applies the underlying event analysis extensively in the English language research, including, modifiers, causatives and inchoatives, tenses and temporal.

3.1.2.1 Decomposition of Event

David Dowty (1979) gives an analysis of causative and inchoative structure within the symbolism of Montague Grammar. His logic form of (11a) is (11b):

(11) a. Mary closes the door.

    b. (∃P)[P(Mary) CAUSE(BECOME(The door is closed))]

In (11b), 'CAUSE' connects two propositions: (∃P) [P (Mary)] and [BECOME (The door is closed)], and indicates the causal relation between these two propositions. 'BECOME' maps the proposition "the door is closed" into the proposition "the door became closed". Parsons took over the idea behind this proposed analysis, and incorporated this idea into a framework with underlying events.

> (12) a. Mary closes the door.
>   b. ∃e [Close(e) ∧ Cul(e) ∧Th(e)= door ∧Agt(e)= Mary]
>
>   Parsons (1990: 117)
>
>   c. ∃e [Cul(e) ∧ Agt(e)= Mary ∧ ∃e' [Cul(e')∧ Th(e')=door
>   ∧CAUSE(e, e') ∧ ∃s[Being-closed(s) ∧ Th(s)= door
>   ∧Hold(s) ∧ BECOME(e', s)]]]
>
>   Parsons (1990: 120)

Parsons (1990) argues that the (12b) is an incorrect analysis of (11a), because it leaves out the notion of causality and does not explain the ambiguities caused by causative verbs. He holds that causative-inchoatives are transitive verbs that are derived from a related adjective with meaning "cause to become ADJ", so the analysis he prefers is (12c), in which the causative-inchoative verb *to close* denotes an action *e* performed by agent *Mary* on the theme *the door*, and this action causes an event e'— *the door* entering a holding state *s* of being closed. From this analysis, we can find that the causative-inchoative verb is decomposed into three underlying event variables. The advantages of Parsons to decompose event are:

Firstly, the nature of causative verbs is explained more accurately. The relation between these extra sub-events or states derived from event decomposition can reflect the nature of the causative verbs more directly and disambiguate the causative verbs and common transitive verbs.

Secondly, a more explicit explanation is provided for modification. These extra underlying events and states are subject to modification by modifiers.

3.1.2.2 Thematic Roles

Thematic role or thematic relation refers to the role that an argument plays in relation to the state or event described by a verb. Dowty (1991:

572) lists the following properties of proto-agent and proto-patient respectively:

(13) Contributing properties for the Agent Proto-Role:
a. volitional involvement in the event or state
b. sentience and/or perception
c. causing an event or state in another participant
d. movement (relative to the position of another participant)
e. exists independently of the event named by the verb

(14) lists the contributing properties for Proto-Patient-Role:
a. under change of state
b. incremental theme
c. causally affected by another participant
d. stationary relative to movement of another participant
e. does not exist independently of the event, or not at all

Dowty (1991: 572)

Before introducing thematic roles into the logic form, Parsons does use the relational symbols as predicate to relate NP to the underlying event.

(15) a. Brutus stabs Caesar.
b. $\exists e[\text{Stab}(e) \wedge \text{Cul}(e) \wedge \text{Subj}(e)=b \wedge \text{Obj}(e)=c)]$

Parsons (1990: 72) claims that 'Subj' and 'Obj' just dummy placeholders for more specific "deep" thematic relations such as Agent and Theme. From the following chart, we can find that there is no one-to-one correspondence between the thematic role and its syntactic function. So Parsons advocates that thematic roles could be treated as event predicates to relate event participant to the event argument, which is a prominent trait of neo-Davidsonian approach. He assumes there are six possible thematic roles for DPs in English:

Role	Typical Position in Active Sentence
agent	subject
theme	direct object; subject of 'is'
goal	indirect object, or with 'to'
benefactive	indirect object, or with 'for'
Instrument (=performer)	subject; object of 'with'
Experiencer	subject

(Parsons 1990: 73-74)

Besides these thematic roles, Parsons (1990: 78-80) investigates the possibility that a participant in the underlying form might be classified as both Agent and Theme., and proposes that in certain cases an NP can have more than one thematic role.

(16) a. Sam will swim to Catalina.   (Agent-Theme)
     b. Bill will run behind the house.   (Agent-Theme)
     c. The cup rolled under the sofa   (Performer-Theme)

There are also Agent-Theme, Experiencer-Theme, and Performer-Theme. "Agent-Theme (a,x)" is an abbreviation for "Agent (a, x) & Theme (a, x)".

There are two reasons for introducing thematic role into the underlying event analysis. First, it provides a convenient way to describe verb extensions in purely semantic terms. The terms, such as subject, object, are rigidly stipulated names for the syntactic position, and the functions of the NPs under such umbrella terms are heterogeneous. Second, thematic roles provide a flexible and direct identification of the individuals that are involved in the verbs' denotation to replace the practice of depending on the order of NPs to determine their function in traditional predicate logic and Davidsonian approach. In fact, one of the major reasons for the popularity of neo-Davidsonian analyses is that it explicitly indicates the relationship between eventualities and their participants via thematic roles or by some kinds of event-decomposition.

3.1.3 A Comparison between these Two Approaches

Neo-Davidsonian approach is regarded as a new stage of Davidsonian approach out of the following reasons:

Firstly, the domain of the distribution of event argument is different. Davidson just applies his underlying event analysis in action sentences, and he denies that states should be treated as Davissonian individuals. Katz (2000, 2003) also expresses similar idea about the distribution of the e-argument. In the neo-Davidsonian stage, the event variable has been applied to all four groups of situation types in Vendler's classification. Later on, all predicates, including adjectives, nouns and even prepositions, introduce the event variable. However, Parsons (1990) states clearly that noun predicate should not take an underlying argument event.

Secondly, these two approaches account the participants of the event in different ways (Bayer, Samuel Louis 1996). Just like the traditional predicate logic, Davidsonian approach still depends on the order of the participants in the logic form to indicate their functions. However, neo-Davidsonian approach adopts a radically innovative strategy. Verbal predicate just denotes set of events, and every participant forms a relatively independent formula with the event variable e, then all these formulas are combined as conjuncts to form the logic form of a sentence.

Thirdly, thematic roles are introduced into the logic form in Neo-Davidsonian approach, and thematic roles appear as separate relational conjuncts relating event variable *e* to their participants (Parsons 1980, 1985, 1990; Landman 2000, 2004; Rothstein 2001, 2004). In Davidsonian approach, the verb contributes a multi-place predicate to logical form, with a place for the event, and others for NPs, and all the thematic roles disappear into the meaning of the verb.

Fourthly, the combination of all the formulas in terms of intersection with an existential quantifier at the end is a compositional process in (11), and exhibits the entailment relation directly in the classical diamond entailment pattern in (12).

(17) a. [agent]= $\lambda x[\lambda e[Agt(e)=x]]$
     b. [theme]= $\lambda x[\lambda e[Th(e)=x]]$

    c. [stab]= λe[Stab(e)]

    d. [(ag) Sam]= λe[Agt(e)=Sam]

    e. [(th) Cindy]= λe[Th(e)=Cindy]

    f. [Sam kiss Cindy]=(11c) $\wedge$ (11d) $\wedge$ (11e)

    g. [Sam kissed Cindy]= $\exists$e[(11c) $\wedge$ (11d) $\wedge$ (11e)]

(18) Sam kissed Cindy passionately in the classroom.

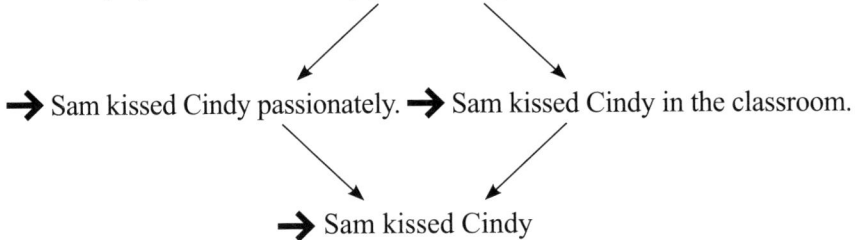

➡ Sam kissed Cindy passionately. ➡ Sam kissed Cindy in the classroom.

➡ Sam kissed Cindy

    Fifthly, Davidson (1967) just treats some of the prepositional phrases as the predicates of underlying events, and doubts the feasibility of analyzing "attributives" in the same way, which means that the theory just has a very narrow application. Parsons (1990) extents the application of the theory into the analysis of "attributes" such an "slowly", "violently", "gently".

3.1.4 The Properties of Event

    As LePore (1985: 151) puts it, "[Davidson's] central claim is that events are concrete particulars—that is, unrepeatable entities with a location in space and time". Although neo-Davidsonian paradigm has been undergoing some major or minor variations, both the Davidsonian and neo-Davidsonian paradigms assume the existence of the underlying event variable, and the core assumption of the event is consistent that eventualities are particular spatiotemporal entities in the world. However, such a highly abstract philosophical definition is not very workable for the semantics of natural languages. Just like the comment of Parsons on the Davidsonian approach: this abstract entity is not seen so much as an account of the semantics of natural languages but as a clause in Davidson's metaphysics of event and actions (Parsons 1990: 5).

    In the past decades, great efforts have been exerted to explore the precise and workable identity criteria for eventualities. Maienborn (2005) puts forward such questions concerning the ontological properties of underlying event argument: What does it mean for a predicate to have a Davidsonian eventuality argument? What linguistic properties follow from its presence? And what means are available to detect these hidden arguments? Of course, none of these questions has so far received anything like a definite answer, and many versions of the Davidsonian approach have been proposed, with major and minor differences between them.

Maienborn (2005: 297) provides a working definition of Davidsonian notion of eventualities:

> (19) Eventualities are particular spatiotemporal entities with functionally integrated participants.

Following this working definition, three ontological properties that are generally accepted are summarized in (20):

> (20) a. They are perceptible.
>   —Event expressions can be infinitival complements of perception verbs.
>   b. They can be located in space and time.
>   —Event expressions combine with locative and temporal modifiers.
>   c. They can vary in the way they take place.
>   —Event expressions combine with manner adverbials, instrumentals, comitatives, etc.
>   Maienborn (2005: 280)

The effectiveness of the diagnostics in (20) varies from language to language, especially the (20a). In Mandarin Chinese, there is no overt tense markings in morphology to distinguish finiteness from non-finiteness systematically (Hu, Pan & Xu 2001), so the first diagnostic is not reliable in Madarin Chinese.

3.2 Theory of Predication

As Kratzer (1996) discusses, a neo-Davidsonian approach to logical form does not entail that the syntax must be neo-Davisonian. Maintaining that the agent and the theme are syntactic arguments does not contradict with the idea that we consider representations in conceptual structure to be neo-Davidsonian. The derivation of the sentence is the process of building up the meaning semantically and syntactically. The linear logical form analysis can be realized as the syntactic tree diagram which contains different layers. A sentence is a binary structure including two different kinds of constituents which are traditionally known as subject and predicate. The VP-internal subject hypothesis supposes that the original position of the subject is within VP (Koopman and Sportiche 1991; Pollock 1989; and Fukui & Speas 1986).

(21) a. Tom hit John.
   b. $[_{IP}Tom_i [_{I'}[_{VP} t_i[_{V'}[_V Hit] John]]]]$

Syntactically, all arguments of the verb appear within the VP; the subject appears in the Spec of VP and moves to the surface subject position, with a trace left there at the original position. The VP-internal hypothesis assumes a different model of combination of elements, so the semantic representation will be changed accordingly. After the VP-internal subject hypothesis has been put forth, attempts have been made to give the corresponding semantic representation (Chierchia 1989; Wyner 1994).

(22) a. Tom hit John
   b. $[_{IP}(Tom) [_{I'} \lambda z[_{VP} (z)[_{V'}[_V \lambda y [\lambda x [Hit(x,y)](John)]]]]]]$
   c. $[_{IP}(Tom) [_{I'} \lambda z[_{VP} (z)[_{V'} \lambda x[Hit(x,John)]]]]]$
   d. $[_{IP}(Tom) [_{I'} \lambda z[_{VP} Hit(z, John)]]]$
   e. Hit (Tom, John)

In the semantic translation of the sentence in (16b), the verb takes two bounded variables as its arguments. With the introduction of the internal argument *John* and the λ-reduction operation, the verb is a relation which takes as its arguments *John* and a trace of the moved argument which is translated into a variable. As we can see in (16d), before the subject *Tom* entering into the semantic representation, the θ-grid of the verb has been saturated. In order to get the subject *Tom* into the relation, the saturated VP will be reopened by an operation of λ-abstraction. Finally, the semantic representation (16e) is derived.

In the neo-Davidsonian version of underlying event theory, as argued for in Higginbothan (1985), Parsons (1990), and Landman (1995, 2000), the verb *kiss* in (23b) binds an event variable *e*, and these two participants are variables bounded by lambda operators. (23a) has the representation in (23c):

(23) a. Mary kissed John.

b. $\lambda y[\ \lambda x[\lambda e\ [Kiss(e) \wedge Agt(e)= x \wedge Th(e)= y]]]$

c. $\exists e[Kiss(e) \wedge Agt(e)= Mary \wedge Th(e)= John\ ]$

In Rothstein (2001, 2004), she doesn't assume the VP-internal subject hypothesis. She assumes that the subject is base-generated in [Spec, IP] position, instead of being generated in [Spec, VP] and then moves to [Spec, IP]. She writes:

The grammatical theory of predication assumes that a predicate is a structurally open syntactic constituent; predication is relation between a predicate and a structurally closed constituent in which the latter closes the former by filling the open position in it. The element which closes a predicate is its subject

Rothstein (2001: 42)

She agrees that a set of thematic roles of a lexical head can be empty and keeps the neo-Davidsonian underlying event variable *e* in the semantic formula. In Rothstein's predication theory, (24a) is represented as (24b):

(24) a. Mary kissed John.

b. $\lambda y[\ \lambda e\ [Kiss(e) \wedge Agt(e)= x \wedge Th(e)= y]](John)$

In (24b), the subject is a free variable, which means that a constituent of type <e, t> will form after applying the verb to all the arguments inside its VP[①]. However, there is a typical mismatch, for VPs should be unsaturated and functional, while the expression which results from combing the verb with its internal argument is saturated. In order to absorb the subject, Rothstein introduces the predicate formation rule, which is equal to the operation of lambda abstraction.

> (25) Predicate Formation:
>   If α is the translation of a syntactic predicate then
> $\alpha \rightarrow \lambda x.\alpha$
>
>   Rothstein (2001: 138)

Such a lambda abstraction operation, which introduces bounded variable, is an operation which occurs automatically at the XP predicate level, and it occurs independently of whether the expression α contains a free variable x or not. The operation means that it permits vacuous λ-abstraction operation. The predicate formation rule is triggered by the category of the node and not by any thematic properties of the lexical head. Different from the expressions in type theory, in the event semantic analysis, the type of individual is marked as *d*; *e* is for the type of event; and t is truth value. Based on the predicate theory of Rothstein, (26) will be taken as a sample to illustrate the event semantic derivation process:

> (26) The derivation tree:

$\exists e\ [Kiss(e) \wedge Agt\ (e)=Mary \wedge Th(e)= John \wedge PAST(e)]$

(Existential quantification)

$IP\ \lambda e\ [Kiss(e) \wedge Agt(e)=Mary \wedge Th(e)=John \wedge PAST(e)]$

DP Mary $VP\ \lambda x[\lambda e[Kiss(e) \wedge Agt\ (e)=x \wedge Th(e)=John]]$

(predicate formation)

$V'\ [\lambda y[\lambda e[Kiss(e) \wedge Agt(e)=x \wedge Th(e)=John]]]$

$V\ \lambda y[\lambda e[Kiss(e) \wedge Agt(e)=x \wedge Th(e)=y]]$ John

Mary   kiss $< \theta_{Ag}, \theta_{Th}>$ John

---

① Here e stands for event.

It is usually assumed that the syntactic rules by which constituents are combined together are what syntacticians should care about. Semanticists should care more about the process of interpretation. However, in any meaningful structures, there is a systematic correspondence between syntax and semantics, or the set of syntactic structures and that of semantic structures are isomorphic to each other, which is obviously presented in the derivation process proposed by Rothstein. Such a dynamic and incremental derivation process is very valuable for the analysis of DPC, for that the semantic interpretation of possessive relation is unspecified. It will get specified incrementally with the derivation process going on.

3.3 Application of Event in Analyzing Possession

The combination of neo-Davidsonian analysis and syntactic theory has been throwing new light on the study of the argument structure.

3.3.1 Voice Proposed by Kratzer (1996)

Kratzer (1996) argues that the external argument is introduced not by the verb but by a separate predicate, which Kratzer calls Voice. Voice is a functional head denoting a thematic relation that holds between the external argument and the event described by the verb; it combines with the VP by a rule called Event Identification. *Voice* is used by Kratzer to add the condition that the event has an agent or experiencer or whatever one considers possible thematic roles for external arguments. Event Identification is stated in (27) (Kratzer 1996), "s" is the semantic type for eventualities:

(27) Event Identification

$$<e,<s,t>> <s, t> \rightarrow <e, <s, t>>$$

(28) a. Brutus stabbed Caesar

    b. Voice P

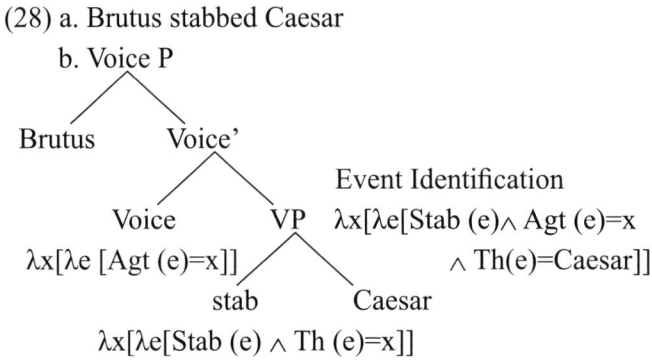

The proposal that external arguments are not true arguments of the verb was first made in Marantz (1984). Kratzer's proposal builds on Marantz's insight and develops a theory about how Marantz's idea can be executed in the syntax without sacrificing traditional assumptions about semantic composition and projection. In other words, Kratzer's theory is an account of how external arguments are syntactically introduced even though they are not projected by the verb.

Hole (2005) takes in the idea of VoiceP proposed by Kratzer and Binding Theory to explore the syntactic and semantic features of non-core arguments in German, Mandarin and English.

3.3.2 Functional Heads in Pylkkänen (2002, 2008)

Pylkkänen (2002, 2008) studies argument structure from the perspective of neo-Davidsonian analysis, in which a verb names a property of an eventuality, which is a cover term for events and states, and the syntactic arguments of the verb name event participants, that is, individuals who stand in thematic relations to the eventuality.

Pylkkänen (2002, 2008) proposes the mechanism of introducing the non-core argument via a functional head. There are seven kinds of functional heads to introduce different non-core arguments

The contrast between a core argument and a non-core argument is illustrated with the following examples in Pylkkänen (2008):

(29) a. The ice melted.

    b. John melted the ice.

c. John melted me some ice.

Pylkkänen (2008: 1)

The verb *melt* only needs to combine with an argument describing an entity undergoing the melting rpocess. In this sense, *the ice* is the core argument of the verb. However, as is indicated in (23b) and (23c), some other arguments such as the causer *John* and the beneficiary of the melting event *me* also get the access into the argument structure. Pylkkänen mainly focuses on how these non-core arguments are introduced into the argument structure. One of the main contributions of her is that she provides a new empirical argument for separating the external argument from its verb: even through external argument are obligatory in some syntactic environments, they are "additional" in that they involve an argument introducer that is separate from the verb. The so-called argument introducers in Pylkkänen's sense are functional heads. Pylkkänen labels functional heads according to their meanings.

(30) Functional heads to introduce arguments

Functional heads	Meaning
1 High applicative	thematic relation between an applied argument and the event described by the verb
2 Low recipient applicative	transfer-of-possessive relation between two individuals: asserts the direct object is *to* the possession of the indirect object.
3 Low source applicative	transfer-of-possessive relation between two individuals: asserts the direct object is *from* the possession of the indirect object.
4 Root-selecting Cause	relate a causing event to a category-free root
5 Verb-selecting Cause	relates a causing event to a verb
6 Phase-selecting Cause	relates a causing event to a phase
7 Voice (Kratzer 1996)	thematic relation between the external argument and the event described by the verb

As is shown in the table, functional heads proposed by Pylkkänen are not constrained in introducing subject. They are employed to introduce "non-core" arguments which are not selected by the predicate verbs but are related with either the event or the elements contained in the event semantically.

3.3.3 Possessive Relation DOC form Pylkkänen's Perspective

Based on the semantic difference, Pylkkänen divides applicative heads into two groups: high applicative and low applicative. The high applicative head, which is not related to the possessive relation, just denotes a thematic relation between an individual and the event described by the verb. Low applicative head, which doesn't involve in an event, combines with the direct object and denotes a transfer-of-possessive relation between the direct object and the applied argument.

(31) a. High applicative

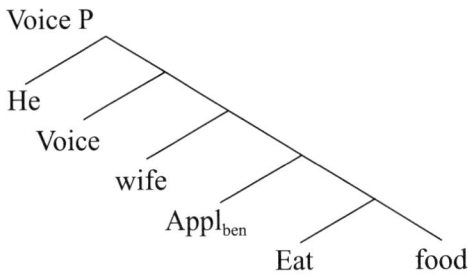

$$\text{Voice P}$$

```
Voice P
├── He
    └── Voice
        ├── wife
            └── Appl_ben
                ├── Eat
                └── food
```

b. Low applicative

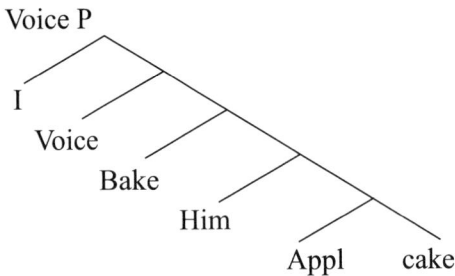

```
Voice P
├── I
    └── Voice
        ├── Bake
            └── Him
                ├── Appl
                └── cake
```

Pylkkänen (2002) differentiates possessor datives from traditional double objective constructions. It is possible to analyze these two constructions in a same syntactic pattern. If the possessive relation is taken into consideration, the alternation of the direction of the possessive relation, which is traditionally marked by "to" and "from", will be illustrated. Therefore, Pylkkänen uses "Pseudo-possessive Interpretation" to express the semantic difference between these two constructions. In the possessor-dative construction, the dative must be the possessor of the direct object, or at least be somehow responsible for it, while in the traditional Double Object Construction, possessiveness is not asserted. In other words, a double object construction is feliticious even if the indirect object does not end up "possessing" the direct object. "From" someone's possession, certainly means the person must have had the entity.

Such analyzes and formalization of possessive relation reveals the subtle semantic variation that is masked by the roughly similar syntactic structures.

3.4 Possessive Relation Illustrated in Wu Ping (2014)

Wu Ping (2014) studies Existential Construction in the event semantic perspective, and points out that Existential Construction in a broad sense is the intersective part of PSPO construction and Existential Construction. In Wu (2014), verbs are subdivided into *gua-type* and *fang-type*. The former type stipulates a location argument in the lexicon, while the latter type requires a location argument introduced by a functional head. This method has something similar to that in Pylkkänen (2002, 2008). The differences in function and position between these two kinds of location arguments are illustrated in (32):

(32) a. $\exists e[\text{ Fang}(e) \wedge \text{Loc}(e)=\textit{zhuozishang} \wedge \text{ Th}(e)= \textit{yibenshu}]$
$\quad\quad\quad|\quad\quad\quad\quad\quad\quad\quad\quad$ Existential closure
$\quad$ EventP $\lambda e[\text{Fang}(e) \wedge \text{Loc}(e)=\textit{zhuozishang} \wedge \text{ Th}(e)= \textit{yibenshu}]$

zhuozishang $\quad\quad\quad\quad\quad\quad\quad\quad$ predicate formation
$\quad\quad\quad\quad$ VP $\lambda e[\text{Fang }(e) \wedge \text{Loc}(e)=x \wedge \text{ Th}(e)= \textit{yibenshu}]$

$\quad\quad\quad\quad$ V $\quad\quad$ *yibenshu*
$\quad\quad$ $\lambda y[\lambda e[\text{Fang }(e) \wedge \text{Loc}(e)=x \wedge \text{ Th}(e)= y]]$

b. $\exists e[Loc(e)=qiangshang \wedge \exists e'[Gua (e') \wedge Th(e')= \textit{liangding maozi}]$

| Existential closure

EventP $\lambda e[Loc(e)=\textit{qiangshang} \wedge \exists e'[Gua (e') \wedge Th(e')= \textit{liangding maozi}]]$

qiangshang   Event'$\lambda x[\lambda e[Loc(e)=x \wedge \exists e'[Gua (e')$
$\wedge Th(e')= \textit{liangding aozi}]]]$

Event$_{LOC}$ VP $\lambda e[Gua (e) \wedge Th(e)= \textit{lingding maozi}]$

$\lambda P[\lambda x[\lambda e[Loc(e)=x \wedge \exists e'[P(e')]]]$

V   liangding maozi

$\lambda x[\lambda e[Gua (e) \wedge Th(e)= x]]$

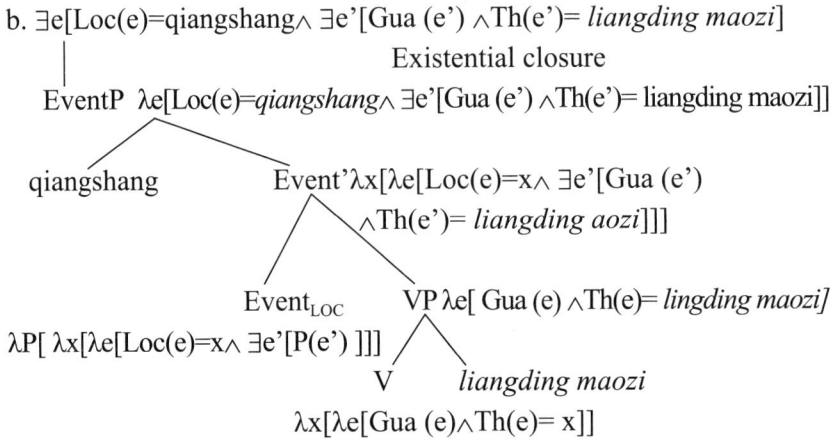

Possessive relation is another focus in Wu (2014). He explains the cognitive mechanism, by which the possessor-subject and possessum-object construction can be interpreted as Existential Construction in a broad sense. He further states that the subcategory of Existential Construction expressing disappearing is not the same as the other two subcategories of Existential Constructions. By the addition of the predicate "Having" into the functional head, the semantic derivation process is dicpicted in great details as in (33):

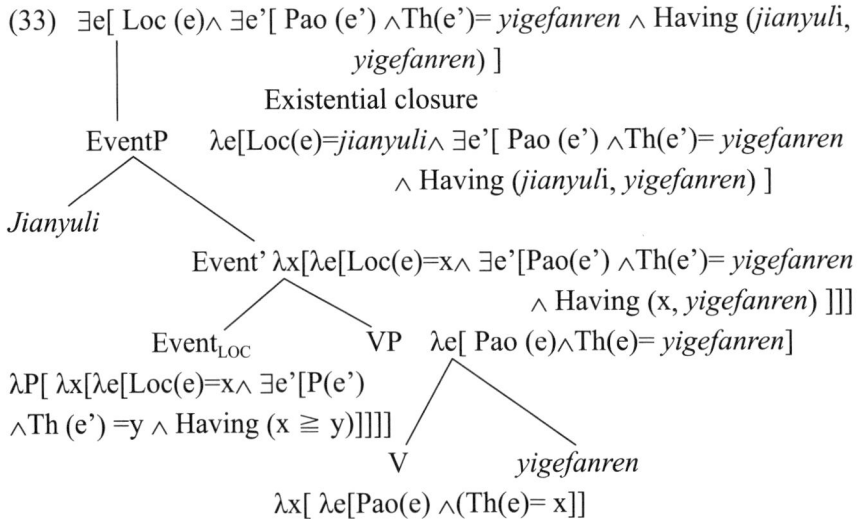

(33) $\exists e[Loc (e) \wedge \exists e'[Pao (e') \wedge Th(e')= \textit{yigefanren} \wedge Having (\textit{jianyuli}, \textit{yigefanren})]$

| Existential closure

EventP $\lambda e[Loc(e)=\textit{jianyuli} \wedge \exists e'[Pao (e') \wedge Th(e')= \textit{yigefanren}$
$\wedge Having (\textit{jianyuli}, \textit{yigefanren})]$

Jianyuli

Event' $\lambda x[\lambda e[Loc(e)=x \wedge \exists e'[Pao(e') \wedge Th(e')= \textit{yigefanren}$
$\wedge Having (x, \textit{yigefanren})]]]$

Event$_{LOC}$ VP $\lambda e[Pao (e) \wedge Th(e)= \textit{yigefanren}]$

$\lambda P[\lambda x[\lambda e[Loc(e)=x \wedge \exists e'[P(e')$
$\wedge Th (e') =y \wedge Having (x \geqq y)]]]]$

V   *yigefanren*

$\lambda x[\lambda e[Pao(e) \wedge (Th(e)= x]]$

As we can see, there is an EventP at the top of the derivational tree, by which Wu could include all the nodes in the tree into the framework of the event semantics. Here, the Event P is totally different from that in syntactic analysis, which is mainly concerning about the verb. The EventP in Wu (2014) roughly equals to a proposition, including the constituents and the tense and aspect feature of the sentence. The EventP in Wu's theory is the layer above the VP and includes the tense since the event occupies space and time. Our analysis will base on the EventP theory and is confined to the Event P. Usually the EventP doesn't go beyond the IP layer.

3.5 Summary

The syntactic/semantic mismatch embodied on the non-core argument in the discontinuous possession constructions is the focus of this dissertation. After the analysis of the basic property of the construction, we try to find out the syntactic mechanism that is capable of introducing the non-core argument and obtain a reasonable explanation for the possessor semantically.

We adopt the eventuality analysis to analyze the DPCs. From the perspective of the event, each argument may have the predicate of its own and what is more, there can be relation between the events as well as the relation between arguments. In a sense, there is no "non-core" argument in the construction. That's the contribution made by Parsons by proposing subatomic semantics. Parson's theory can be employed to analyze the event and it can also illustrate the connection between the event and the eventuality, which enables the theory to cover more language phenomenon. The approach can be applied to describe and account for different kinds of constructions. The description of the eventuality makes it possible for us to demonstrate the role of each element in the combination of the structure. The eventuality can be divided into atom event and the atom event can be further decoded into subatomic event, until the meaning generated at each layer gets interpreted.

The analysis of the eventuality is to decode the whole event into smaller component parts, but the semantic analysis can not take place of syntactic derivation. The approach to introduce functional node proposed by Pylkkänen paves the way to show the function of the syntax playing in generating the meaning. Xiong (2014) proposes functional categories to introduce arguments as well. The process is just the opposite to the eventuality analysis. It is the process to establish the meaning. Wu (2014) has already applied the functional node to the broad-sensed Existential Construction. We will follow his approach and try to apply the analysis to possessive constructions in Mandarin Chinese. According to different sources and features of the possession, we will take eventuality analysis and describe the constructions in Logic Form. In order to make our analysis more clearly, we also turn to type theory and other formal semantic means when it is necessary.

Chapter Four

Possessive Relation Triggered by Relational Nouns

The possessive relation is a kind of semantic relationship between two nominal terms in nature. It denotes the relation between two entities and it is a kind of structure by itself in the language structure. The "Belonging_to" relationship between two nominals is represented by different positions the possessor and the possessum occupy in possessive constructions.

As the result, possessor and possessum nominals behave differently when used independently. The degree that they depend on each other is quite different, which decides their performance in the construction. Some possessum nominals depend so much on possessive relation that they are a kind of argument-taking nouns which require its possessor to function independently as its argument. Section 4.1 will illustrate the definition, the classifications of inalienable possession and try to describe the relational nouns in a formal way. 4.2 proposes the type-raising analysis to ensure the semantic derivation of the construction since in functional application computation, the type of predicate verbs and the type of relational nouns do not go with each other. The Extended Logic Semantic Analysis is introduced because we need to deal with complex language constructions.

4.1 Inalienable possession

In the former part, we talk about the function of PR in satisfying the unsaturated meaning of the sentence in those with possessive relation as (1a) and (1b). With the PR and the possessive relation existing in the sentence, both sentences in (1) are well-formed sentences. While without the PR and possessive relation, (2a) is an independent sentence and (2b) is not a good sentence to be used independently. The degree to which the PM is attached to PR is different. Inalienable possession requires the PR in the sentence in order to ensure the status of the sentence both at syntactic level and at the semantic level. Alienable possession doesn't impose so strict requirements on PR.

(1) a. 张三丢了钱包。
   Zhangsan diu-le   qianbao.
   Zhangsan lose-Perf wallet
   "Zhangsan has lost the wallet."

   b. 张三丢了弟弟。
   Zhangsan diu-le   didi.
   Zhangsan lose-Perf brother
   "Zhangsan lost his brother."

(2) a. 钱包丢了。
   Qianbao diu-le.
   wallet lose-Perf
   "The wallet was lost."

   b. ? 弟弟丢了。
   ?Didi diu-le.
   brother lose-Perf
   "Brother was lost."

Possession is divided into two kinds: alienable possession and inalienable possession according to the inherent relationship between two entities. As the PM in inalienable possession, it presupposes the existence of the PR semantically. If there is no PR coexisting in the sentence, the sentence containing only PM is usually not an independent sentence. That is to say, it is compulsive for the PR to coexist with the

PM in a sentence with inalienable PM. The inalienable noun carries its PR information in the lexicon, which is in the form of a variable. PR variable must get satisfied in the conversation. The inalienable noun is a two-place argument predicate.

The following sentences are well-formed sentences with possessive relation.

(3) a. 张三喜欢汤姆的妈妈。

Zhangsan   xihuan Tom de mama.

Zhangsan   like Tom   De mother.

"Zhangsan likes Tom's mother."

b. 张三喜欢妈妈。

Zhangsan xihuan mama.

Zhangsan like   mom.

"Zhangsan likes his mom/speaker's mom."

(4) a. 张三打了李四的弟弟。

Zhangsan da-le   Lisi de didi.

Zhangsan beat-Perf Lisi De didi.

"Zhangsan beat Lisi's younger brother."

b. 张三把弟弟打了一顿。

Zhangsan   ba didi   da-le yidun.

Zhangsan   Ba brother beat-Perf one CL.

"Zhangsan beat his brother once."

With the possessive marker *de* to go between Tom and *ma ma*, the constitute of possessive phrase shows the possession clearly with the head word PM and the modifier PR. The mother is definitely "Tom's mother" in (3a). In (3b), there is no such internal possessive constitute to clearly denote the possession. *Mama* has three possible interpretations: the first is "Zhangsan's mother", which means Zhangsan likes his own mother. The second interpretation is that *mama* is the speaker's mother, which means Zhangsan likes speaker's mother. The third interpretation is that *mama* is a generic term. *Mama* must be interpreted to be the social status of being a mother. In (4a) *didi* is Lisi's brother and in (4b), the subject *Zhangsan* again is interpreted to be the possessor of *didi*. The variable carried by kinship relational nouns should be fulfilled within the sentence. Besides kinship terms, the body part-whole nominals impose the same constrains on the semantics of the nominal. For example, in (5a) and (5b), body-part nominals are the relational nouns which occupy object positions.

> (5) a. 李四伤了手。
>   Lisi shang-le shou.
>   Lisi hurt-Perf hand.
>   "Lisi had his hands hurt."
>   b. 张三打断了李四一条腿。
>   Zhangsan daduan-le Lisi yi-tiao tui.
>   Zhangsan break-Perf Lisi one CL leg.
>   "Zhangsan has broken one of Lisi's legs."

The hand in (5a) must be "Lisi's hand" and the leg belongs to Lisi in (5b). *Shou* and *tui* are the nominals which denote the body parts and they seek for the whole body nominal to realize the full interpretation. The relationship of being the body part and the whole is the typical inalienable possession.

As for what is inalienable possession, a wealth of alternative terminologies and characterizations has been proposed. The inalienable category has been called "intimate", "inherent", "inseparable", or even "abnormal" while the alienable categories have been labeled "non-intimate", "accidental", "acquired", "transferable", or "normal" (Nichols 1988, 1992; Chappell and McGregor 1996).① All these terms show the different features of the two kinds of possession from different aspects. In the meanwhile, The scope of inalienable possession is quite different according to different definitions.

Guéron (2006: 590) holds that inalienable possession is a construal associated with certain structures which contain two nominals: one that denotes a body part and the other that denotes the possessor of the body part. These two nominals form a single constituent when a DP denoting

---

① Inalienable possession can be shown at lexical level. For example we have compound adj as "heart breaking" and "hear-broken". In both the constructions the relation between heart and the possessor remained the same.

the possessor is embedded in a DP denoting the body part.

Heine (1997-10) tries to list the definite types of the nouns. Items belonging to any of the following conceptual domains are likely to be treated as inalienable relationship:

(a) Kinship roles

(b) Body-parts

(c) Relational spatial concepts, like "top", "bottom"

(d) Parts of other items, like "branch", "handle"

(e) Physical and mental states, like "strength" "fear"

(f) Nominalizations, where the "possessee" is a verbal noun,
for example: "his singing", "the planting of bananas"

In addition, there are a number of individual concepts in a given language that may be treated inalienably, such as "name, voice, smell, shadow, footprint and property etc".

Chappell and McGregor (1996) propose the following four kinds of relationship that tend to be associated with inalienability:

(a) A close biological or social bond between two people (kin)

(b) Integral relationship (body-parts and other parts of a whole)

(c) Inherent relationship (spatial relations)

(d) Essential for one's livelihood or survival

Nichols (1988,1992) proposes the following implicational hierarchy for the semantic membership of inalienable classes:

(i) kin terms and/or body-parts;

(ii) part-whole and/or spatial relations and

(iii) culturally basic possessed items.

Heine's definition is more specific with the lists of the kinds of items which can form relationships. Chappell and McGregor's (1996) definition is general and wide and is more like a tool to delimit the domain and to define its status. What is more, the way inalienability is defined in a given language is largely dependent on culture-specific conventions. Among the definitions, we can identify three core domains: (a) kinship; (b) body-parts and (c) spatial relations. Kinship and part/wholes and body-parts are considered to be typically included in inalienable possession. Such kind of relationship is "permanent contact", but there is no "control" between the two entities. In fact, as far as the whole body is concerned, body-parts nominals also compose a kind of "part-whole" relation with the functional whole.

In Mandarin Chinese, we all acknowledge that kinship terms and part-whole nominals are relational nouns with PR in the lexicon. Other kinds listed in Heine (1997) are treated in Mandarin Chinese quite differently. Words like *ding* "top", *di* "bottom", b*ashou* "handle" can be listed under the category of par-whole category. For example, *ba shou* "handle" should be part of a physical entity. *Men Bashou* "the handle of the door", *chouti bashou* "the handle of the drawer". The abstract nouns as *li liang* "strength", *kongju* "fear" don't need the PR information to be used independently. They belong to common nouns with abstract concept. There is no PR information attached to these abstract concepts in the lexicon. Whether the Nominalizations should be treated as a sub-type of possessive construction is still a hot issue in Mandarin Chinese study. Some nouns denoting property are considered to be relational nouns, such as *jiage, zhiliang*.

Therefore, we propose a definition for the inalienable possession in Mandarin Chinese in this dissertation. The inalienable possession in Mandarin Chinese includes two types:

(i) Kin terms denoting the kinship relation like *baba, mama.*
(ii) Part-whole relation (including body-parts) like *yezi, shou, jiage.*

The concepts of the "part" and "whole" in the definition are confined to the noun with physical identity forms, that is, they denote physical objects in the real world. Here the entity serving as the whole can not be an abstract or psychology concept. For example: *zhuozitui men bashou. Zhuozi* and *men* are physical objects that function as the whole.

Inalienable noun terms are called relational nouns as well. According to Taylor (2000), just as the verb denotes "syntactic gap" which can be fulfilled by arguments in the sentence, relational nouns contain "semantic gap" in nature. Words like *qizi,tui* need its PR to be fully interpreted semantically. These kinds of nouns are stored in the lexicon in the form of *x de qizi*. For example, *tou* as a body-part nominal and body-parts are standardly assumed to be relational or functional nouns. They not only have referential arguments, but also are loaded with arguments for the possessor of the body-part.

Partee (2001) argues that both common nouns and relational nouns characterize the entities filling their "referential role" as belonging to a certain "sort". Relational nouns differ from simple sortal nouns in having an additional argument place. They describe their referents not only as being of a certain "sort" but as standing in a certain relation to some other entity or entities. Using "Thing" as a place-holder for a sortal property and "Related-to" as a place-holder for a relation, the basic scheme of the interpretation of a simple sortal N is as in (6a) and that of a relational N as in (6b)

(6) a. $\lambda x[\text{Thing}(x)]$

    b. $\lambda y [\lambda x [\text{Thing}(x) \& \text{Related-to-y} (x)]]$

Rothstein (2004) mentions that $<d, t>$ and $<d,<d, t >>$ are types of one and two place functions from individuals to truth-values. The first is the type of simple common nouns like "book" and the second the type of the relational nouns like "mother of".

The interpretation of the relational nouns in this way means that there will be two arguments in the frame of the logical form. For example, the lexical entry for "head" is given in (7).

(7) Head: $\lambda x[\lambda y [\text{head}(x) \& \text{body-part of y} (x)]]$

We use "Belonging_to (y,x)" as the predicate to denote the inalienable possessive relation in the dissertation. The lexical meaning of verbal phrase "belong to" is to denote the relationship between the part and the whole. "Belonging_to" functions as the logical predicate denoting the abstract possessive relation. This kind of possessive relation does not emphasize the controlling power that the whole has over the part, instead, it focuses on the dependence and attachment that the part has towards the whole. Kinship relation to some degree is a kind of "Belonging_to" relation. An individual is a member of a social group and in a sense, he/she belongs to that social group. We can revise (7) into (8):

(8) Head: $\lambda x[\text{Belonging\_to (head, x)}]$

It is evident that "Belonging_to" is the predicate of two-place arguments denoting inalienable possessive relation between two arguments. This kind of relationship should be fulfilled compulsively in the construction.

A basic sortal noun of type $<e,t>$ has a referential role and a characterizing property. A relational noun's referential role is characterized as one term of a relation. Alienable nouns are of one-place argument predicates. Words like *shu*, *diannao*, *qiche* do not entail possessive relation by themselves. Sentence like *yi zhi bi diule* can be independent syntactically, but it tells almost nothing specific and does not contain enough information to be used in the real communication. It is not sufficient semantically and needs to be further defined to denote the referential entity in order to be used in the communication. The task can be fulfilled by *zhe* or *na* "this or that", PR nominal or the context. When the possession is the option to change an indefinite NP to definite NP, the information about PR is not part of *yi zhi bi*. The possessive relation is triggered not by the noun itself but by other elements.

(9) a. 我丢了钱包。
　　Wo diu-le　qianbao.
　　I　lose-Perf　wallet.
　　"I have the wallet lost"
　b. 我的钱包丢了。
　　Wo de　qianbao diu-le.
　　I　De　wallet　lose-Perf.
　　"My wallet is lost".

(9a) entails (9b) and the possessive relation between *wo* and *qianbao* is triggered by the verb *diu* in Existential Construction.

The observations show that the PR variant contained in the inalienable possession noun must be fulfilled in the sentence. Generally speaking, the identification and interpretation of the PR is clear in a simple sentence like (9). When the sentence structure becomes complex with embedded clause, the identification and interpretation of the PR give rise to some difficulties. For example:

(10) a. 张三给弟弟打了电话。
　　　　Zhangsan gei didi da-le dianhua.
　　　　Zhangsan give didi do-Perf phone call.
　　　　"Zhangsan called his brother."
　　 b. 张三让李四给弟弟打了电话。
　　　　Zhangsan rang Lisi gei didi da-le dianhua.
　　　　Zhangsan ask Lisi give didi do-Perf phone call.
　　　　"Zhangsan asked Lisi to give a phone call to his brother."
　　 c. 张三让李四把弟弟叫来。
　　　　Zhangsan rang Lisi ba didi jiaolai.
　　　　Zhangsan ask Lisi Ba brother call come.
　　　　"Zhangsan let Lisi call his brother to come."

In (10a)-(10c), there is a relational noun *didi* that asks for the PR nominal. In (10a), it is quite clear that *didi* is "Zhang San's brother", while in (10b) and (10c) , both *Zhangsan* and *Lisi* are able to serve to be the possessor of *didi*. In these two sentences, *didi* tends to be "Lisi's brother", since *Lisi* is closer to *didi*.

According to Croft (1990), "Adjacency Principle" [①]works at all grammatical levels, ranging from sentence, phrase and lexicon. This rule requires the components which are closely related syntactically and semantically occupy nearest positions in syntactic structure. *Didi* lies in the same syntactic constitution with *Lisi* so that it gains priority in the interpretation. We may add pronoun to further illustrate the point.

---

① Adjacensy principle is used in GB to set the order of the complement. According to the rule, the complete which receives the case can lie before the complement that without the case. That is to make sure the complete is adjacent to it functional head.

(11) a. 张三 ᵢ 让李四 ⱼ 给他 ᵢ/ⱼ 弟弟打了电话。

　　　Zhangsan$_i$ rang Lisi$_j$ gei ta $_{i/j}$ didi da-le dianhua.

　　　Zhangsan let Lisi give him brother do-Perf phonecall.

　　　"Zhangsan$_i$ let Lisi$_j$ give his$_{i/j}$ brother a phone call."

　　b. 张三 ᵢ 让李四 ⱼ 他 ᵢ/ⱼ 自己弟弟打了电话。

　　　Zhangsan$_i$ rang Lisi$_j$ gei ta $_{i/j}$ ziji didi da-le dianhua①.

　　　Zhangsan let Lisi give himself brother do-Perf phonecall.

　　　"Zhangsan$_i$ let Lisi$_j$ give his$_i$ brother a phone call."

(11a) may have two kinds of interpretations, since the personal pronoun can refer to both *Lisi* and *Zhangsan*. In (11a), *didi* just goes with *ta* to form the possessive relation. *Didi* in (11b) takes *Zhangsan* to be its possessor since if *Zhangsan* is the priority interpretation, then *ziji de* will become redundant. This is the evidence for the conclusion we reach for (10b) and (10c).

When inalienable relational nouns exist in the sentence, the PR as a semantic variant should be realized as an overt lexical element. It is the nature of the inalienable possession that brings possessive relation into the sentence. In this chapter, we first focus on the derivation of the sentence with relational nouns.

4.2 Type-raising analysis

The possessive relation in the construction can be introduced by relational nouns right from the lexicon. From the surface structure of the construction, there is no difference between the constructions with relational nouns and those without. For example, in (12), we get the same linear structure as "NP$_1$+VP+NP$_2$". The same syntactic structure doesn't ensure the same interpretation of the structure. In (12a), besides the grammatical meanings to be agent and theme, there is additional possessive relation interpretation between *Zhangsan* and *fuqin*. The possessive relation is absent in (12b). The logic forms of the two sentences may help us tell the difference of the contributions.

---

① The example is discussed in the class to check the interpretation of possession

(12) a. 张三喜欢父亲。

   Zhangsan xihuan fuqin.

   Zhangsan like father.

   "Zhangsan likes his/speaker's father."

  b. 张三喜欢这本书。

   Zhangsan xihuan zheben shu.

   Zhangsan like this-CL book.

   "Zhangsan likes this book."

If we do not take the speaker into the consideration, *baba* in (12a) must be Zhangsan's father while the book does not necessarily belong to *Zhangsan*. What implies in fact is that there is no possessive relation between *Zhangsan* and the book. The difference should be included in their logic forms:

(13) a. ∃s [Xihuan(s)∧ Experiencer(s)=*Zhangsan* ∧ Th(s)= *zhebenshu*]

   b. ∃s [Xihuan(s)∧ Experiencer(s)=*Zhangsan* ∧ Th(s)=*fuqin* ∧Belonging_ to (*fuqin, Zhangsan*)]

When we compare (13a) with (13b), the difference lies in the additional part denoting possessive relation. "Belonging_to (*fuqin, Zhangsan*) " part is added to the logic form to represent the possession property demonstrated in the construction.

Since *Zhangsan* is a proper noun and *zhebenshu* is a definite noun phrase with "this" to be its determiner, both *Zhangsan* and *zhebenshu* are of the type <d> arguments[①]. The transitive verb *xihuan* 'like' is of the type <d,<d, t>>, which takes two arguments. It follows natural step in functional application computation.

[①] Following Rothstein, we use <d> to denote entity; <e> for event and t stands for truth,which is the semantic type for sentence.

(14) EventP $<t>$ $\exists s[Xihuan(s) \wedge Exp(s)=Zhangsan \wedge Th(s)= zhebenshu]$

Existential closure

$<e,t>$

Zhangsan $<d>$ Event' $\lambda x[\lambda s\ [Xihuan(s) \wedge Exp(s)=x \wedge Th(s)= zhebenshu]]$

Predicate formation $<d,<e,t>>$

$<e,t>$

VP $\lambda s\ [Xihuan(s) \wedge Exp(s)=x \wedge Th(s)= zhebenshu]$

V $<d,<e,t>>$ *zhebenshu* $<d>$

$\lambda y\ [\ \lambda e[Xihuan(s) \wedge Th(s)=y \wedge Exp =x\ ]]$

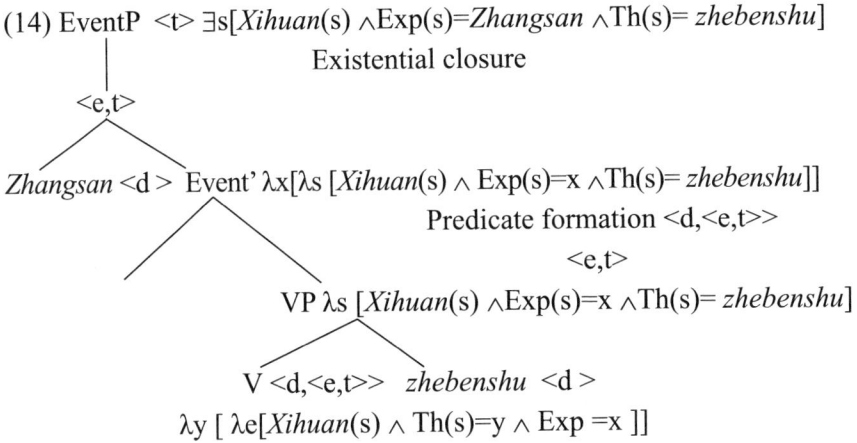

When the object noun is the proper noun of the type $<d>$, it is taken by the predicate verb of $<d,<e,t>>$ as the argument, then the VP node will be of the type $<e,t>$, which can not take in any variable. According to Rothstein (2004), the predication is formed at VP layer, which enables the variable in VP to be bounded and the semantic type of the VP to be raised to be $<d,<e,t>>$. *Zhangsan*, as the subject, is the last argument to be incorporated into the structure. After the event closure, we get the sentence of semantic type of $<t>$. There is no possessive relation added to the construction during the process.

When the object is the relational noun of the type of $<d, t>$, the possessor information is loaded with the possessum nominal in the semantic meaning in the form of a variable. The variable is unsaturated and needs to be fulfilled in the construction. The relational noun has different semantic type from the common noun and proper noun.

When we come to the derivation of (12b), functional application can not be conducted directly to the predicate verb of type $<d,<e, t>>$, since the type of the relational noun of is $<d, t>$. We adopt type raising analysis to raise the semantic type of the verb to ensure the derivation of the structure. That is, the verb of the type $<d,<e, t>>$ is raised to the type of $<<d, t>, <d,<e, t>>>$. In order to ensure the Functional Application[①], we propose the semantic type raising rule for the verb in taking relational nouns as the argument in this dissertation:

---

① Functional Application is the computation conducted in deriving the construction. It is the logic predicate that takes in argument.

(15) Type raising rule for the verb in taking relational nouns:

V	N	VP
$<d,<e,t>>$	$<e,t>$	$<d,<e,t>>$
$<<d,t>, <d,<e,t>>>$	$<e,t>$	$<d,<e,t>>$

With the rule to ensure the application, we can express the derivation process of (12a) in (16):

(16) a. $\exists s$ [Xihuan(s)$\wedge$ Exp(s)=$Zhangsan\wedge$Th(s)=$fuqin$
$\wedge$Belonging_ to($fuqin$, $Zhangsan$)]

   b. [xihuan]$_V$ $\rightarrow$ $\lambda y[\lambda s$[Xihuan (s) $\wedge$Exp(s)=x$\wedge$Th(s)=y]]

   c. [xihuan fuqin]$_{V'}$$\rightarrow$[$\lambda y[\lambda s$[Xihuan(s) $\wedge$Exp(s)=x$\wedge$Th(s)=y]
($fuqin$[λx [Belonging_to($mama$, x)])
=λs[Xihuan(s) $\wedge$Exp(s)=x$\wedge$Th(s)= $fuqin$[λx [Belonging_
to ($fuqin$, x)]]

   d. [xihuan fuqin]$_{VP}$$\rightarrow$$\lambda x[\lambda s$[Xihuan(s) $\wedge$Exp (s)=x $\wedge$Th(s)= $fuqin$
[Belonging_to ($fuqin$,x)] (by type raising)

   e. [Zhangsan xihuan fuqin]$_{IP}$$\rightarrow$ $\lambda x[\lambda s$[Xihuan(s)$\wedge$Exp (s)=x
$\wedge$Th(s)= $fuqin$[Belonging_ to ($fuqin$,x)] (Zhangsan)
=λs[Xihuan(s)$\wedge$Exp (s)=$Zhangsan\wedge$Th(s)= $fuqin$
[Belonging_to ($fuqin$, Zhangsan)]

   f. Existential quantification leads to: $\exists s$ [Xihuan(s)
$\wedge$Exp (s)=$Zhangsan\wedge$Th(s)= $fuqin$ $\wedge$ Belonging_
to($fuqin$, Zhangsan)]

EventP $\exists s$[Xihuan (s) $\wedge$ Exp (s)=$Zhangsan$ $\wedge$ Th(s)= $fuqin$
$\wedge$ Belonging_ to($fuqin$, Zhangsan)]

Existential closure

EventP λs[Xihuan (s) $\wedge$ Exp (s)=$Zhangsan$ $\wedge$ Th(s)= $fuqin$
$\wedge$ Belonging_ to (fuqin, $Zhangsan$)]

Zhangsan <d>   VP λx [λs [Xihuan(s) $\wedge$ Exp(s)=x $\wedge$ Th(s)=λx
$\wedge$ Belonging_to(*fuqin*,x)]]
$<d,<e,t>>$

V

λP [λy[λs[Xihuan(s) $\wedge$ Exp(s)=x   *fuqin* λx [Belonging_ to (*fuqin*, x)]
$\wedge$ Th(s)= y$\wedge$ P(y,x)]]] $< d, t >$
$<<d,t>, <d,<e,t>>>$

"There was a singular event *Zhangsan xihuan fuqin*, in which Zhangsan is the agent, *fuqin* is the theme." In the derivation process, the experiencer is a free variable x, and it is unbounded until the operation of type raising of the verb. The motivation for the verb to raise the type is due to the possessive relation carried by relational nouns. After the operation, the agent noun becomes bounded since all the arguments are involved in the same event. The underlying event argument is always bounded by the lambda operator, until the last existential quantification operation. At the IP level, the event existential closure over the event argument takes place, and type< *t* > is finally brought out. The "Existential Closure" is a type-shifting operator applied in order to produce a sentence of type< *t* > (Landman 2000). Sentences come to describe eventualities via an operation over an unsaturated event variable.

When relational noun *fuqin* serves as the argument to go with type-raised verb *xihuan* in functional application, λy is substituted and possessive relation is introduced into the construction. The key point in this step is that the variable becomes bounded and the VP node is of the type <d,<e,t>> with the bounded variable for both the agent of the event and the possessor of the theme. The reason for the type raising of the verb is the possessive relation that is carried by relational nouns. After the verb raises its type, it is of the most complicated semantic type <<d,t>, <d,<e,t>>> and becomes the predicate for the whole construction. It is loaded with all the information that the construction needs and there is no free variable in the construction until the agent nominal takes the place of both the subject position and the bounded variable of possessor. The motivation for the change is to build up the possessive relation between the subject and the object during the normal derivation of the sentence.

4.3 Extended Logic Semantic Analysis

The proposal to raise the semantic type of the verb is to follow the

"Extended Logic Semantic Analysis" in Wu (2007).① The key point of the analysis is to extend the usage of Logic Semantic Analysis to describe the language phenomenon found in Mandarin Chinese. In semantic analysis, the classical formal method is as the following: the semantic interpretation corresponds to syntactic structure. Besides the basic rules, two principles are applied to the analysis: one is to reset the semantic type of a certain element; the other is Logic Predicate Principle. ②

The Combination Principle should be obeyed when we describe and analyze the semantics in the classical formal semantics represented by Montague. The calculation of the semantic expression is corresponding with the lexical elements and the way they combine to form phrases. This kind of corresponding relation is represented in type theory by the rule that each syntactic category is given a particular semantic type and the same semantic type can be assigned to different syntactic categories. For example, <e, t>is used to denote Common nouns, VPs and intransitive verbs. What the function relation shows is the homomorphic relation between semantic type and syntactic category. The purpose to employ type re-arrangement is for the derivation of more complicated constructions.

Logical Predicate Principle is the idea that the basic logic semantic information for a sentence is determined by the logic predicate contained in the sentence. Logical predicate is the basic idea employed in formal semantics. It mainly refers to those that can take in arguments in the logic form. The logic predicate includes not only the verb which serves as the predicate in syntax but also the modified elements in syntax such as the adjectives, nouns and prepositions etc. They are all common logic predicates in logic form. A logic predicate is different from a syntactic predicate in that the former is the semantic concept while the latter is the syntactic concept.

The significance of the ELSA is as follows:

The first is that the formal semantic derivation basically depends on syntactic theory. Non-transformation syntactic theory is adopted to be the base for semantic analysis. The syntactic rules are reduced to the

---

① Wuping (2007) propose the analysis in order to better account for the complicated construction.

② The predicate in logic sense is different from predicate in syntax. Predicate in logic form refers to those which can introduce argument into the construction. Besides verbs, adj,noun and preposition can be predicate.

most basic Phrase Structure grammar[①]. By means of the combination and calculation of the semantic type, we can calculate and limit the generating process of the semantic meaning. Under the guidance of such logical semantic analysis, the generation of the meaning may partially adopts non-combination principle. From the perspective of generative power, the semantic analysis in fact confines the generative power in the semantics. On the other side, because of the type re-arrangement, the derivation of the semantic meaning can be ensured at the most extent, particularly in the derivation of the complicated construction.

Secondly, there may be some differences between the basic information contained in the lexical items and the actual qualities they acquire in specific syntactic constructions. Construction Grammar (Fillmore 1988, Goldberg 1995; Kay 1995) holds that the construction by itself should have the construction meaning of their own, therefore, when the lexical items enter into the syntactic construction, they may take on some different qualities.

Thirdly, from the point view of the formal semantic approaches, both the lexical items functioning as logical predicate and the lexical items functioning as arguments can be the starting point and the center to study the construction meaning. From the generative production of the meaning in the logical form, Logical predicates are more suitable to be the focus in semantic study. Compared with semantic type of the arguments, the logical predicate is the most complicated in semantic type.

In the constructions with the possessive relation, possessive relation becomes an indispensable component of the meaning. The logic predicate indicating possessive relation should be added to the logic form of the construction. Together with the possessive relation brought by relational nouns, the construction by itself should adjust itself to incorporate the relation into the construction meaning.

4.4 Summary

As the most typical possessive relation, the inalienable possession

---

① PS-rules is employed in TG to restrict the generating power. The original form of PS-rule is a set of rewriting rules: sentence: NP+VP. VP: V+NP etc.

has different features in different languages. It is considered to be the core prototype of the possession. In Mandarin Chinese, we give inalienable possession a new definition including two kinds of relationships: the kinship terms and the part-whole relation (including body-part nominals). The point is that the mention of the PM may require the coexistence of the PR to get full interpretation. To serve the purpose, the nominal denoting the whole should be a physical object existing in the objective world. That is, they must have referent entities. The inalienable possessive relation between the two entities is represented by "Belonging_ to". The predicate is the two-argument predicate and denotes inalienable possession between the two arguments. In order to ensure the semantic derivation of the construction, we maintain that the semantic type of the verb to be raised from $<d,<e,t>>$ to $<<d,t>,<d,<e,t>>>>$. The motivation to raise the semantic type is the possessive relation contained in relational nouns. The possessive relation is introduced into the construction together with the object inside the VP and is carried along in the computation until it finds its possessor.

Chapter Five

Possessive Relation Introduced by Verb Frame

In Chapter 4, we focus on relational nouns, which carry the possessive relation in lexical meaning. That is, relational nouns are loaded with the possessor variables together with them and carry the possessor information into the construction. Partee (2001) terms the property as "R"[①].The possessor information is stored in the lexicon together with relational nouns. It is the compulsory information that should be represented in the construction. In addition to the fact that relational nouns carry the possessor information, the argument structure of the verb may have possessive relation information as well. Based on the existence of the possessive relation in languages, there are constructions that are used to denote the discontinuity of the possessive relation. Double object construction (DOC) is the construction employed to denote the transfer of the possession in Mandarin Chinese. Section 5.1 points out that possessive relation is the semantic center of double object construction. Section 5.2 is to put the focus on *depriving-type* DOC.

5.1 Possessive relation in DOC

In recent years, Green (1974), Kayne (1993), Pesetsk (1995), Harley

---

① Partee's puzzle is about the diversity of the relations and their sources in possession. She proposes a single rule plus coerced type-shifting, depending on whether the head N is relational or not.

(1995,2002), Beck and Johnson (2004) all contribute to the study on DOCs under the framework of generative grammar. Harley (1995, 2002) proposes "CAUSE to HAVE" relation in the construction. At home, there are also much study concentrating particularly on the possessive property contained in DOCs. Li (1996), Wang (2005), Li (2006) and Si (2014) illustrate the transfer of the possessive relation in DOC from different perspectives.

As the DOC shows the transfer of the possession, its direct object must have the features of [+disposable] and [+alienable].

Lin (2013) proposes three kinds of relationships contained in "possession transfer event" presented by the prototype DOC:

(1) Spatial relationship: the transferred object is in receiver's hand or within his reach. DOC means that under the external force, the transferred object moves from starting point to the ending point. The giver (the former possessor) is the starting point and the receiver is the ending point (the new possessor). At the end of the event, the object is at the ending point.

(2) Time relationship: the transfer of the possession has been completed. Together with the spatial relationship, there is time span. The time relationship represents the state of the time, that is, the completion of the movement. The verb should have the semantic features of [+telic] and [+accomplish] features.

(3) Possessive relation: the receiver possesses the transferred object. The accomplishment of a dynamic specific transfer event means the accomplishment of a static abstract possession event. The movement of NP_3 is not just a simple motion of matter but a kind of "transfer of the ownership".

The semantic contents of the DOC center on the transfer of possessive relation. From the perspective of argument structure, the verb must carry at least three arguments: NP_1, serving as the external force; NP_2, the possessor; and NP_3, denoting the entity. The eventuality of the DOC should not only show the transfer event but also the possessive relation. Since the possessive relation by itself is a kind of relation between two entities, it is possible that the language may take advantage of the semantic relation when a certain construction is needed to express the eventuality involving in possession.

5.2 *Depriving-type* Double Object Construction

5.2.1 Defining features of *depriving-type* DOC

There are two types of DOCs in Mandarin Chinese. One is *giving-type* Double Object construction, which is represented by *gei* in Chinese. Typical verbs include *gei, song, mai, jiaogei, jigei*. The other is *depriving-type* Double Object Construction, which is represented by *qiang*. Typical verbs found in this type are *tou, na, da, chi*, which have the referents of indirect objects losing something, or that exempt them from something. The status of *depriving-type* DOC is still a controversial topic in grammatical research.

Zhu (1979) illustrates the definition of the *giving-type* DOC:

(1) There exists both "giver" and "receiver"
(2) There exists "the object" that is given and received.
(3) The "giver" intentionally makes the object transfer from the "giver" to the "receiver".

The definition for *depriving-type* DOC is quite similar:

(1) There exists both "obtainer" and "loser";
(2) There exists the object that is obtained or lost.
(3) The "obtainer" intentionally makes the object transfer from the "loser" to the "obtainer".

Zhu (1982) uses the following examples to illustrate *depriving-type* DOC:

(1) a. 买了他一所房子。
     Mai-le   ta   yi-suo   fangzi.
     buy-Perf him   one CL   house.
     "Buy one of his houses."

b. 偷了他一张邮票。

Tou-le   wo yi-zhang   youpiao.

steal-Perf me one-CL   stamp.

"Steal one of my stamps."

c. 娶了他家一个闺女。

Qu-le   ta-jia   yige guinv.

marry-Perf his-family one-CL daughter.

"Marry one of his daughters."

d. 收了你两百块钱。

Shou-le   ni   liangbai   kuaiqian.

take-Perf   you two-hundred CL money.

"Take your hundred 200 yuan."

Zhu suggests that if there is a genitive marker *de* between the two objects, or even if there is no *de* but demonstrative expressions such as *na-suo*, *na-zhang* precede the final nominal, the construction is a single object construction; while if there is no *de* between the two objects, and the final nominal is preceded by numerical expressions, this construction is treated as a double object construction, however, he does not further explore the reason.

As far as the possessive relation is concerned, the establishment and the deprivation of the possessive relation are represented by *giving-type* DOC and *depriving-type* DOC respectively. They are a pair of constructions and share the same linear sequential structure: $NP_1+VP+NP_2+NP_3$.

(2) a. 张三给了李四三个苹果。

Zhangsan gei-le Lisi san-ge pingguo.

Zhangsan give-Perf Lisi three-CL apple.

"Zhangsan has given Lisi three apples."

b. 张三吃了李四三个苹果。

Zahngsan chi-le Lisi   san-ge pingguo.

Zhangsan eat-Perf Lisi   three-CL apple.

"Zhangsan has eaten three of Lisi's apples."

The meanings of these two sentences are just contradictory to each other. First, the properties of the predicate verbs are quite different. For *giving-type* DOC, both the direct object and indirect object should co-exist to form the construction. For *giving-type* event, people want to know "to whom" and "what" is given, since the function of *giving-type* DOC is to establish the relationship between two entities. Usually, the possessive relation is established after the event. We can not say (3a) or (3b):

> (3) a. * 张三给了李四。
>   *Zhangsan   gei-le   Lisi.
>   Zhangsan   give-Perf Lisi
>   *"Zhangsan has given Lisi."
> b. ? 张三给了三个苹果。
>   ?Zhangsan gei-le   san-ge   pingguo.
>   Zhangsan give-Perf three-CL apple.
>   "Zhangsan has given three apples."

In (2b), *chi* is a transitive verb which takes two arguments. It is quite normal to say (4b), but (4a) is not permitted.

> (4) a. * 张三吃了李四。
>   *Zhangsan   chi-le   Lisi.
>   Zhangsan   eat-perf Lisi.
>   *"Zhangsan has eaten Lisi."
> b. 张三吃了三个苹果。
>   Zhangsan chi-le   san-ge   pingguo.
>   Zhangsan eat-Perf three-CL apple.
>   "Zhangsan has eaten three apples."

It is not necessary to involve in possessive relation in the construction in (4b). The second difference is the relationship between the direct object and indirect object in DOC. The function of the *giving-type* DOC is to build up the possessive relation between the two objects. The problem is that it does not ensure the established relationship. For example, we can deny the possessive relation between the direct object and indirect object.

> (5) a. 张三给了李四三个苹果，但李四没收到。

Zhangsan gei-le   Lisi   sange   pingguo, dan Lisi mei
nadao.

p.n   give-Perf Lisi three-CL apple, but Lisi not receive

"Zhangsan has given Lisi three apples but Lisi does not
receive them."

b. 张三寄给李四两千块钱，但李四一直没有收到。

Zhangsan jigei Lisi lingqian kuaiqian dan Lisi yizhi
mei shoudao.

p.n post to Pn two thousand CL money but Lisi always
not receive

"Zhang post two thousand yuan to Lisi but Lisi never
receive it"

The relationship between *Lisi* and p*ingguo* fails and in literature, the
scholars use the idea of "to" to indicate the final goal of the possessum.
We may find that the thematic role of "goal" is assigned to indirect
object in *giving-type* DOC. But in *depriving-type* DOC, the possessive
relation between the two objects is definite. It is impossible to deny
the possessive relation. For example, we can not say (6a) since there is
presupposed possessive relation.

(6) a. * 张三吃了李四三个苹果，但李四没有三个苹果。

*Zhangsan chi-le   Lisi   san-ge   pingguo,

Zhangsan eat-Perf Lisi three-CL apple

danshi Lisi meiyou san   ge   pingguo.

but   Lisi not have three CL apple

*"Zhangsan has eaten three apples of Lisi's, but Lisi
doesn't have three apples."

b. 李四至少有三个苹果。

Lisi zhishao you san-ge   pingguo.

p.n at least have three CL apple

"Lisi has at least three apples."

In (6), if "*Zhangsan chile Lisi sange pingguo*" is true, then (6b) must
be true. We know that the possessive relation must exist before the event
happens.

Giving-type DOC shows that the possessive relation is coming into being and the entity that is going to be transferred is not controlled by the possessor yet. The construction focuses on the process of the event and there is no possessive relation between the direct object and indirect object before the event.

The *depriving-type* DOC shows the process of depriving someone of his control over some entity. The possessive relation between the possessor and the possessum is clear and definite before the sentence is uttered. What the speaker focuses on is not the possessive relation itself any more but the external force or the deprived entity. The definiteness in *depriving-type* DOC is stricter than any other kind of possession splitting construction. The indirect object in *depriving-type* DOC is usually a proper noun or pronoun and the direct object should be in the form of "Number+Classifier+Noun" construction. The possessive relation between the two objects exists before the event happened.

Si (2015) suggests that we should employ different deriving ways to get the interpretation of the possessive relation included in DOC. For *giving-type* DOC, the possessive relation is realized by entailment derivation. For *depriving-type* DOC, it is a kind of presupposition derivation.

The entailment and the presupposition are different. The definitions are listed here to help account for the difference.

Following the formal semantic approach, the entailment is defined as (i) and is exemplified in (7):

(i) Proposition p entails q, if and only if, when p is true, q must be true; when p is false, q is not necessarily false.

(7) a. 张三给了李四三个苹果。(p)
        Zhangsan gei-le   Lisi san-ge   pingguo (p).
        Zhangsan give-Perf Lisi three-CL apple.
        "Zhangsan has given Lisi three apples."
    b. 李四有了三个苹果。(q)
        Lisi you-le   san-ge   pingguo (q).
        Lisi have-Perf three-CL apple.
        "Lisi has got three apples."

When (7a) is true, (7b) must be true. That is, if *Zhang san gave Lisi three apples* is true, the proposition that *Lisi has three apples* must be true. If the proposition in (7a) is false, (7b) can be either true or false.

Presupposition is defined as (ii), and is exemplified in (8):

(ii) Proposition p presupposes proposition q, if and only if: When p is true, q must be true; when p is false, q is still true.

(8) a. 张三吃了李四三个苹果。(p)

    Zhangsan chi-le   Lisi san-ge   pingguo. (p)

    Zhangsan   eat-Perf Lisi three-CL apple.

    "Zhangsan has eaten three apples of Lisi's."

  b. 李四有三个苹果。(q)

    Lisi   you   san-ge   pingguo. (q)

    Lisi   have-Pre three-CL apple.

    "Lisi has three apples."

When (8a) is true, (8b) is true as well; when (8a) is false, (8b) is still true. That is no matter whether (8a) is true or false, (8b) is true. The denial of (8a) does not result in the denial of (8b). The possessive relation between *Lisi* and *sange pingguo* is presupposed information in the construction.

We hold the view that it is this presupposed possessive relation between the two objects that makes it possible for the common transitive verb to be used in *depriving-type* DOC. Lu (2002) lists four conditions for the common transitive verbs to enter into the DOC:

(i) There must be possessive relation between post-verbal NP$_2$ and NP$_3$;

(ii) NP$_2$ is the theme argument of the predicate verb semantically;

(iii) NP$_3$ must be in the form of "Number+Classifier+Nominal" phrase;

(iv) They can be modified by *Zonggong/yigong*.

His focus is to prove the status of *depriving-type* DOC and he does not explain how the possessive relation between the two entities is generated and what function it plays in the construction.

Pylkkanen (2008: 49-52) illustrates the difference between the possessor dative construction and double objection construction, which may help us better understand the *depriving-type* DOC. In the possessor-dative construction, the dative must be the possessor of the direct object, or at least be somehow responsible for it, while in the traditional Double Object Construction, possessiveness is not asserted. In other words, a double object construction is felicitous even if the indirect object does not end up "possessing" the direct object. For an entity to be from someone's possession, that person must have had the entity. In other words, a possessor dative construction entails that the direct object in some sense belongs to the dative for the same reason that the English sentence in (9) entails the sentence in (10):

(9) He stole the keys from Mary.

(10) Prior to the event of stealing, Mary had the keys.

According to Pylkkanen (2008), the meaning of a possessor dative differs from that of its genitive counterpart in exactly the same way as (9) differs from (10):

(11) Possessor dative: I stole the keys from Mary's possession.

(12) Genitive: I stole Mary's keys.

Example in (11) asserts that Mary loses something while (12) does not. The sentence with the genitive possessor simply indicates that Mary is the owner of the keys; it does not assert that Mary, at the time of the stealing, had the keys. (11) asserts that the individual named by the dative, in certain sense, lost something.

(13) *I stole the keys from Mary's possession when she didn't have them.

(14) I stole Mary's key when she didn't have them.

5.2.2 Eventuality analysis of *depriving-type* DOC

Depriving-type DOC is a single clause in Mandarin Chinese. The eventuality is quite simple, which includes only one event. In this event, there is only one object that can bear thematic role of the theme. The theme is closely related with the verb and the indirect object is the entity that is labeled as the theme. The indirect object is labeled as the "source" in the logic form and together with it, possessive property of the construction also becomes overt in the logic form, which is part of the contents of the eventuality. *Depriving-type* DOC is based on the presupposed possessive relation existing between the two objects. The focus is on the loss of the direct object or the deprivation of the control over the direct object. The possessor is not necessarily included in the core arguments of the verb and can be omitted in the argument structure in the sentence construction. More examples of *depriving-type* DOC are as following:

> (15) a. 张先生拿了老李一本书。
> Zhang xiansheng na-le   Laoli yi-ben   shu.
> Zhang Mr   na-Perf Laoli one-CL book.
> "Mr Zhang has taken one of Laoli's books."
> b. 小偷偷了他五百块钱。
> Xiaotou tou-le   ta   wubai   kuaiqian.
> Thief   steal-Perf him   five hundred CL money.
> "The thief has stolen five hundred yuan from him."
> c. 张三抢了敌人一把枪。
> Zhangsan   qiang-le diren yiba   qiang.
> Zhangsan   rob-Perf enemy one-CL gun.
> "Zhangsan robbed the enemy of a gun."

The possessive relation exists for sure between the indirect objects *ta, Lisi, diren* and the direct objects *yikuai dangao, wubai kuaiqian* and *yibaqiang*. The source argument can be omitted as well. And if the source argument is omitted, correspondingly, there is no possession property in the construction any more. For example:

(16) a. 张先生拿了一本书。

　　Zhang xiansheng na-le　　yiben　　　shu.

　　Zhang Mr　　　take-Perf one-CL　book.

　　"Mr Zhang has taken one book."

b. 小偷偷了五百块钱。

　　Xiaotou　tou-le　　wubai　　　kuai qian.

　　Thief　　steal-Perf　five hundred　CL money.

　　"The thief has stolen five hundred yuan."

c. 张三抢了一把枪。

　　Zhangsan　qiang-le　　yiba　　　qiang.

　　Zhangsan　rob-Perf　　one-CL gun.

　　"Zhangsan rob a gun."

Examples in (16) are normal SVO constructions, in which the predicate verbs behave as the common transitive verbs. They take the two arguments with one being the agent subject and the other being theme object. There is no possessive relation involved in the construction. It is a single event with just one atom event. We have the logic forms shown in (17a) and (17b) for them.

(17) a. ∃e [Na(e) ∧ Agt(e) = *Zhangxiansheng* ∧ Th(e)= *yibenshu*]

b. ∃e [Tou(e) ∧ Agt(e) = *xiaotou* ∧ Th(e)= *wubai kuaiqian*]

c. ∃e [Qiang(e) ∧ Agt(e) = *diren* ∧ Th(e)= *yibaqiang*]

(17a) states that "there was a singular event *zhangxiansheng nale yibenshu*, in which Zhangxiansheng is the agent, *yibenshu* is the theme".

(15a) and (15b) in fact entail (16a) and (16b) respectively. The possessor *Laoli* and *diren* are more like the location than the possessor itself. They are in fact the "source" of the direct object. (15a) and (15c) mean (18a) and (18b) respectively.

(18) a. 张三（从 / 在）老李（那里 / 书架上）拿了一本书。

       "Zhangsan has taken a book from Laoli's book."

       nale   yi ben   shu.

       Zhangsan (cong/zai) Laoli (jiali/shujiashang)

       take-Perf   one-CL   book.

       Zhangsan (from/at) Laoli (house/bookshelf)

b. 张三（从）敌人（手里 / 仓库里）抢了一把枪。

       Zhangsan (cong) diren (shouli/cangkuli) qiangle yi

       ba qiang.

       Zhangsan (from) enemy (hand/warehouse) rob-Perf

       one CL gun

       "Zhangsan robbed the enemy of a gun."

The "source" meaning is more obvious with the location noun serving to be the indirect object. For example:

(19) a. 张三吃了盘子里三块饼干。

       Zhangsan chi-le panzili san kuai   binggan.

       Zhangsan eat-Perf dish in three-CL biscuit.

       "Zhangsan has eaten the three biscuits in the plate."

b. 张三偷了公司一张支票。

       Zhangsan tou-le gongsi yi zhang zhipiao.

       Zhangsan steal-Perf company one-CL check.

       "Zhangsan has stolen a check from the company."

We can predict that "source" information should be included in the lexical information of the *depriving-type* verbs. It is nature that what is stolen or robbed doesn't belong to the one who performs the action. The entity must be from somewhere. Together with the "source" information, possessive relation between the entity that is stolen and the nominal denoting "source" is triggered.

Together with the source, the possessive relation is triggered to be part of the construction meaning. We can have logic form in (20) for (19):

(20) a. $\exists e$ [$Na(e) \wedge Agt(e) = wo \wedge Th(e) = yibenshu$

       $\wedge$ Source(e)=*Laoli* $\wedge$ Having (Laoli,ibenshu)]

b. ∃e [Qiang(e)Agt(e)=*wo* ∧ Th(e)=*yibaqiang*
∧ Source(e)=*diren* ∧ Having (*diren, yibaqiang*)]

(20a) states that "there was a singular event *wo cong Laoli nale yibenshu*, in which *wo* is the agent, *yibenshu* is the theme *Laoli* is the possessor who has the book when the taking event happened".

Compared (17) with (20), we find that the difference lies in the "source". In (20), the source is clearly indicated in the form of indirect object while in (20), the source is not illustrated clearly. In fact, when we talk about the *stealing-type* or *robbing-type* event, the entity that is stolen or robbed must be from somewhere and belong to someone else rather than the agent subject himself. In (9), the source is indicated in the lexical meaning of the verb but it is a convert element because of the SVO construction. Once the *depriving-type* verbs enter into Double Object Construction, the possessive relation will be triggered to be an overt element. Therefore, we have the logic form for the *depriving-type* DOC in (15):

(21) λy [λz [λx[λe[Depriving-verb(e) ∧ Agent(e)=x ∧
Th(e)= y ∧ Source(e)=z ∧ Having (z,y)]]]]

We have already known that the event must be a *depriving-type* event, the agent is "x" and the theme is "y". In the event, "y" is from the possession of "z". We apply "Having" to be the predicate introducing the possessive relation since it denotes the ownership. The number of the books that *laozhang* has must be more than three and the number of the guns that the enemy has is likely to be more than one. We see the defining conditions for triggering the possessive relation in DOC is: the semantic properties of the verb should be of depriving type and the source part is overt in the construction. In the logic form, we use " ∧ " to connect source to other parts to show the addition of the information. In fact, the function of the part is just like the function of the preposition phrase or locative adverb.

The properties of the "source" possessor in *depriving-type* DOC are also shown in the transfer among possession splitting constructions. *Giving-type* DOC behaves differently from *depriving-type* DOC when they are transformed into *Bei* construction and *Ba* construction.

(22) a. 张三给了我一本书。
　　　Zhangsan gei-le　wo yi-ben　shu.
　　　Zhangsan give-Perf me one-CL　book.
　　　"Zhangsan has given me a book."
　　b. * 张三把我给了一本书。
　　　* Zhangsan ba wo gei-le yiben　　shu.
　　　Zhangsan BA me give-Perf one-CL book.
　　c. 我被张三给了一本书。
　　　* Wo bei Zhangsan gei-le　yi-ben　　shu.
　　　I　BEI Zhangsan give-Perf one-CL book.
　　　"I was given a book by Zhangsan."

　　　The indirect object in *depriving-type* DOC can transform with *Ba-*DPC and passive DPC. *Depriving-type* DOC can be treated as a variant of *Ba* DPC and it can be expressed by *Bei* DPC.

(23) a. 张三偷了我两百块钱。
　　　Zhangsan tou-le　wo liangbai kuaiqian.
　　　Zhangsan steal-Perf me two hundred　CL money.
　　　"Zhangsan has stolen two hundred yuan from me"
　　b. 张三把我两百块钱偷了。
　　　Zhangsan ba wo liangbai kuaiqian　　tou-le.
　　　Zhangsan ba met wo hundred　CL money steal-Perf.
　　　"Zhangsan has stolen two hundred yuan from me"
　　c. 我被偷了两百块钱。
　　　Wo bei tou-le　liangbai　kuai　qian.
　　　I bei steal-Perf two hundred CL　money.
　　　"I was stolen two hundred yuan."

　　　In (23), the sentences take different forms, but the possessive relation between *wo* and *liangbai kuaiqian* remains the same.

　　　Usually the possessive relation is alienable possession in DPC since the entity that can be deprived from others is likely to be material items, but sometimes we may find inalienable possession as well like Zhu's example about marriage.

Possessive relation information can be part of the lexical meaning of the verb and the *depriving-type* verbs can form Double Object Construction. Double Object Construction enables the verb to obtain particular argument structure. It is the argument structure that brings about the possessive relation in the construction. DOC is the common construction in Mandarin Chinese and *depriving-type* DOC shares the similarity with the typical *giving-type* DOC. The construction has its own characteristic since the possessive relation is brought in through the indirect object as the source. In *depriving-type* DOC, the indirect object, which is brought in by the verb frame, has direct semantic relation with the argument structure of the predicate verb.

Chapter Six

The Possessive Relation Triggered by Construction

Possessive relation is triggered by the lexical meaning of either the relational nouns or the predicate verb frame in *depriving-type* DOC. The possessor information is predetermined in the construction. The possessor in the construction is not extra and should co-exist with the possessum so that the possessive relation can be built and interpreted. Relational nouns reflect the features of the PM for its dependence on the possessive relation. The characteristic of the possessor also enables the construction to be understood as the Topic Construction and we find possessive relation in Topic Construction, *disappearing-type* Existential Construction, PSPO, *Bei* DPC and *Ba* DPC. What is the function of the construction in triggering the possessive relation? How does the possessor enter into these constructions? These two questions are what we need to cover in this chapter. Topic Construction will be analyzed first and we assume the possessive relation is triggered by the initial topic nominal.

6.1 Properties of the Possessor to be the Topic

Taylor (1996) focuses on the possessive relation in English. Based on "reference-point" analysis, he illustrates the individuality and definiteness of the English attributive possession and proposes the topic property of the possessor. It follows Langacker's (1993) assertions about possessor as "reference point" for their "targets". Possessor as sentence topic hypothesis assumes that a special construction that foregrounds the possessor nominal by expressing it outsider the possessive phrase must signal the status of the possessor as a sentence-level topic. The rest of the utterance would function as a comment on this topic.

Within a Cognitive Grammar framework, Langacker (1993, 1995) develops a Reference-Point model for understanding possessive constructions generally. Langacker argues that conceptually, there is not really an "extra" argument. The reference point model is based on "our basic cognitive ability to invoke one entity (the PR) as a reference point for establishing mental contact with another (PM) (1995b: 27). He proposes that reference point constructions are isomorphic to topic/comment constructions. Maslova and Bernini (2006) push this connection further and draw a parallel between constructions involving reference points and "hanging topic" construction. (Maslova and Bernini 2006: 28:).

Besides the property of being reference point, possessor nominals have the semantic property to be the topic. The first and most important property is the definiteness of the possessor. The possessor noun in a possessive relation is normally definite. The definiteness property of the noun signals that the topic is being shared by both participants in the communication.

According to Lyons (1999), familiarity hypothesis shows that : "the" signals the entity denoted by the noun phrase is familiar to both speaker and hearer. Furthermore, many linguists prefer to see definiteness as being about identifiability. The hearer matches the referent of the definite noun phrase with some real-world entity which he knows to exist.

In Mandarin Chinese, the possessor nouns are mainly proper nouns, pronouns and the definite noun phrase with "this or that". These possessor nouns are definite without the context. Bare noun can also be the possessor and the context may help to fix the definiteness of the nominal. Bare noun stands for the generic use as well. The function of the possessor in a sense is an efficient way to locate the entity in a definite set.

6.2 Topic Construction

6.2.1 Features of Topic Construction

Scholars have different ideas about what kind of sentence can be qualified as *zhuwei weiyu ju*. It is agreed that those with possessive relation between the initial noun and the noun contained in predicate part are *zhuwei weiyu ju* as shown in (1)-(3). More than often, this type of sentences in (1)-(3) are referred to as the constructions with subject-predicate phrases to be their predicates. In Mandarin Chinese, *daxiang, zhajian fangjian, Zhangsan* and *shuiguo* generally are treated as the topics.

(1) a. 大象鼻子很长。

    Daxiang bizi henchang.

    elephant nose very long.

    "The elephant's nose is very long."

  b. 这间房间门小，窗户大。

    zhejian fangjian men xiao chuanhu da.

    this CL room door small window big.

    "The door of the room is small and the window of the room is big."

(2) a. 张三头发白了一大半。

    Zhangsan toufa bai-le yida ban.

    p.n hair white-Perf one half.

    "Half of Zhangsan's hair is white."

  b. 这盆花叶子掉了好几片。

    Zhe pen hua yezi diao-le haojipian.

    this-CL flower fall-Perf several leaves.

    "Several leaves of the flower falls off."

(3) a. 水果，我喜欢苹果。

    Shuihuo wo xihuan pingguo.

    fruit I like apple

    "As for fruits, I like apples."

  b. 晚饭张三吃面条。

    Wanfan Zhangsan chi miantiao.

dinner p.n   eat noodle.
"As for the dinner, Zhangsan eats the noodle."

The possessive relation between two entities is quite clear in (1)-(3). The possessor nominal can be animate nouns like *Zhangsan* and *wo*. It can also be locational nouns like *zhejian fangjian* and *zhepenhua*. The possessive relation can be realized into *de* phrase: *Zhangsan de qianbao* and *zhege fangjian de men*.

As for (3), we can not use *shuiguo de pingguo* "* fruit's apple" or *wanfan de miantiao* "* dinner's noodle". *pingguo* is just a kind of fruits and *miantiao* is a kind of food for the dinner. This kind of possession is not the same as *de* phrase, instead, it belongs to hyponymy semantic relation. "Fruit" and "dinner" are superordinate nominals, which denote a larger concept category. "Apple" and "noodle" are just one specific type of the "fruit" and "dinner". This kind of nouns with hyponymy relation is also a kind of possessive relation. In such kind of possession, the initial noun is a concept of generic nominal. The possessor generic nominal is usually in the form of bare noun. NP_1 and NP_2 are in the relation of type and token relation. Generic nominal denotes a set and the token nominal denotes a sub-set included in the set. We have the structure in (4) for Topic Construction.

(4) a. $NP_1+[NP_2+VP]$
   b. $NP_1+[NP_2+VP+NP_3]$

In (4a) and (4b), NP_1 and NP_2, NP_1 and NP_3 form the possessive relation separately. NP_2 is the core argument of the verb and the distinguishing feature for Topic Construction is that the predicate constitute is an independent sentence.

6.2.2 Properties of the Topic

Li & Thompson (1981) propose that languages can be classified according to two parameters: topic-prominent and subject-prominent. English belongs to subject-prominent languages and Mandarin Chinese is topic-prominent. Topic and subject are two different concepts, which belong to different levels. One is a syntactic element and the other is a pragmatic element, but they are both components of the sentence (Li & Thompson 1981; Huang1982; Li 1990). Usually, either the topic or the subject occupies the initial position of the sentence.

Chao (1968) proposes that Mandarin Chinese is characterized by its prominence of the Topic Constructions. He thinks that the Chinese construction "describes the state or characteristic, less commonly an event, about the main subject". That is, the function of Topic Constructions is to describe a state or characteristic of something. Describing a state or a characteristic is typically the discourse-pragmatic function of an unaccusative intransitive clause, which has only a subject, and not of a transitive clause, which permits an object.

Li and Thompson (1976) list the following features of the topic:

1. The topic is definite.
2. The topic is not necessarily chosen by the predicate verb in the sentence.
3. The topic is not decided by the verb.
4. The function of the topic can be summarized as "attention center."
5. There is no agreement between the topic and the verb.
6. The topic always occupies the initial position.

NP_1 in the above examples meet most of the features listed by Li. Xu (1999) tries to define the topic in Mandarin Chinese from both syntactic and semantic perspectives. The semantic features are:

(i) Topic is the entity involved in the following comment. The semantic element is what is stated, which is "aboutness".
(ii) Topic may have the thematic relationship with the verb as agent, theme or other kinds or it can be non-core arguments of VP and embedded element in semantic structure. Topic can even be the time and location which denotes the context of the sentence.

In Mandarin Chinese, a topic may have no direct argument relation with its main predicate verb or may not be embedded in other verbs. Instead, there can be some elements that are related with the contents of the sentence via common sense or background information. As for syntactic features, the topic occupies the initial position and should be put before the comment.

The construction of "subject-predicate" fits most of the features mentioned above. The initial nominal has no semantic relation with the predicate verb, since its predicate part by itself is in the form of "subject+predicate" , which is an independent constitute on its own. In Mandarin Chinese, such construction is the typical Topic Construction. There is a distinguishing feature about such construction. It is without exception that the possessive relation is required between the topic and the element contained in the comment.

Usually, topics are derived via a syntactic operation. Certain arguments can move forward to the sentence-initial position to become the topic. These kinds of Topic Constructions are called *moved-type* topic constructions. The topics are usually the arguments of the verb and are related to syntactic positions. This syntactic position may be occupied by either a resumptive pronoun referring to the topic nominal or a syntactic gap, which means that we can put the topic back to the original syntactic position. For example:

(5) a. 苹果我吃了。
Pingguo wo chi-le.
apple　I　eat-Perf.
"As for the apple, I ate it."
b. 苹果我把它吃了。
Pingguo wo ba ta chi-le.
apple　I　BA it eat-Perf.
"As for the apple, I ate it."

In (5a), "apple" serves as the object and the sentence can be treated as its original order "I eat the apple"; In (5b), the resumptive pronoun "it" and the topic nominal "apple" share the same reference entity. This kind of Topic Construction is shared by all the languages. Movement of a certain element is the commonly used mechanism to make topic constructions

As a topic-prominent language, Chinese differs from other languages in that it not only has English-style topics related to a syntactic position inside the comment, but also has what Chafe (1976) termed as "Chinese-style" topics.

Li & Thompson (1976)①point out that the topic in Mandarin Chinese is not necessarily related to a syntactic position within the comment or is decided by the predicate verb in the comment. Once the comment satisfies "aboutness" condition, the Topic Construction will be well formed. It is one of the distinguishing features of Mandarin Chinese and is the semantic ground for such "Chinese Topic Construction".

6.2.3 Formation of Topic Construction

The sentence-initial elements mentioned above are treated as canonical topics and the rest of the sentence as the comment which is about the topic in question. They are formed not by movement but base-generated at its original position. In such kind of construction, the comment by itself is a clause. The comment clause has neither an open syntactic gap nor an extra theta-role to apply to the topic. In a sense, they are no longer unsaturated syntactic predicates that can function as predicate of their subject syntactically. The key idea is that the topic can not be put back to the comment directly.

Pan & Hu (2002) and Lu & Pan (2014) further develop such views and maintain that topics in Mandarin Chinese can be licensed either in syntax or at the semantic-pragmatic interface. When a topic is licensed in syntax, a syntactic gap or a resumptive pronoun in the comment clause is related to the topic in question. When it is licensed at the semantic-pragmatic interface, a semantic variable will be detected in the comment clause.

What we are concerned with is a type of canonical position Topic Construction with possessive relation. When we analyze the sentences, we treat them as their original forms, which are typical normal constructions

---

① Tompson (1976) called this construction 'double subject'. The example is *ta yanjing jinshi* or *nachangdahuo xingkui xiaofangyuan laide jishi*.

in Mandarin Chinese. Hu (2009) proposes the possessive relation as the constrains for the Topic Construction. The significance to distinguish Topic Construction lies in that not all constructions are Topic constructionss. For example:

(6) a. 我吃了一个苹果。

Wo chi-le yige pinguo.

I eat-Perf one-CL apple.

"I ate an apple."

b. 苹果，我吃了。

Pingguo, wo chi-le.

apple, I eat-Perf.

"As for the apple, I ate it."

c. 苹果，我吃了个小的。

Pingguo wo chi-le ge xiaode.

apple I eat-Perf CL small one.

"As for the apple, I ate a small one."

d. 水果我吃了个苹果。

Shuiguo wo chi-le ge pingguo.

fruit I eat-Perf CL apple.

"As for the fruits, I ate an apple."

(6a) is just a simple sentence with "SVO" construction. (6b)-(6d) are Topic Constructions, among which, (6b) is derived by syntactic movement. (6c) and (6d) are what interest us. In (6c) and (6d), the initial nominal and the nominal in comment clause compose set-subset relation, which is a kind of possessive relation. It is this kind of semantic relation that connects the topic with the comment clause.

6.2.4 Aboutness Condition

For the Topic Construction in Mandarin Chinese, the "aboutness" is of vital importance, but "aboutness" is quite vague and needs further explanation. Xu & Liu (1998) illustrate the idea from three aspects. Firstly, the topic delimits the scope or a certain field within which the communications are carried on. Secondly, the topic offers the index related with semantic interpretation to help the hearer fully interpret the sentences. Thirdly, the topic is the starting point in the discourse, which indicates there should be something to follow, specifically, the comment. The aboutness constrain is instantiated by the possessive relation in Mandarin Chinese. It is the semantic skeleton that lies under the surface structure.

6.2.5 Eventuality Analysis

The eventuality analysis will demonstrate the relationship more clearly. In a Topic Construction, the comment is a syntactically independent clause. It can be treated as an event and equals to a proposition. To be specific, the topic is "extra", which lies at external layer of the comment proposition. For example:

> (7) a. Shuiguo wo xihuan pingguo.
>   fruit   I   like   apple.
>   "As for truits, I like the apple."
>   b. $\exists s$ [Xihuan (s)$\wedge$ Exp (s)= *wo* $\wedge$ Th(s)= *pingguo*]

When there is a topic in the sentence, the topic requires the "aboutness" relation between the topic and the element in the comment proposition. The relationship between the two entities is represented as possessive relation. Therefore, the possessive relation in Topic Construction is triggered by the topic. Possessive relation is the semantic component for Topic Construction. (8) is the logic form of (7):

> (8) $\exists s$[Top-possessor(s)= *shuiguo*$\wedge\exists s$'[Xihuan(s')$\wedge$ Agt(s') = *wo* $\wedge$ Possessee (s')=*pingguo* $\wedge$ Included_in (*pingguo*, *shuiguo*)]

When the extra topic is added, (7b) is switched to (8). That is, the sentence becomes Topic Construction and it is reflected by Topic Event. It also brings about the possessive relation between the topic and the element in the comment. The possessive relation is reflected in the element contained in s and s' respectively. s' is an embedded state. There are two significances for s' to be embedded with the Topic s: one is that two nominals follow the order of the PR+PM and the direction is from PR to PM. The other is that the contents of the s' is about PM, which offers more specific information instead of enlarging or exceeding the limit set by the topic PR. In the Topic Construction, the "aboutness" condition is reflected as possessive relation.

To sum up, possessive relation exists in the Topic Construction and it is triggered by initial topic nominal.

6.2.6 Semantic Derivation

The Topic Construction is a compound event, which is composed of e_1/s_1 and e_2/s_2. "e_1/s_1"denotes topic event and "e_2/s_2" denotes comment event. "e_2/s_2" should be an embedded event in the compound event. What connects these two events is the possessive relation. In the logic form of the Topic Construction, the occurrence of the topic nominal brings along with it the functional node to introduce the "non-core" argument as well as the possession meaning as is shown in (9a):

> (9) a. 鞋我喜欢运动鞋。
> Xie wo xihuan yundongxie.
> shoes I like   sports shoes.
> "As for shoes, I like sports shoes."

The logic form of (9a) is as following:

> (9) b. e: xie wo xihuan yundongxie
> e_1: λs[Top (s) $\wedge$ Possessor(s)= xie]
> e_2: λs[Xihuan(s)$\wedge$ Exp(s)= *wo* $\wedge$ Th(s)= yundongxie]
> e_3: Included-in (yundongxie,xie)

First of all, we know from the analysis that the comment proposition is an individual event, which realizes as e_2/s_2 in (9). The atom event is a normal SVO construction. We can see the Logic form of e_2 in (10):

(9) c. a. e_2: λs[Xihuan(s)$\wedge$ Exp (s)= *wo* $\wedge$ Th(s)= yundongxie]

    b. [Xihuan]$_V$ $\rightarrow$ λy[λs[Xihuan (s) $\wedge$Exp(s)=x$\wedge$Th(s)=y]]

    c. [Xihuan yundongxie] $_{V'}$ $\rightarrow$ λy[λs[Xihuan(s)

    $\wedge$Exp(s)=x$\wedge$Th(s)=y]] (yundongxie)

    =λs[Xihuan(s) $\wedge$Exp(s)=x$\wedge$Th(s)= yundongxie]

    d. [Xihuan yundongxie]$_{VP}$ $\rightarrow$$\lambda x$[$\lambda s$[Xihuan(s) $\wedge$Exp

    (s)=x $\wedge$Th(s)= yundongxie] (by predicate formation)

    e. [wo xihuan yundongxie]IP$\rightarrow$ λx[λs[Xihuan(s)

    $\wedge$Exp (s)=x $\wedge$Th(s)= yundongxie](wo)

    =λs[Xihuan(s)$\wedge$Exp(s)=wo$\wedge$Th(s)= yundongxie]

    f. Existential quantification leads to: $\exists s$ [Xihuan(s)

    $\wedge$Exp(s)=wo $\wedge$Th(s)= yundongxie]

The derivation of the construction follows the normal step and there is no possessive relation existing in the construction. But when a possessor topic is added, the event changes from a single event to a compound event with possessive relation. The derivation tree for (9a) is (9d):

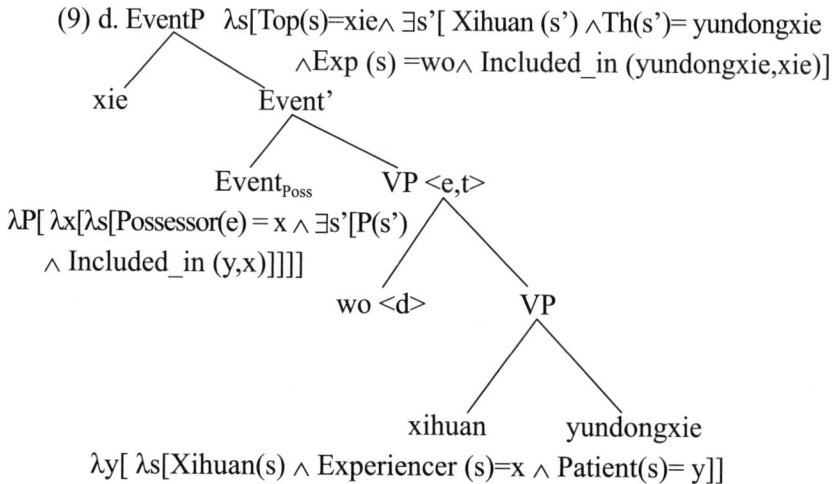

(9) d. EventP λs[Top(s)=xie$\wedge$ $\exists s'$[Xihuan (s') $\wedge$Th(s')= yundongxie

                 $\wedge$Exp (s) =wo$\wedge$ Included_in (yundongxie,xie)]

        xie   Event'

                  Event$_{Poss}$ VP <e,t>

λP[λx[λs[Possessor(e) = x $\wedge$ $\exists s'$[P(s')

  $\wedge$ Included_in (y,x)]]]]

                    wo <d>   VP

                              xihuan   yundongxie

λy[λs[Xihuan(s) $\wedge$ Experiencer (s)=x $\wedge$ Patient(s)= y]]

The significance of the Topic Construction is that there is possessive relation restriction existing in the construction without exception. If we do not admit the Topic Construction in MC, we may not offer a better account for the phenomenon. From the perspective of possession, the construction in (9) is not double subject construction[①] at all, but is a typical Topic Construction with PR as the topic and PM in comment proposition. The possessive relation is not introduced by the comment proposition but is triggered by the topic nominal in order to form the Topic Construction. The initial nominal of the topic sentence should be related to the comment to satisfy "aboutness" condition and in the comment, there should be a specific element to correlate with the topic. What fulfills this task is the abstract possessive relation.

There seems to be a "possession chain", one end of which is the topic nominal and the other end of which is the PM.

Eventuality analysis can help us to accurately describe the kind of information mentioned above, which is not included in syntax. Eventuality analysis is a better and richer means to show relation between the event and its participants as well as the inter participants relationship. By Eventuality analysis, we can give account for the production of the possessive relation, the interdependence of the elements and the interaction fully and more clearly. From the eventuality, the nature of the possession is demonstrated in details. There is an asymmetry relation between PR and PM, where PM is restricted by PR. PR is involved in the main event, which is the external element. PM participates in embedded event and is closely related with the predicate verb semantically. As the syntax is concerned, the syntactic position of PR is higher than PM, which is in accordance with the common possessive relation construction. What is more, the order of the PR and PM is fixed and PR is put before PM. Or else, the opposite order may lead to ungrammatical sentence as in (10).

> (10) * 香蕉我喜欢水果。
> 　　　*Xiangjiao wo xihuan shuiguo.
> 　　　banana　I　like　fruit.
> 　　　* "as for banana, I like fruit."

---

① Teng (1974);Tsao (1978), Chappell (1995) call the construction Double nominative construction. Chen (2004); Sun(2012) also use this term. The focus is on the syntactic status of the two nominals.

6.3 *Disappearing-type* Existential Construction

6.3.1 Two types of Arguments

From the perspective of event semantics, each type of a certain special construction in Mandarin Chinese represents a particular event structure, which also expresses particular semantic meanings. Generally speaking, Existential Construction can be divided into three types-existence, occurrence and disappearance, as shown below:

(11) a. 墙上挂着两张地图。

Qiangshang gua-zhe liangzhang ditu.

on the wall hang-Pre two-CL map.

"Two maps hang on the wall."

    b. 书桌上放着一台电脑。

Shuzhuoshang fangzhe yitai diannao.

on the desk   lie-Pre one-CL computer.

"A computer lies on the desk."

(12) a. 家里来了三位客人。

Jiali   lai-le   sanwei   keren.

in house come-Perf three-CL guest.

"Three guests come to the house."

    b. 脸上长了四个疙瘩。

Lianshang zhang-le sige   geda.

on face grow-Perf four-CL pimple.

"Four pimples grow on the face."

(13) a. 钱包里少了二百块钱。

Qianbaoli shao-le erbai kuaiqian.

In the wallet miss-Perf two hundred CL money.

"Two hundred yuan in the wallet is missing."

    b. 监狱里跑了一个犯人。

Jianyuli pao-le yige fanren.

in the prison flee-Perf one-CL prisoner.

"A prisoner fled from the prison."

The word order of Existential Construction can be represented as $NP_{Loc}+$

V+NP. The property of verbs differs a lot in Existential Constructions. According to their different features, that is, whether the verb can get access to the construction "NP+V" or not, verbs are grouped into two categories. One type can enter into this construction grammatically, such as *gua* "hang" in (11a), *lai* "come" in (12a), *shao* "disappear" in (13a) and *pao* "escape" in (13b). The other type does not have the corresponding usage, just like the verb *fang* in (11b) and *zhang* "appear" in (12b). For instance:

(14) a. 两张地图挂着。

　　　 Liangzhang ditu gua-zhe.

　　　 two-CL   map hang-Present.

　　　 "Two maps are hanging."

　 b. 一台电脑放着。

　　　 Yitai   diannao   fang-zhe.

　　　 one computer   put-Pre.

　　　 *"a computer puts."

(15) a. 三位客人来了。

　　　 Sanwei keren   lai-le.

　　　 three-CL guest come-Perf.

　　　 "Three guests came."

　 b. 四个疙瘩长了。

　　　 *Sige geda zhang-le.

　　　 tour-CL pimple grow-Perf.

　　　 *"four pimples grew."

(16) a. 二百块钱少了。

　　　 Erbai kuaiqian shao-le.

　　　 two hundred CL money miss-Perf.

　　　 "Two hundred yuan is missing."

　 b. 一个犯人跑了。

　　　 Yi ge fanren   pao-le.

　　　 one CL   prisoner flee-Perf.

　　　 "A prisoner fled."

As far as the semantic relation between sentences is concerned, examples (11a), (12a), (13a) and (13b) entail (14a), (15a), (16a) and (16b) respectively. From the perspective of verb type, verbs like *gua, lai, shao* and *pao* all belong to unaccusative verbs, which take only one argument. On the other hand, verbs like *fang* and *zhang* are transitive verbs taking two arguments. From the perspective of event semantics, sentences in (11), (12) and (13) express the event of existence, appearance and disappearance respectively. Take (11a) as an example, the event structure can be presented as the following in (17):

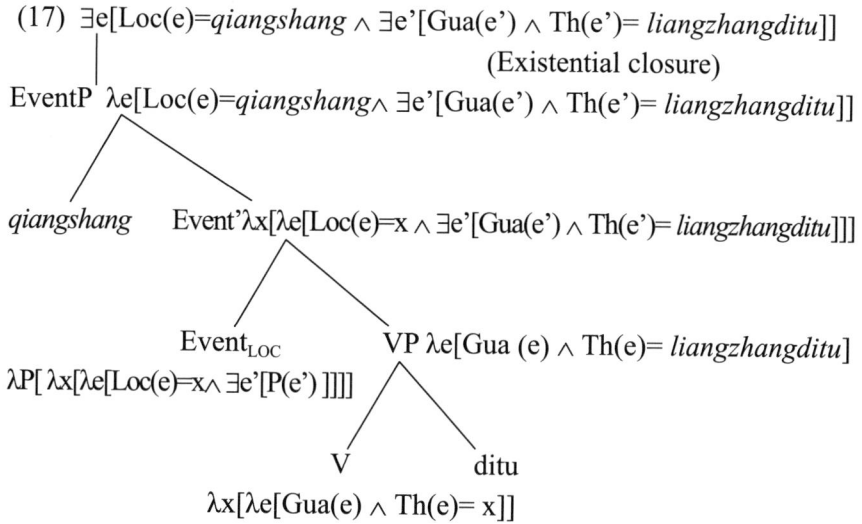

(17) $\exists e[Loc(e)=qiangshang \wedge \exists e'[Gua(e') \wedge Th(e')= liangzhangditu]]$

(Existential closure)

EventP $\lambda e[Loc(e)=qiangshang\wedge \exists e'[Gua(e') \wedge Th(e')= liangzhangditu]]$

qiangshang   Event'$\lambda x[\lambda e[Loc(e)=x \wedge \exists e'[Gua(e') \wedge Th(e')= liangzhangditu]]]$

Event$_{LOC}$ VP $\lambda e[Gua (e) \wedge Th(e)= liangzhangditu]$
$\lambda P[\lambda x[\lambda e[Loc(e)=x\wedge \exists e'[P(e')]]]]$

V   ditu
$\lambda x[\lambda e[Gua(e) \wedge Th(e)= x]]$

As is shown in the sentences, verbs like *fang* and *zhang* normally require locative arguments. The existential meaning of the sentence is always carried out by verbs, while the locative argument is contained within the lexical information of the predicate verbs. We can examine example (11b), the event structure of which is shown in (18):

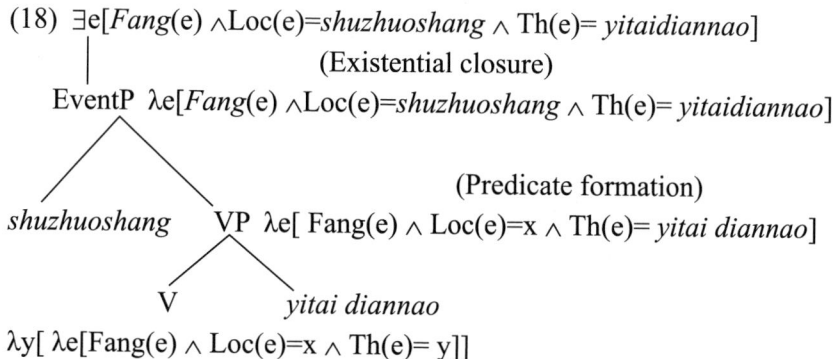

(18) $\exists e[Fang(e) \wedge Loc(e)=shuzhuoshang \wedge Th(e)= yitaidiannao]$

(Existential closure)

EventP $\lambda e[Fang(e) \wedge Loc(e)=shuzhuoshang \wedge Th(e)= yitaidiannao]$

(Predicate formation)

shuzhuoshang   VP $\lambda e[Fang(e) \wedge Loc(e)=x \wedge Th(e)= yitai diannao]$

V   *yitai diannao*
$\lambda y[\lambda e[Fang(e) \wedge Loc(e)=x \wedge Th(e)= y]]$

On the basis of the entailment of (17), we can clearly depict the entailment relation between (11a), (12a), (13a), (13b) and (14a), (15a), (16a) and (16b). However, in accordance with the entailment of (18), the entailment relation between these sentences will disappear. That's the reason why verbs of *gua-type* and *fang-type* will have different performances in the construction of "NP+V". *Gua* is an intransitive verb in "*liang ding mao zi gua zhe*", which represents the basic semantic meaning of the verb. When the locative argument is introduced by function parameters, it will be converted into an Existential Construction, meaning "*mou chu gua zhe liang zhang di tu*". We should analyze the sub-event of *gua* as embedded event, thus, it may seem that the intransitive verb *gua* has been transformed into a two-argument verb. In fact, this phenomenon of increased-valence is the requirement of the semantic and pragmatic meanings. Therefore, the locative argument in these Existential Constructions is obligatory by the semantic meaning of the sentence themselves. In other words, the meaning of existence is reflected by increasing valence of a locative argument. Besides, this locative argument is usually not contained within the lexicon by the predicate verb and introduced by function parameters. Meantime, locative arguments in Existential Constructions with verbs such as *fang* and *zhang* are generally introduced by lexicon of the verbs.

The argument structure, brought by predicate verbs from lexicon, aims at introducing the core argument. Meanwhile, other non-core arguments are introduced by function parameters.

(19) 张三有一只猫。

Zhangsan you yizhi mao.

Zhangsan have one-CL cat.

"Zhangsan has a cat."

(20) 黑板上有字。

Heiban shang you zi.

blackboard on have character.

"There are characters on the blackboard."

Firstly, we will explore the argument of the predicate verb. As we can see, both (21a) and (21b) are ungrammatical.

(21) A. 有一只猫。
    You   yizhi   mao.
    have/there be one-CL cat.
    "There is a cat."
  b. * 张三有。
    *Zhangsan you.
    *Zhangsan have.

Whether (21a) is grammatical depends on the lexical meaning of *you*. If there is some context and *you* represents the existential meaning, then (21a) is applicable. Such utterance is usually used for reminding the listener that *mou chu you yi zhi mao*. Nevertheless, if *you* means *yongyou* (POSSESS), then we can't utter a sentence like (21a). From the perspective of event structure, *you* is a predicate representing two-argument relations and therefore, requires taking two arguments. (22) is the logical expression of the example (21).

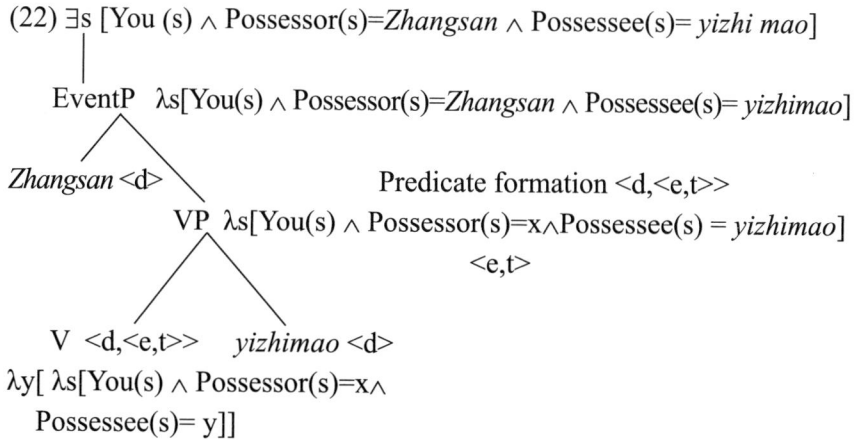

(22) $\exists$s [You (s) $\land$ Possessor(s)=*Zhangsan* $\land$ Possessee(s)= *yizhi mao*]

EventP λs[You(s) $\land$ Possessor(s)=*Zhangsan* $\land$ Possessee(s)= *yizhimao*]

Zhangsan <d>   Predicate formation <d,<e,t>>

VP λs[You(s) $\land$ Possessor(s)=x$\land$Possessee(s) = *yizhimao*]
                                          <e,t>

  V <d,<e,t>>   *yizhimao* <d>
λy[λs[You(s) $\land$ Possessor(s)=x$\land$
    Possessee(s)= y]]

The semantic representation of *heibang shang you zi* can be shown as follows:

(23) ∃s [*You* (s) ∧possessee(s)=*zi* ∧ Location(s)= *heibanshang*]
|
EventP λs[*You*(s) ∧Possessee(s)=*zi* ∧ Location(s)= *heibanshang*]

heibanshang   predicate formation

VP   λs[*You*(s) ∧ Possessee(s)=*zi* ∧ Location(s) = x]

V   *zi*

λy[λs[*You*(s) ∧ Possessor(s)=x∧
        Possessee(s)= y]]

Observed from the perspective of event structure, both sentences are singe events. The semantic meaning of (21) is: There is a possessive state, in which *Zhangsan* is the possessor of "the cat" and "the cat" is the possessum. The semantic meaning of (22) is: There is an existential state, in which *zi* is the existential object and *heibanshang* is the existential location. The information of "possession" and "existence" are both contained in the lexical information of the predicate verb and are introduced by the predicate verbs directly. The possessive relation between two entities is just what the verb tends to express. This kind of semantic derivation of the possessive relation is what the predicate possession represents in Mandarin Chinese.

6.3.2 Argument Introduced by Function Node

From the discussion above, we can figure out that the way arguments enter into sentences differs a lot. Each sentence only picks one way to introduce their arguments. We'll focus on sentences in which non-core arguments are introduced by function parameters, that is, Existential Constructions with verbs like *gua, lai, shao* and *pao*, also called *disappearing-type* Existential Constructions.

(24) a. 墙上挂着两张地图。
Qiangshang gua-zhe liangzhang ditu.
wall on hang-Pre two-CL map.
"Two maps hang on the wall."

      b. 家里来了三位客人。

      Jiali lai-le sanwei keren.

      house in come-Perf three-CL guest.

      "Three guests came to the house."

      c. 监狱里跑了一个犯人。

      Jianyuli pao-le yige fanren.

      prison in flee-Perf one-CL prisoner

      "A prison fled from the prison."

Example (24) expresses a compound event, in which the first is the activity event of hanging the map and the second is a state of two maps hanging on the wall. We can reach a conclusion of the entailment relation according to the analysis of (15) and (16) as the following:

(25) a. 墙上挂着两张地图。

      Qiangshang gua-zhe liangzhang ditu.

      wall on hang-Pre two-CL map.

      "Two maps hang on the wall."

      b. 两张地图挂着。

      Liangzhang ditu guazhe.

      Two-CL   map gua-Pre.

      "Two maps are hung."

(26) a. 家里来了三位客人。

      Jiali   lai-le   sanwei keren.

      house in come-Perf three-CL guest.

      "Three guests came to the house."

      b. 三位客人来了。

      Sanwei   keren laile.

      threee-CL guest come-Perf.

      "Three guests came."

(27) a. 监狱里跑了一个犯人。

      Jianyu li pao-le yige fanren.

      Prison in flee-Perf one-CL prisoner.

      "A prison fled from the prison."

      b. 一个犯人跑了。

      Yige   fanren pao-le.

one_CL   prisoner   flee-Perf

"A prisoner fled."

In these instances, (25a) (26a) and (27a) entail (25b) (26b) and (27b) respectively. Taking (25) as an example, its logical representation is as the following:

(28) a. ∃e [Loc(e)= *qiangshang* ∧ ∃e'[*Gua* (e')

    ∧ Pm(e')= *liangzhang ditu* ∧ Having(*qiangshang, ditu*)]]

  b. ∃e [*Gua*(e) ∧ Th(e)= *liangzhang ditu*]

According to the analysis of Parsons, one simple sentence can be regarded as a singleton. That is to say, all these sentences such as *liang zhang di tu gua zhe, san wei ke ren lai le* and *yi ge fan ren pao le* represent a complete event. Therefore, the example (24) embodies a larger major event comprising of several atom events, the feature of which is a compound event. The locative phrase is the argument of the major event, which is introduced by functional node and is not associated with the predicate verb of the sub-events. Information of locative phrase is not maintained within the lexicon of predicate verbs. From the perspective of predicate verbs, it is so-called "extra argument". In this sense, the functional node is equal to a two-place predicate and introduces the "extra argument" and event respectively. The type of the functional node is <<d,<e,t>, <d,<e,t>>>. A grammatical sentence requires the functional node introducing both an entity and an event as input arguments. When the event is converted to a sub-event and combined with a new argument, a novel meaning is created containing the possessive meaning. From the view of the sentence structure, the sentence-initial argument is an essential element. The newly-increased argument expresses the meaning of location-*qiang shang, jia li and jian yu*. Thus, the construction becomes the locative Existential Construction, emphasizing the result after the event happens. Meanwhile, the construction containing the increased argument also entails the sentences in example (29):

(29) a. 墙上有了两张地图。

    Qiang shang you-le   liangzhang ditu.

wall   on   have-perf two-CL   map.

"There are two maps on the wall as the result of an event."

b. 家里有了三位客人。

Jia   li   you-le   sanwei   keren.

House   in   have-perf three-CL   guest.

"Three guests are in the house now."

c. 监狱里有一个犯人。

Jianyu li   you   yige   fanren

prison in   have   one-CL prisoner

"There is at least one prison in the prison".

As is shown above, example (29) clearly indicates that there is a possessive relation between the increased argument and the object following the predicate verb. Obviously, this possessive meaning is beyond the lexical meaning of the predicate verb *gua, lai, shao* and *pao* from the lexicon. On the other hand, the possessive meaning is obtained from this particular syntactic structure, in which arguments are introduced by functional node. Along with the added arguments, the abstract meaning and the possessive relation are both aroused in the construction. Therefore, the logical representation of example (24) can be expressed as follows:

(30) a. $\exists$e [Loc(e)=*qiangshang* $\wedge$ $\exists$e'[Gua(e') $\wedge$Possessee(e')= *liangzhangditu* $\wedge$ Having (qiangshang, *liangzhang ditu*)]

b. $\exists$e [Loc(e)=*jiali* $\wedge$ $\exists$e'[Lai (e') $\wedge$possessee(e')= *sanwei keren* $\wedge$ Having(*jiali, sanwei keren*)]

c. $\exists$e [Loc(e)=*jianyuli* $\wedge$ $\exists$e'[Pao(e') $\wedge$Possessee(e')= *yige fanren* $\wedge$ Having (*jianyuli, yige fanren*)]

Correspondingly, the deduction of this sentence should be modified as (31):

(31) EventP λe[Loc(e)=*qiangshang*∧ ∃e'[Gua(e') ∧Th(e')= *liangzhangditu*]
        ∧ Having (*qiangshang, liangzhang ditu*)]

Qiangshang   Event'λx[λe[Loc(e)=x∧ ∃e'[Gua(e')
                    ∧Possessee(e')= *liangzhangditu*
                      ∧ Having (x, *liangzhang ditu*)]]

        Event$_{LOC}$ VP λe[Gua (e) ∧ Possessee(e)= *liangzhang ditu*]
λy[λP[λx[λe[Loc(e)=x ∧ ∃e'[P(e')
∧ Th (e') =y ∧ Having (x, y)]]]]]
                        V   *liangzhang ditu*
                    λx[λe[Gua(e) ∧ Th(e)= x]]

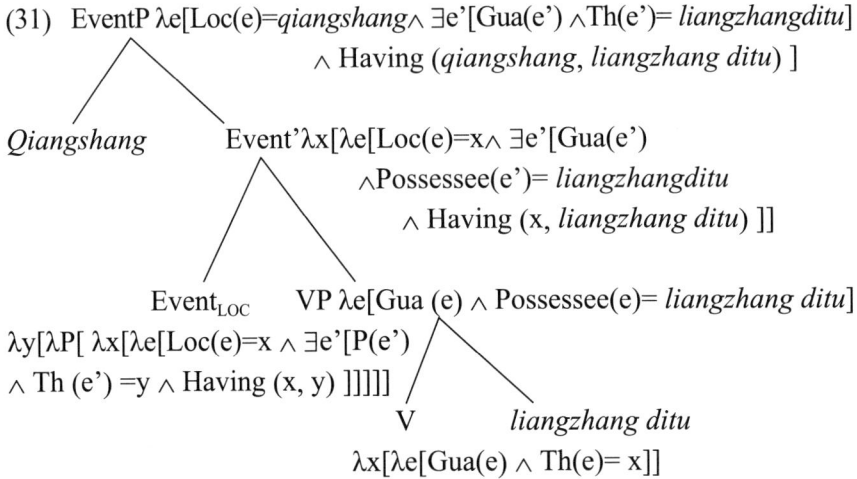

We can observe that there is difference between Existential Consrtuctions of disappearance and appearance.

> (32) a. * 墙上挂着两张地图，还有一张。
>   *Qiangshang guazhe liangzhang ditu, hai you yizhang.
>   wall on   hang-Pre two-CL map, still have one-CL.
>   *"Two maps hang on the wall and there is one more."
>   b. * 家里来了三位客人，还有一位。
>   * Jiali laile sanwei keren, haiyouyiwei.
>   house in three-CL guest, more one-CL
>   *"There are three guests in the house and there is one more."
>   c. 监狱里跑了一个犯人，还有一百个。
>   Jianyuli paole yige fanren, haiyou 100 ge.
>   prison in flee-Perf one-CL prisoner, more 100 CL.
>   "One prisoner fled, and there are still100 more in the prison."

As is shown in example (32), it is forbidden to change the number of quantitative phrases in Existential constructions of appearance, while for those of disappearance, the number is subject to change. In (32a), it indicates that the exact number of the maps on the wall is not more than two, but exact two. Likewise, (32b) indicates that the number of guests coming to the house is three, not more than three. However, what indicates in (32c) is quite different, which means that there is at least one prisoner in the prison. The greater likelihood is that there are more than one prisoner in the prison. Therefore, it is inapplicable for the entailment of (29). The correct entailment relation should be represented as (33):

(33) 监狱里跑了一个犯人。
　　　Jianyuli pao-le yige fanren.
　　　prison in flee-Perf one-CL prisoner.
　　　"One prisoner fled from the prison."
　→ 监狱里至少有一个犯人。
　　　Jianyu li zhishao you yige fanren.
　　　prison in at least have one-CL prison.
　　　"There are at least one prisoner in the prison."

It is generally represented the relation of entailment of two sentences by symbol "→". If the meaning of sentence p is true, then the meaning of sentence q is necessarily true. Thus, we can say p→q. If we want to express the entailment relation during the process of the semantic deduction, we need to further modify the semantic functional node of *disappearing-type* Existential Constructions. That is, the deduction form of (31) should be changed into (34), as is shown below:

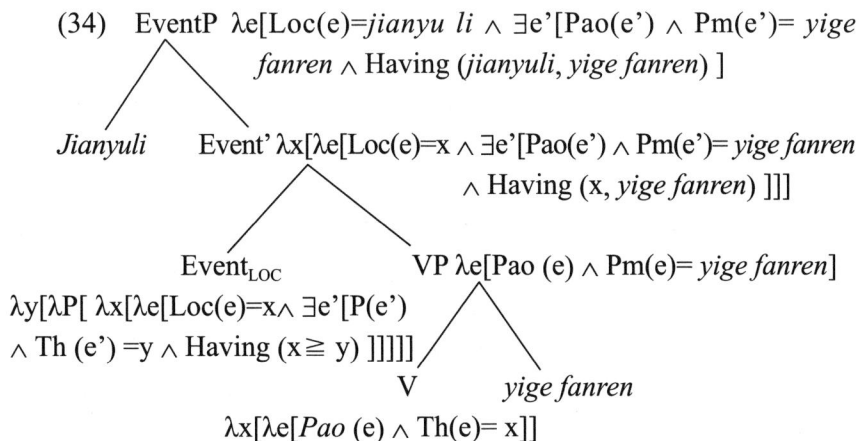

(34)　EventP $\lambda e[Loc(e)=jianyu\ li \wedge \exists e'[Pao(e') \wedge Pm(e')= yige\ fanren \wedge Having\ (jianyuli, yige\ fanren)\ ]$

Jianyuli　　Event' $\lambda x[\lambda e[Loc(e)=x \wedge \exists e'[Pao(e') \wedge Pm(e')= yige\ fanren \wedge Having\ (x, yige\ fanren)\ ]]]$

Event$_{LOC}$　　　　VP $\lambda e[Pao\ (e) \wedge Pm(e)= yige\ fanren]$
$\lambda y[\lambda P[\ \lambda x[\lambda e[Loc(e)=x \wedge \exists e'[P(e') \wedge Th\ (e')\ =y \wedge Having\ (x \geqq y)\ ]]]]]$

V　　　　*yige fanren*
$\lambda x[\lambda e[Pao\ (e) \wedge Th(e)= x]]$

The possessive relation in example (29) belongs to different types of possession. Both (29a) and (29b) focus on the meaning of "existence" while (29c) shows the possession, which means the prisoners belong to the prison.

> (35) a. 店里来了一位顾客。
>   Dianli   lai-le   yiwei   guke.
>   store in come-Perf one-CL customer.
>   "A customer came to the store."
>   b. 箱子里放着一把枪。
>   Xiangzili fang-zhe yiba qiang.
>   case in lay-Pre one-CL gun.
>   "There is a gun in the case."

As is shown above, the customer doesn't belong to the shop in (35a). Likewise, the gun doesn't belong to the suitcase either. However, there must exist certain possessive relation in Existential Constructions with "disappearance" meaning. Taking (33) as an example, the escaped prisoner must belong to this specific prison.

Then the question arises—how does the possessive relation come into existence in *disappearing-type* Existential Construction. In other words, which element triggers the possessive relation in *disappearing-type* Existential Construction?

In the above discussion, we have emphasized that the abstract structural information brought by the functional node, the meaning of which is not contained in the lexical meaning of the predicate verb from the lexicon. The sentence-initial locative argument brings about two changes: on the one hand, the construction is converted into a *disappearing-type* Existential Construction. On the other hand, it establishes the possessive relation between the sentence-initial locative argument and the theme of the sub-event of the sentence.

The contrast in semantic meaning between *disappearing-type* Existential Construction and *appearing-type* Existential Construction share the same syntactic structure, is that both share the common semantic basis. The essence of "appearance" is:

(i) There is an existing location, that is *"mou chu"*.
(ii) There is something existing in someplace, that is, *"mou wu"*.
(iii) There is something that appears at someplace.

The essence of "disappearance" is

(i) There is an disappearing location,that is *"mou chu"* .
(ii) There is something that disappears, that is*"mou wu"*.
(iii) Something disappears from somewhere.

From the process of the existence, there are three stages that the entity may undergo: appearance, change and disappearance. The "change" and "disappearance" of the entity are based on the "appearance" of the entity. That is, the disappearance of the entity presupposes the existence of the entity. The entity occupies space if it exists in the real world. The possessive relation between the space and the entity exists before it disappears. People may take different perspectives, when they observe and describe "appearance" and "disappearance" phenomenon. When people describe the appearance event, they should take the location into the consideration. When it comes to the disappearance event, the perspective is different. What disappears is not the place but the "object". Xuan (2011) proposes two typical constructions to express "appearance" and "disappearance" events in Mandarin Chinese:

(i) Typical *appearing-type* construction:
Locative NP+verb with appearance meaning+NP denoting entity.
(ii) Typical *disappearing-type* construction:
NP denoting entity+verb with disappearance meaning.

When the verbs with the meanings of "change" or "disappearance" are employed in Existential Construction, they co-exist with the locative noun, which usually occupy the initial positions of the constructions. In such constructions, the locative NPs and the disappearing entities have the possessive relation. It is the lexical meaning of the verbs and the Existential Construction together trigger the possessive relation. Verbs with disappearance meaning adjust the argument structure by way of function node in order to take the locative NP argument. The establishment of the possessive relation in *disappearance-type* Existential Construction is the interaction of both the syntax and the lexical layer and is triggered by the particular kind of *disappearing-type* verbs in the Existential Construction.

The elements denoting the location are likely to be the topics of the conversation in Mandarin Chinese. When the locative phrase occupies the initial position of the sentence, it usually becomes the topic. As is shown in (36):

> (36) a. 山上架着一门炮。
>
> Shanshang jiazhe   yimeng pao.
>
> mountain on put-up-Pre one-CL cannon.
>
> "There is a cannon in the mountain."
>
> b. 台上唱着梆子戏。
>
> Taishang yanzhe   bangzixi.
>
> stage on   perform-Pre opera.
>
> "The opera is being performed on the stage right now."

For the full interpretation of the sentence, the "mountain" should be definite. As the topic of the sentence, the definiteness of the nominal is of prime importance. It is the information shared by both the speaker and the listener. *Yi meng Pao* is the new information the speaker wants to inform. (36b) means that "the opera is being performed on the stage right now". The focus is what is going on in some place.

In Chinese, there are a large number of constructions denoting the "location". From the linear structure construction, these constructions are in the form of "NP_1 +VP+NP_2". Many nominals can be used to denote the locations directly. As the result, "NP_2 +VP" construction is formed. The NP in "NP+VP" construction is not always the subject in the strict sense, it is more like a locative topic. Because of the possessive relation, the status of the topic is clear and it is indisputable to be identified as the topic with the existence of the possessive relation. In *disappearing-type* Existential Construction, possessive relation between the location and disappearing entity exists for sure. "The location" in *disappearing-type* Existential Construction is a broad-sensed concept, including locative words and the nominals denoting people. The possessive relation is introduced into the construction by the combination of the lexical meaning and the Existential Construction. Therefore, this kind of construction belongs to a sub-type of Existential Construction as well as to a sub-type of Topic Construction.

Existential Construction is a normal construction in Mandarin Chinese. Its function is to show that there is something at some place. The point is that in *disappearing-type* Existential Construction, possessive relation exists simultaneously. Neither the disappearance verbs nor Existential Construction has the information of possessive relation by itself. *Disappearing-type* verbs in lexicon do not contain possessive information, but when they enter into Existential Construction, the location nominal and the disappearing entity acquire possessive relation.

We can analyze the eventuality of the *disappearing-type* Existential Construction in a new perspective. It should be treated as the Topic Construction. The initial nominal serves as the topic for the construction. It indicates an atom event to go after the topic. There are at least two atom events in this compound event.

(37) $\alpha = \exists e[\text{Top}(e)=jianyuyi]$
$\beta = \exists e'[Pao\ (e') \wedge \text{Possessee}(e')=yige\ fanren]$

As far as (37) is concerned, the possessive relation is missed in the construction. If the initial element is treated as the topic, there must be "aboutness" relation between the topic and the comment. In this construction, the "aboutness" relationship is instantiated as possessive relation. We use "Having" as the predicate to indicate the possessive relation, "Having (x,y)" means that possessive relation exists between "x" and "y". It is a kind of connection in meaning and is contained in the construction. Therefore, we should add possessive relation to the eventuality as well. When we form the "$\alpha+\beta$" construction, possessive relation is generated in this specific situation. (38) is the representation of "$\alpha+\beta$" construction.

(38) α +β= ∃e [Top(e)= *jianyuli* ∧ ∃e'[Pao (e') ∧ Pm(e')=

yige fanren ∧ Having (*jianyuli, yige fanren*)]

EventP λe[Loc(e)=*jianyuli*∧ ∃e'[Pao(e') ∧Pm(e')= *yige fanren*

∧ Having (*jianyuli, yige fanren*)]]

jianyuli   Event'λx[λe[Loc(e)=x∧ ∃e'[Pao(e') ∧Pm(e')= *yige fanren*

∧ Having (x, *yige fanren*)]]]

Event $_{Top}$ VP λe[Pao (e) ∧ Pm(e)= *yige fanren*]

λy[λP[λx[λe[Loc(e)=x∧ ∃e'[P(e')

∧Pm (e') =y ∧ Having (x ≧ y)]]]]]

V   *yige fanren*

λx[λe[Pao(e) ∧Pm(e)= x]]

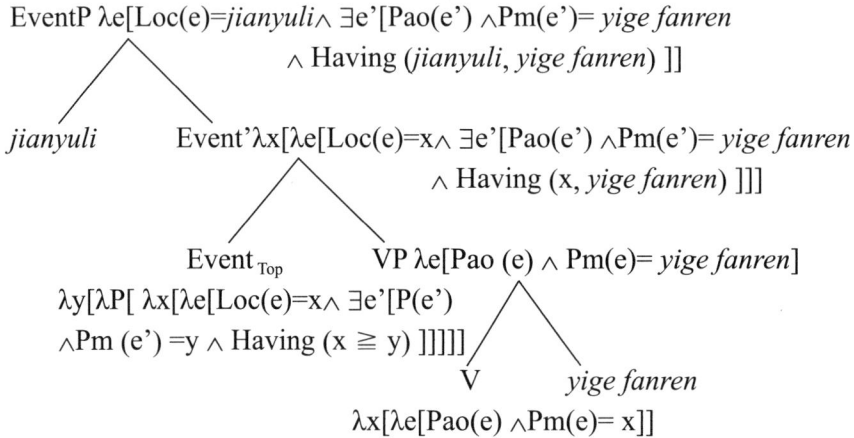

The function node contains all the information needed in the construction. It is like a complicated predicate which takes in a proposition and an entity as its arguments. At the same time, abstract meaning is triggered in the combination. The delicate description of the meaning pays its costs. It doesn't obey strictly the functional application rule, which can be shown in (39):

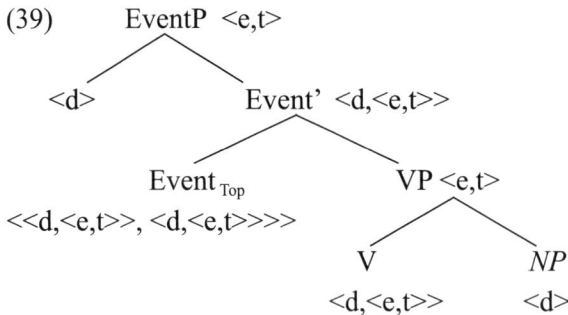

(39)   EventP <e,t>

<d>   Event' <d,<e,t>>

Event $_{Top}$ VP <e,t>

<<d,<e,t>> ,<d,<e,t>>>>

V   NP

<d,<e,t>>   <d>

We see that the type of the functional node is the most complicated type. It is of the type of <<d,<e,t>> ,<d,<e,t>>>, but we can not do functional application directly when it combines with "VP", which is of the type of <e,t>. Here we should employ the type-raising mechanism to ensure the derivation to go smoothly. The rule for type-resetting is as follows:

(40) <<d,<e,t>,<d,<e,t>>>   <e, t> → <d,<e,t>

It is just because the Topic Construction and the possessive relation that motivate the type-raising. The rule is applied to other types of Topic Constructions, which will be further illustrated in the next Chapter.

6.4 Possessor Subject and Possessum Object Construction

6.4.1 PSPO & *disappearing-type* Existential Construction

The term of PSPO is first used by Guo (1990). His point lies in the syntactic and semantic features of the construction. The term not only manifests the fact that the subject and the object that the two nominals occupy respectively but also indicates the possessive relation between them. Huang (2007) argues about the term since he notices there is not always possessive relation between the two nominals and some propose other terms with different focus they have on the construction. Xiong (2012) argues that the subject is assigned a causer role by the cause, and it can establish a possessive relation with the causee. The arguments of the verb are selected by the functional categories, hence the arguments can be loose with the verb semantically. From the point of the possessive relation, the construction does contain possessive property in the construction. Maybe some of the possessive relations are not so typical as the prototype possession. The typical examples listed in the literature are repeated in (41):

(41) a. 王冕七岁上死了父亲。
　　　　Wangmian qisuishang si-le fuqin.
　　　　Wangmian seven-year-old die-Perf father.
　　　　"Wangmian's father died on him when he is seven years old."
　　　b. 他白了头发。
　　　　Ta bai-le   toufa.
　　　　he white-Perf hair.
　　　　"His hair becomes white."

c. 他已经烂了五筐橘子，记得饭都不想吃了。

ta yijing lan-le   wukuang juzi,

he already go-rotten-Perf five basket orange

ji-de   fan ye buxiang chi-le.

anxious DE dinner not want eat-Perf.

"Five baskets of his oranges have gone rotten and he is too anxious to eat."

d. 上个星期，动物园跑了一只狗熊，

shang ge xingqi, dongwuyuan pao-le yizhi gouxiong,

last CL week zoo   run-Perf one CL bear

在市民中引起了恐慌。

zai shiming zhong yinqi-le   yixie huangluan.

among inhabitant   arouse-Perf some panic

"last week, a bear ran away from the zoo, which aroused some panic in the inhabitants."

e. 老张丢了两百块钱。

Laozhang diu-le   liangbai kuai qian.

Laozhang lose-Perf two hundred-CL money.

"Laozhang lost two hundred yuan."

The surface structure of PSPO construction can be formalized as "NP_1+Vi+NP_2". From the examples, we see that both the alienable and inalienable possession can be demonstrated in the construction. *Wang mian* and *fuqin* are kinship relation; *toufa* and *ta* are in body-part relation. The possession type in (41a)-(42e) are inalienable possession.

Ren (2009) illustrates the possibility to treat PSPO construction as a kind of Existential Construction, which she terms as "broad-sensed" Existential Construction. Her illustration is based on cognitive perspective. Other scholars share her opinion in that the initial nominal should be treated as the location where the event occurred. Lin (2008) treats *Wang mian* as location subject. They all put emphasis on the function the initial nominal plays in the construction. Wu (2014) points out that the exact meaning of the subject in PSPO is more likely to be a location closely related with the subject. It is by means of the metonymy that the subject can be treated as the location. We take (41e) as the example. Although *Lao zhang* takes the syntactic position of the subject, it does not have the typical features shared by typical subject. *Lao zhang* is not the agent of the verb. From the point of view of canonical intransitive uses of the predicate verb, NP$_2$ is expected to appear in subject position. *Lao zhang* is the "extra argument" if one considers the canonical valency properties of the verb as well as the thematic relations typically associated with eventualities encoded by the verb.

Laozhang has no volition to initiate the event either. *Lao zhang* himself doesn't want to lose the money. He is the experiencer of the "losing" event. The feature of no volition is shared by all the examples in (41). Adverbs can be applied to test the ability for the construction to show the intention of the subject. Adverbs such as *zhudong de, teyi de* (intentionally) are employed to check the grammaticality and the sentences are not good sentence any more.

> (42) a. * 王冕 特意地 / 故意地 / 专门地死了父亲。
> *Wangmian teyi-de/zhudong-de si-le   fuqin.
> Wangmian intentionally/willingly die-Perf father.
> *"Wangmian intentionally experienced the event of his father's death."
>
> b. * 他特意地 / 故意地 / 专门地白了头发。
> *Ta teyi-de/zhudong-de   bai-le   toufa.
> he intentionally/willingly white-le hair.
> * "His hair intentionally/willingly becomes white."
>
> c. * 他已经特意地 / 故意地 / 专门地烂了五筐橘子，急得饭都不想吃了。
> *ta yijing teyi-de/zhudong-de   lan-le.
> he already intentionally/willingly go-rotten-Perf
> wu kuang juzi,   ji-de   fan ye buxiang chi-le.
> five basket orange anxious DE dinner not want eat
> *"Five baskets of his oranges have intentionally/ willingly gone rotten and he is too anxious to eat."
>
> d. * 上个星期动物园 特意地 / 故意地 / 专门地跑了一只狗熊，在市民中引起了一些慌乱。
> *Shang ge xingqi, dongwuyuan teyi-de/zhudong-de pao-le last CL week zoo   intentionally/willingly run-Perf yizhi gouxiong, zai shiming zhong yinqi-le yixie huangluan.

one CL bear among inhabitant arouse-Perf some
panic
*"last week, a bear intentionally/willingly ran away
from the zoo, which aroused some panic in the
inhabitants."

e. * 老张特意地 / 故意地 / 专门地丢了两百块钱。

*Laozhang teyi-de/zhudong-de diu-le liangbai kuai
qian.

p.n   intentionally/willingly lose-Perf twohundredCL
money.

*"Laozhang intentionally/willingly lost two hundred
yuan."

Lao zhang in this construction is more like an entity without life
denoting a location or a place. In fact, the concept of the initial nominal
Lao zhang in (41e) has a wider range than *Laozhang* as a possessor
entity. It equals to mean that "*Lao zhang de shenshang/koudaili/jiali diu-
le 100 kuaiqian*". We can use *laozhang* to replace lao zhang's pocket.
More examples can be found to illustrate the situation.

(43) a. 夹克少了一粒扣子。

Jiake shao-le yili kouzi.

jacket miss-Perf one-CL button.

"two buttons are missing from the jacket."

b. 监狱里跑了一个犯人。

Jianyu   pao-le yige fanren.

prison flee-Perf one-CL prisoner.

"One prisoner fled from the prison."

(44) a. Tom 丢了二百块钱。

Tom diu-le   200 kuai qian

Tom lose-Perf 200 CL money

"Tom lost 200 yuan"

b. 李四跑了一个厨师。

Lisi pao-le yige chushi

Lisi leave-office-Perf one-CL cook.

"Lisi had a cook leave Lisi's restaurant."

(43) and (44) can be revised as (45) and (46) respectively. The location can be an overt locative phrase.

> (45) a. 夹克（上）少了一粒扣子。
>   Jiaoke (shang) shao-le   yili   kouzi.
>   jacket (on)   miss-Perf   one-CL button.
>   "Two buttons are missing from the jacket."
> b. 监狱里跑了一个犯人。
>   Jianyu (li) pao-le   yige   fanren.
>   prison in flee-Perf   one-CL prisoner.
>   "One prisoner fled from the prison."
> (46) a. Tom 的（钱包里 / 身上 / 口袋里 / 家里）丢了 200 块钱。
>   Tom (de qianbaoli/shenshang/koudaili/jiali) diu-le
>   200 kuaiqian.
>   Tom 's (wallet/pocket/house)   lose-Perf 200 CL yuan.
>   "Tom lost 200 yuan in his pocket."
> b. 李四的（店里 / 饭馆里）离开了一位厨师。
>   Lisi (de dianli/fanguanli) likai le   yige   chushi.
>   Lisi ('s store/restaurant) leave-office-Perf one-CL
>   cook.
>   "Lisi's cook left office from the (store/restaurant)."

The possessive location of the possessum can be default, as in (45a), the button is pinned on the clothes; the possessive location may not be default. For example, the money can be put in the pocket along with the owner; it can also be put somewhere at home. Sometimes, the possessive relation involves context to help to fully interpret the relation between the possessor and the possessum. For example, in (46b), *Lisi* should be the boss or the manager who is in charge of the store or restaurant.

Ren (2009) proposes the idea of "broad-sensed" Existential Constructions which includes PSPO construction. She notices that under a certain condition, the initial location nominal can interchange with possessor. If PSPO is analyzed the way we analyses the *disappearing-type* Existential Construction, the transformation of these two constructions indicates that they are closely related in meaning. There is one more reason for the transformation: they both can be treated as Topic

Construction for the location.

What differs PSPO construction from the *disappearing-type* Existential Construction illustrated above is that the properties of the initial argument introduced by the functional node. In *disappearing-type* Existential Construction, it is the locative nominal. In PSPO construction, it is the nominal denoting the person or the name of the institution. Wu (2014) propose that they stand quite close to each other in the continuum. There are constructions as (47)-(49) to go between the two constructions.

(47) a. 村子里住着一位名人。

Cunzi li zhu-zhe yiwei mingren.

town   in live-Pre one-CL famous person.

"A famous person is living in the town."

b. 办公室放着一排书架。

Bangongshi fang-zhe yipai shujia.

office   lay-Pre one-CL bookshelf.

"A row of bookshelves stand in the office"

(48) a. 学校来了三位记者。

Xuexiao lai-le   sanwei jizhe.

school come-Perf three-CL journalist.

"Three journalists came to the school."

b. 中国出了个毛泽东。

Zhongguo chu-le   ge Maozedong.

China   appear-Perf CL Maozedong.

"there is Maozedong in China."

(49) a. 裤子少了一条拉链。

Kuzi shao-le yige   lalian.

pants miss-Perf one-CL zip.

"A zip is missing from the pants."

b. 监狱跑了一个犯人。

Jianyu pao-le yige   fanren.

prison flee-Perf one-CL prisoner.

"A prisoner fled from the prison."

In the examples here, the initial nominals are not directional phrases, but locative phrases. Directional phrase is usually made by combining the locative nominal with position nominal. Therefore, locative words are more like typical noun phrase. Compared with the subject in PSPO, the subject in PSPO is the typical noun phrases.

Yang (2004) holds that the interpretation of the constitution in the construction "NP$_1$ you NP$_2$" is ambiguous in meaning. The constitution is made up of the human members. It is entitled with a certain rights and can perform a certain function. It shows a certain animate properties. If this kind of properties is involved in the construction, the construction is PSPO construction. When the constitution name is used to denote the location of the constitution, it is a typical inanimate theme. Animate property is greatly reduced while the space propertity is increased. In the sense, it has the typical semantic properties for Existential Construction. She lists a continuity for the possession and existence relation.

(50) possession   existence
       animate property   space property
   human being> animals>common objects>constitution>locati
on>position

Xuan (2011) gives the hierarchy of the noun phrases according to the degree of the locative properties they denote after he gives a thorough description about the relation between the two constructions. His hierarchy is listed in the following chart:

(51)

Locative feature degree	strong	medial	weak
Semantic relation	Spatial relation	either	Possessive relation
syntactic construction	Disappearance EC	either	PSPO

From the illustration above, we can draw the conclusion that there is semantic connection between PSPO construction and *disappearing-type* Existential Construction. PSPO is the least typical *disappearing-type Construction*.

6.4.2 Verb in PSPO and *disappearing-type* Existential Construction

First, we observe the properties of the verbs in the construction by the test to find out whether the predicate verb can enter "NP+V" construction.

(51) a. 他已经烂了五筐橘子。

　　　ta yijing lan-le　　wukuang　juzi.

　　　he already go-rotten-Perf five-CL basket　orange.

　　　"Five baskets of his oranges have gone rotten."

　　b. 五筐橘子烂了 / 烂了五筐橘子。

　　　Wu kuang juzi　lan le/lan-le wukuang juzi.

　　　five basket orange go-bad-Perf.

　　　"Five baskets of oranges have gone bad."

(52) a. 上个星期，动物园跑了一只狗熊。

　　　shangge xingqi, dongwuyuan pao-le　yizhi　gouxiong.

　　　last week,　zoo　run-away-Perf one-CL　bear.

　　　"Last week, a bear ran away from the zoo."

　　b. 一只狗熊跑了。

　　　Yizhi　gouxing pao-le.

　　　one-CL　bear　run-away-Perf.

　　　"A bear ran away last week."

(53) a. 他来了三位客人。

　　　Ta lai-le　sanwei　keren.

　　　he come-Perf three-CL guest.

　　　"Three guests came to visit him."

　　b. 三位客人来了 / 来了三位客人。

　　　Sanwei　keren lai-le/lai-le sanwei keren.

　　　three-CL guest　come-Perf.

　　　"Three guests came."

From (51b), (52b) and (53b), the objects can be used to form an independent sentence. The nominal phrases *juzi, gouxing* and *keren* can occupy either the subject or object syntactic position. It represents an event. In this event, some changes happen to the theme. This kind of change is autonomic, one-way relation and usually there is no external force. Guo (1990) first mentions the [+one-way] characteristic of PSPO construction. The properties make the intransitive verbs differ from other kind of intransitive verbs. They are unaccusative verbs.

Under the framework of Relational Grammar, Perlmutter (1978) first proposes that intransitive verbs can be further divided into two sub-categories: unaccusative verbs and unergative verbs. They both belong to one-argument verbs and the only argument usually occupies the subject position before the predicate verbs in the surface structure, but the logic relationship between the predicate verbs and other argument are different in nature. The final subject is the initial direct object for unaccusative verbs. That is, the subject in surface structure is the logic object in deep structure while for unergative verb, the final subject in surface structure is its initial subject. They remain in subject position both in surface and deep structures. This is "Unaccusative Hypothesis". Burzio (1986) shares and develops the hypothesis. Burzio further points out that the transitive verbs should also be on parallel with intransitive verbs and be divided into "transitive" and "causitive" categories:

(54) a. unergative verbs: cry. laugh, talk, sneeze, jump
     b. unaccusative verbs: exist, appear, come, be, arrive
     c. transitive verbs: eat, drink, hit, critic, kick, discuss
     d. causative verbs: break, sink, move, open, close

From the perspective of GB, there is only one logic subject with one thematic role for unergative verbs. It is the construction without object in deep structure, while for unaccusative verbs, they just have logic object and there are no logic objects in deep structure. According to Williams (2002), the only argument carried by an unergative verb is the external argument. The unaccusative verbs lack external arguments and the only argument for them is the internal arguments.

In Mandarin Chinese, scholars find the same contrast in intransitive verbs. Pan (2005), Xu (1999) and Yang (1999) illustrate the division in Mandarin Chinese. Pan & Han (2005) propose that in Mandarin Chinese, the unaccusative verbs show overt syntactic features. This kind of verbs in Mandarin Chinese are not only generated in object position but also can remain in situ as the other kind of objects, which show the features of the unaccusative verbs clearly. Most of the time, we can distinguish unaccusative verbs from others just from their syntactic position. Existential verbs as *lai* and non-causative verbs as *chen* and *po* are typical unaccusative verbs. The existential verbs are decoded to show the appearance, disappearance and existence of the entities. The non-causative verbs denote the change of the state. The normal constructions containing accusative verbs include:

    i) existential constructions;

    ii) non-causative construction with corresponding causative equivalence;

    iii) passive construction. Typical examples are listed below:

(55) a. 来了客人。

      Lai-le   keren.

      come-Perf guest.

      "The guest come."

   b. 沉了三艘货船。

      Chen-le   sansou huochuan.

      sink-perf three-CL cargo ship.

      "Three cargo ships sank."

   c. 被偷了一辆摩托车。

      Bei tou-le   yiliang motuoche.

      bei-steal-Perf one-CL   motorcycle.

      "A motorcycle has been stolen."

From the source of the unaccusative verbs, they are not of the same kind. The existent verbs belong to the basic unaccusative verbs. They are basic vocabulary in the lexicon. The unaccusative verbs like *chen* and *po* are derived vocabulary. They are derived from the corresponding transitive causative verbs. That is to say, these verbs function as both intransitive verbs and transitive verbs. They can form the "construction pairs" as shown in (56) and (57):

(56) a. 敌人毁灭了城市。

    Diren huimie-le   chengshi.

    enemy destroy-Perf city.

    "The enemy destroyed the city."

  b. 城市毁灭了。

    Chengshi huimie-le.

    city   destroy-Perf

    "The city was destroyed."

(57) a. 北语出版了这本书。

    Beiyu chuban-le   zheben shu.

    BLCU publish-Perf this-CL book.

    "BLCU has published the book."

  b. 这本书出版了。

    Zheben shu chuban-le.

    this book   publish-Perf.

    "This book has been published."

Chengshi and *shu* occupy object position in (56a) and (57a) and they can occupy the subject position in (56b) and (57b) respectively. The causative relationship introduces the subjects as *diren* and *beiyu* into the construction.

(51)-(53) share the same features as (56) and (57). The post-nominal can be put both before and after the predicate verb without much change of the meaning. What differs (51)-(53) from (56) and (57) is that NP_1 has different semantic relationship with the NP_2. In (56) and (57), it is the causative functional node that introduce the external argument into the construction while in (51)-(53), it is the possessive relation between two entities, namely NP_1 and NP_2, that combines all the elements into the construction.

The characteristics of the unaccusative verbs fit the semantic features of discontinuous possession constructions in that the semantic focus of the construction is to illustrate the changes happened to the possessum. The possessum undergoes some non-autonomy changes by itself. The changes either happened without any external force or the changes resulted from the external force. In the construction, the focus is not on the agent and sometimes it is impossible to know clearly who is the agent. Since agent is not the most salient element in the construction. Huang (2007) shares the same idea that the unaccusative/unergative dichotomy in its essence represents two types of events. The events represented by unaccusative verbs and unergative verbs stand for two types of eventuality: the unergative verbs describe the action with the agent to be basic argument, representing agent-centered events. Unaccusative verbs refer to the final state after the action with theme or patient as its basic argument. They are representatives for patient-centered events. In the possessive relation, usually the possessor has a kind of control on the possessum, but it is not always the case. The possessum may undergo the changes against the possessor's volition. In this case, the final result is more concerned than the action by itself.

The unaccusative characteristics of the predicate verbs also satisfy the request to be comment position in Chinese-style Topic Construction. The comment position is an syntacticly independent sentence. In Existent Construction and PSPO construction, the initial elements denote location and have no direct relation with the predicate verb. The theme is the real argument of unaccusative verb and they form syntactically complete sentence. From the perspective of the eventuality, the comment is an atom event embedded in the Topic event.

6.4.3 Eventuality analysis

From the perspective of the eventuality, we know that PSPO construction is a compound event with two atom events. One is the topic event and the other is the atom event represented by the predicate verb. (58) is the typical example of PSPO construction.

(58) a. 王冕丢了钱包。
    Wangmian diu-le   qianbao.
    Wangmian lose-Perf wallet.
    "Wangmian lost his wallet."
  b. 钱包丢了。
    Qianbao diu-le.
    wallet   lose-Perf.
    "The wallet is lost."

In (58b), the verb is *diu* and it can also take a locative subject as in (58a). In this analysis, *diu* is taken to be an unaccusative verb with *qianbao* as its argument. From (58a), the intransitive verb *diu* is used in a "transitive" way. The NP Wangmian is a base-generated topic NP and doesn't have a direct bearing on the verb. The usage of the *diu* is much like the "fly" or "melt" in English. It seems that it can take either one argument or two arguments.

> (59) a. They melt the ice.
>   b. The ice melt.

In Pylkkänen (2002, 2008), "melt" is analyzed as taking one argument and the "ice" is introduced by the verb itself. "They" is the "non-core" argument, which is treated as the causer of the event. Such kind of "non-core" argument is introduced by functional node with causative functional meaning. (58) and (59) both require that the functional node is added to the derivation. The functional node is used to introduce "non-core" argument. They are different in that this functional node brings in causative meaning in (59) and possessive meaning in (58). Therefore, the thematic role the "non-core" argument has is different. We can see the difference clearly from the logic form.

> (60) $\exists e$ [Melting(e) $\wedge$ Th(e)= the ice]
> (61) $\exists e$ [Loc(e) = *Wangmian* $\wedge$ $\exists e'$[*Diu* (e') $\wedge$ Pm(e')= *qianbao*
> $\wedge$ Having (*Wangmian, qianbao*)]]

The thematic role "they" has is the "Causer" of e while *Wangmian* has the thematic role of "Loc".

From the process of the derivation, the Existential Construction and PSPO show no difference. The key is the identification of the initial nominal. We may have two options as in (62) for both Existential Construction and PSPO construction.

(62)   EventP

wangmian   Event'

Event$_{LOC}$ $\lambda e'[Diu(e') \wedge Pm(e')=qianbao]$

$\lambda y[\lambda P[\lambda x[\lambda e[Loc(e)=x \wedge \exists e'[P(e') \wedge Pm(e')=y] \wedge Having(x, \geqq y)]]]]]$

From the eventuality shown in (62), we find the atom event is "*qian bao diu le*". It is a separated syntactic constitute and is a complete clause syntactically. The contribution to the logic meaning is that it is a proposition. *Wang mian* is at the external level to e'. From the syntactic analysis, *Wang mian* is outside of the IP layer. According to Xu (1998), what *Wang mian* occupies is the topic position. *Wangmian* in essence is the initial external clausal topic that looks like the agent. The eventuality of (62) is corresponding to the eventuality of the Topic Construction. The eventP has only one argument *Wangmian*, and the comment proposition is an embedded e'. The possessive relation between *Wangmian* and *qian bao* instantiates the "aboutness" condition for the topic and comment. To sum up, (62) can be treated as a sub-type of Topic Construction. *Wangmian* is the "possessor-topic". The derivation in (62) can be re-analyzed as (63).

(63)   EventP

Wangmian   Event'

Event$_{Top}$ $\lambda e'[Diu(e') \wedge Pm(e')=qianbao]$

$\lambda y[\lambda P[\lambda x[\lambda e[Possessor\text{-}Top(e)=x \wedge \exists e'[P(e')$
$\wedge Pm(e')=y] \wedge Having(x, \geqq y)]]]]]$

We adjust the locative event to Possessor-topic event. From the point of the topic, the possessor in PSPO construction occupies the topic position in the construction. It has possessive relation with the possessum in the comment.The subject position of the position is left empty. It differs from the locative topic in *disappearing-type* Existential Construction in that in this construction, the possessive relation is more obvious.

6.4.4 Passive PSPO

Li (2007) proposes the "passive PSPO construction", which is a special type of PSPO Construction. It is in the form of active voice but indicates passive meaning. The subject and object in the construction maintain possessive relation. This particular type is an ambiguous construction, which may have more than one interpretations. This type of PSPO Construction has already arisen scholars' interest. Here we use examples from Shen (1994).

> (64) a. 他拔了牙。
>   Ta ba-le   ya.
>   He pull-out-Perf teeth.
>   b. "he pulled out (patient's) teeth."
>   c. "Someone pulled out his teeth."
> (65) a. 他修好了自行车。
>   Ta xiuhao-le zixingche.
>   He repair-Perf bicycle.
>   b. "He repaired (Xiaowang's) bicycle."
>   c. "(someone) repaired his bicycle."

(64a) and (65a) may have two ways of interpretations shown in (64b), (64c) and (65b), (65c) respectively. According to Li's (2007) analysis, the primary presupposition that leads to the ambiguity is the possessive relation existing between the subject and the object. In our opinion, the reason for the ambiguous interpretation is just the mismatch between the semantic arguments and the syntactic arguments. *Ba* is a transitive verb which takes two arguments. *Ya* is the relational noun which presupposes the existence of the possessor. Therefore, we need at least three arguments to fully interpretate the meaning the sentence conveys.

We come to the interpretation in (64b) first. If there were no possessive relation between the subject *ta* and the object *ya*, *ya* must have another possessor which is covert. The construction is just an ordinary "SVO" construction. Both the subject *ta* and the object *ya* are introduced by the verb with its lexical information from the lexicon. The derivation of "*ta ba le ya*" is exactly the same as "*ta ba le cao*", which has no possessive relation existing between the subject and the object. The derivation process is as the follows:

(66) 他拔了 (病人的) 牙。

　　　Ta ba-le (bingren de) ya.

　　　He pull-out (someone's) teeth.

　　　"He pulled out (someone's) teeth."

EventP　$\lambda e[$ *Ba* $(e) \wedge$ Agent$(e)=$ *ta* $\wedge$ Patient$(e)=$ *(bingren de) ya*$]$

ta　　　VP $\lambda e[Ba(e) \wedge$ Agent$(e)=he \wedge$ Patient$(e)=(bingrende)$ *ya*$]]$

　　　　V　　　*(bingren de) ya*
$\lambda y[\ \lambda e[Ba(e) \wedge$ Agent$(e)=x \wedge$ Patient$(e)= y]]$

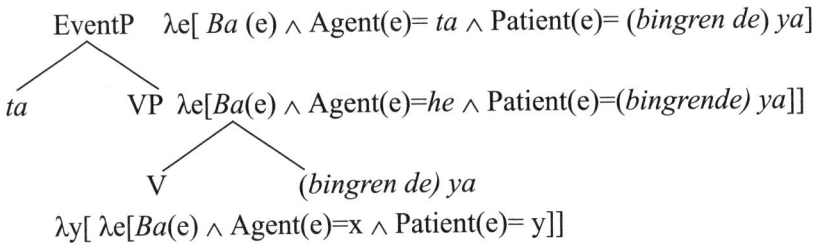

As (66) illustrates, all the arguments are introduced by the predicate verb. The possessor like *bing ren DE* rather than the subject combines with *ya* to form an independent possessive phrase before it occupies the object of the verb.

For (64c), the possessive relation should be interpreted as the relationship between *ta* and *ya*. If there is possessive relation between *ta* and *ya*, it is not likely that he is the agent who performed the action of *ba ya*. There should be another subject which is overt in the construction. Therefore, *ta* is not the argument that is introduced by the verb. *Ta* should be introduced by the functional node and the syntactic position *ta* occupies in the construction is not agent subject but the topic position ahead of the subject. The eventuality also shows that there is a syntactic gap in argument structure of transitive verb *ba*. When there must be the relationship between *ta* and *ya*, the construction is in essence Topic Construction. The derivation of (56c) is shown in (67).

(67) 他拔了（自己的）牙。

      Ta ba-le (ta de) ya.

      "He had his own teeth pulled out."

EventP $\lambda e[Loc(e)=ta \wedge \exists e'[\text{Become-Ba }(e') \wedge Pm(e')=ya]$
$\wedge \text{Having }(ta, ya)]$

Ta   Event'$\lambda x[\lambda e[Loc(e)=x \wedge \exists e'[\text{Become-Ba}(e') \wedge Pm(e')= ya$
$\wedge \text{Having }(x, ya)]$

Event$_{LOC}$ VP $\lambda e[\text{Become-Ba }(e) \wedge Pm(e)= ya]$

$\lambda y[\lambda P[\lambda x[\lambda e[Loc(e)=x \wedge \exists e'[P(e')$
$\wedge Pm (e') =y \wedge \text{Having }(x, y)]]]]]$

Bei-Ba   *ya*

$\lambda y[\lambda e[\text{Become-Beiba }(e) \wedge Pm(e)= y]]$

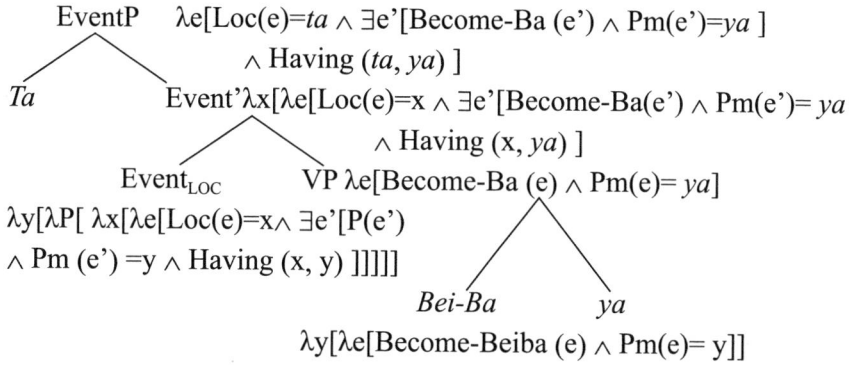

By comparing (66) with (67), we notice two differences. The first is that (66) is a simple event—there is only one event in the eventuality. We can use (68) to illustrate the logic form of (66).

(68) $\exists e[Ba (e) \wedge Agt(e) = ta \wedge Th(e)= ya]$

In (67), the eventuality shows that the Topic Construction is a compound event, which is composed of two atom events.

(69). $\exists e [Loc(e)=ta \wedge \exists e'[\text{Become-Beiba}(e') \wedge Pm(e')= ya \wedge \text{Having}(ta, ya)]]$

The second difference is the voice in the sentence. If the initial nominal is decoded as the agent subject, there is usually no possessive relation between the subject and the object. The construction is in active voice. If the initial nominal is decoded as the topic and there is possessive relation between the topic and the object, the sentence is in its passive voice in meaning. They are two different event types with different properties. (68) is the activity eventuality and (69) is BECOME event.

We see the eventuality analysis can help to distinguish the ambiguous sentences. Treating *"wangmian diu le qianbao"* as the Topic Construction can help us distinguish ambiguous sentences and it can help to analyze those that seem alike from the surface structure. For example:

(70) a. 王冕打碎了窗户。
　　　Wangmian dasui-le　chuanghu.
　　　Wangmian break-Perf window.
　　　"Wangmian has broken the window."
　　b. 王冕丢了钱包。
　　　Wangmian diu-le　qianbao.
　　　Wangmian lose-Perf wallet.
　　　"Wangmian has lost the wallet."

From the linear syntactic position, these two sentences seem to share the same construction "NP$_1$+VP+NP$_2$". In (70a) and (70b), the verbs take two arguments, one taking the subject position and the other taking the object position. In fact, they are of different type. (70a) is SVO construction while (70b) is of Topic Construction. The verb *diu* only carries one argument in the lexicon while *dasui* must get two arguments. The difference can be shown clearly from the derivation process of the eventuality.

(71) 王冕打碎了窗户。
　　Wangmian da-sui-le chuanghu.
　　Wangmian break-Perf window.
　　"Wangmian broke the window."

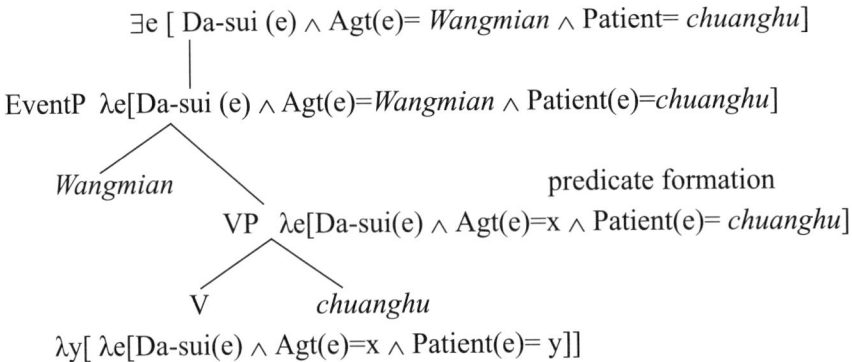

$\exists$e [Da-sui (e) $\wedge$ Agt(e)= *Wangmian* $\wedge$ Patient= *chuanghu*]

EventP λe[Da-sui (e) $\wedge$ Agt(e)=*Wangmian* $\wedge$ Patient(e)=*chuanghu*]

Wangmian　　　　　　　　　　　　predicate formation

VP　λe[Da-sui(e) $\wedge$ Agt(e)=x $\wedge$ Patient(e)= *chuanghu*]

V　　　*chuanghu*

λy[λe[Da-sui(e) $\wedge$ Agt(e)=x $\wedge$ Patient(e)= y]]

In (71), neither the verb *dasui* nor the noun *chuanghu* contains the possessive relation in the lexicon. What is more, there is no other elements that can trigger the possessive relation. *Wangmian* here is the agent of the verb and does not have the possessive relation with *chuanghu*.

The possessive relation illustrated in this chapter is triggered by *disappearing-type* verbs when they enter into Existential Construction. The *disappearing-type* verbs in this chapter include both intransitive verbs and transitive verbs. The intransitive verbs are mainly unaccusitive verbs like *diu,diao,duan* which mean the change of the state. This kind of change or disappearance is usually in autonomy. The verbs denote the reason or the way for the entity to disappear. Neither the intransitive verbs nor transitive verbs in their passive meaning contain possessive information in their lexical meaning from their lexicon. For example, the "subject+Vi" construction as "*diu le liangbai kuaiqian*" or "subject+vt+object" as "*wo beichi le sange pingguo*". No possessive relation exists in both of these constructions. The *disappearing-type* verbs offer the presupposed possessive relation semantically. The disappearance of the entity means that it existed before the disappearing event. The entity must occupy certain space or belong to a particular possessor. This kind of relation exists before the disappearance of the entity. When *disappearing-type* intransitive verbs enter into Existential Construction, the verb and the construction work together to trigger the possessive relation between the two entities. From the surface structure of the construction, we see one more argument, which is the possessor, is added to the construction.

When the intransitive *disappearing-type* verbs enter into Existent Construction, the construction becomes the Topic Construction with the locative nominal to be the topic. The introduction of the extra argument is realized by semantic means, therefore, has no direct relation with the predicate verbs semantically. From the perspective of the eventuality analysis, the event with extra argument and possessive relation entails the event without them. The extra possessor argument is usually more like a broad-sensed location than a possessor entity. The location interpretation of the possessor in the constructions makes it possible to be treated as the topic. When we analyze the eventuality of these constructions, the eventuality of the Existential Construction and PSPO constructions is corresponding with that of Topic Construction, which in turn fortifies the function the possessive relation plays in bridging the extra argument and the other part.

6.5 Passive DPC

6.5.1 Features of DPC

Passive DPC is a special variant of *Bei* construction. Broad-sensed Passive DPC refers to the passive construction in which there is retained object left behind the passive verb. These retained objects are of different types. Some are locative nouns and some are tool objects. Narrow-sensed passive DPC refers to those that exist in the transitive verbs in their passive form constructions. Such construction is special in that not all the objects are positioned before the passive verb. There is a part of the object retained at post-verbal position. Usually, the pretained object and the retained object maintain possessive relation or part-whole relation (Zhou, 2006; Deng, 2009; Ma, 2010) . Examples are as the following:

(72) a. 李四被打断了一条胳膊。
   Lisi bei daduan-le yitiao gebo.
   Lisi BEI break-Perf one-CL arm.
   "One of Lisi's arm is broken."

 b. 张三被杀了父亲。
   Zhangsan beisha-le   fuqin.
   Zhangsan BEI kill-Perf father.
   "Zhangsan's father is killed."

 c. 苹果被削了皮。
   Pingguo beixiao-le   pi.
   Apple   BEI peel-Perf skin.
   "The apple is peeled off the skin."

 d. 我被偷了钱包。
   Wo bei tou-le   qianbao.
   I BEI steal-Perf wallet.
   "My wallet was stolen."

　　e. 小明被妹妹抢走了玩具汽车。

　　　Xiaoming bei meimei qiangzou-le wanjuqichu.

　　　Xiaoming BEI sister rob-Perf toy train.

　　　"Xiaoming was robbed of the toy train by his sister."

f. 那本书被张三撕掉了封面。

　　Nabenshu bei (Zhangsan/pro) sidiao-le femgmian.

　　That book BEI(Zhangsan/pro) tear-off-Perf cover.

　　"That book is tore off the cover by Zhangsan."

In these examples, the initial nominal and the retained object can form the *de* possession as follows: *Lisi de gebo* "Lisi's arm"; *Zhangsan de baba* "Zhangsan's father"; *pingguopi* "the skin of the apple"; *wo de qianbao* "my wallet"; *Xiaoming de wanjuche* "Xiaoming's toy car"; *shu de fengmian* "the cover of the book". The predicate verbs in the construction are transitive verbs in their passive form. *Da xiao, tou, qiang, si* are verbs taking two arguments. The initial nominals are possessors. They are neither the agent nor the patient of the constructions, which means they have no direct semantic relation with the verbs. The "patient", which is really related with the verb, occupies the post-verbal position.

We can summarize the form of the passive DPC to be "NP_1+ [*Bei* (NP_3) +V_2]^1+NP_2", among which NP_1 and NP_2 have possessive relation. Np_3 in the construction can be omitted, which imposes no difference to the structure of the construction. Although the verb itself is transitive verb, the predicate part in the form of [*Bei* (NP_3) +V_2]^1 functions like an intransitive verb.

6.5.2 Properties of the Verb in Passive DPC

6.5.2.1 Syntactic Property

Pan (2005) lists the surface unaccusative verbs in Chinese which include passive verbs. In a sense, passive verbs should be considered as a kind of derived unaccusative verbs. They are derived from corresponding transitive verbs. The passivization refrains the external argument of the original transitive verb and at the same time, the verbs lose the nature of transitivity and become a intransitive-like verb functionally. He notices that the base-generated objects can stay in situ, which will result in examples of (73) and (74).

(73) 被抢了一个钱包。
Bei qiang-le   yi ge qianbao.
Bei robbed-Perf one-CL wallet.
*"was robbed of a wallet."

(74) 被打伤了一条胳膊。
Bei dashang-le yitiao gebo.
bei hurt   one-CL arm.
*"was hurt one arm."

Xujie (2002) also emphasizes the "unaccusativity" of the predicate verb in passive construction and unaccusative construction. He holds that the syntactic features of some unaccusative verbs are introduced from the lexicon but the syntactic features of the passive verbs are the result of "passivization", as shown in the chart:

example	Features from lexicon	Syntactic operation	
		Former Passivization	Latter operation
si	Carry a patient thematic role but can not assign objective case	No syntactic operation	Assign patient role but can not assign case to object
Bei-sha	Carry two thematic roles and can assign objective case	Bei absorb the objective case as well as the Agent thematic role	

Wu (2011) illustrates the properties of the verbs and gives the classifications of the verbs. From the surface form of the construction, we can judge the nature of the verbs.

Intransitive verb(i)	NP+V	* V+NP		Ordinary intransitive verb(unergative)
Intransitive verb(ii) Transitive verb(i)	NP+V NP1+V+NP2	V+NP NP2 +V	unaccusative verb ergative transitive verbs	ergative verbs
Transitive(ii)	NP1+V+NP2	*NP2+V		transitive (unergative)

Different from the passivization account, passive construction in Mandarin Chinese is considered to be base-generated construction. Some hold that strictly speaking, there is no passivization in Mandarin Chinese. The passive construction is not derived but base generated by adding *Bei* to the verb. The construction is used to indicate that the subject undergoes something unhappy. Ma (2013), An (2007) formulate that the passive meaning is just the meaning affiliated with "*Bei*" and passive construction in Mandarin Chinese is not corresponding with the equivalence in English that is derived from active construction. They state that Passive DPC is in fact a special construction in Mandarin Chinese employed to show misfortune experience.

6.5.2.2 Semantic Property

Fan (2006) mentions the result caused by the action when he studies the semantic features of the passive predicates. Action verbs are typical verbs used as predicate in passive construction. Since the passive construction is used to indicate that the theme or patient entity is suffered from a kind of "action" or is in a certain situation (being changed, being moved or being depriving of sth) resulting from the action. [+result] is compulsive feature for the passive DPC in that the result of the action may exert a kind of influence on the object. This feature is not overt in all the verbs in passive construction. In these verbs, [+action] is quite clear but [+result] should be entailed in the meaning of the verb. For example, *chi, zhuang, tou, sha, yao, reng, diu, tou* are mono-syllable verbs, when they are in passive construction, *le* is used to indicate the result and help to make the construction complete.

> (75) a. 老人被车撞了。
>   Laoren   bei che zhuang-le.
>   old man Bei car knock-down-Perf.
>   "The old man was knocked down by the car."
>   b. 牲畜都被敌人杀了。
>   Shengchu dou bei diren sha-le.
>   cattle   all Bei enemy kill-Perf.
>   "All the cattle were killed by the enemy."

c. 孩子被狗咬了。

haizi bei gou yao-le.

child Bei dog bite-Perf.

"The child was bite by the dog."

In these sentences, [+action]in *zhuang sha yao* is overt. These actions must lead to certain results. If an old man is hit by a car, it is quite natural that the accident may impose great influence on the old man. The influence can be physical injure or psychology influence. The knocking event affects the old man. The old man may be in the situation of being *duan shang tong si* as the result of the action. If the sentence is in form of the passive construction, it indicates the action has been completed and the result has come into being. In passive DPC, information about the PM serves as further information to illustrate what specific result or influence has been caused.

(76) a. 老人被车撞伤了腿。

Laoren bei che zhuang   shang-le tui.

old man Bei car knock down-hurt-Perf leg.

"The old man was knocked down and got hurt in the leg."

b. 孩子被狗咬伤了手。

Haizi bei gou yaoshang-le shou.

child Bei dog bite-hurt-Perf hand

"The child was bit by the dog and got hurt in the hand."

(76a) means that the car hit the old man and as a result, the man's leg is hurt. (76b) means the dog's biting the boy leads to the injury on the hand.

We can see that passive DPC in Mandarin Chinese in fact is the construction to emphasize the result of an action. Usually, the possessor in the construction is adversely affected by the event where PR is involved. As the result, the possessor is treated as the malefactive of the event. The construction is considered to be Adversity Passives.

6.5.3 Analyze in Topic-comment Pattern

No matter whether the passive verb is analyzed as the result of the passivization or *Bei* is used to generate the passive DPC construction directly, what matters is that the predicate verb in "*Bei*+Vt" can only take one argument in the construction. Just as Deng (2004) illustrates "ergativization is the strategy to make transitive verbs into intransitive verb". We will see whether the verbs in (77)-(82) can form "NP$_2$+V" construction.

(77) a. 李四被打断了一条腿。

　　　Lisi bei daduan-le yitiao tui.

　　　Lisi Bei break-Perf one-CL leg.

　　　"Lisi suffered from the result that one of his legs was broken."

　　b. 李四的一条腿被打断了。

　　　Lisi de yitiao tui bei daduan-le.

　　　Lisi's one-CL leg Bei break-Perf.

　　　"one of Lisi's legs is broken."

　　c. * 一条胳膊被打断了。

　　　*Yitiao gebo bei daduan-le.

　　　one-CL arm Bei break-Perf.

　　　*"An arm was broken."

(78) a. 张三被杀了父亲。

　　　Zhangsan bei sha-le fuqin.

　　　Zhangsan Bei kill-Perf father.

　　　"Zhangsan suffered from the fact that his father got killed."

　　b. 张三的父亲被杀了。

　　　Zhangsan de fuqin beisha-le.

　　　Zhangsan's father Bei-kill-Perf.

　　　"Zhangsan's father got killed."

　　c. * 父亲被杀了。

　　　*fuqin beisha-le.

　　　father Bei kill-Perf.

　　　"Father was killed."

(79) a. 苹果被削了皮。

　　　Pingguo bei xiao-le pi.

　　　apple   Bei peel-Perf skin.

　　　"The apple was peeled off the skin."

b. 苹果皮被削了。

Pingguopi bei xiao-le.

apple skin Bei peel-Perf.

"The skin of the apple was peeled."

c. * 皮被削了。

*Pi bei xiao-le.

skin Bei peel-Perf.

*"was peeled."

(80) a. 我被偷了钱包。

Wo bei tou-le   qianbao.

I Bei steal-Perf wallet.

"I suffered from the fact that I had my wallet stolen."

b. 我的钱包被偷了。

Wo de qianbao bei tou-le.

I de wallet Bei steal-Perf.

"My wallet was stolen."

c. 钱包被偷了。

Qianbao bei tou-le.

wallet Bei steal-Perf.

"The wallet got stolen."

(81) a. 小明被妹妹抢走了玩具汽车。

Xiaoming bei meimei qiangzou-le wanjuqiche.

Xiaoming Bei sister rob-away-Perf toy car.

"Xiaoming suffered from the fact that his toy car was robbed away by his sister."

b. 小明的玩具汽车被妹妹抢走了。

Xiaoming de wanjuqiche bei meimei qiangzou-le.

Xiaoming De toy car Bei sister rob-away-Perf.

"Xiaoming's toy car was robbed away by his sister."

c. 玩具汽车被抢走了。

Wanju qiche bei meimei qiangzou-le.

toy car Bei sister rob-away-Perf.

"The toy car was robbed away."

(82) a. 那本书被张三撕掉了封面。

Nabenshu   bei Zhangsan sidiao-le fengmian.

that-CL book Bei Zhangsan tear-off-Perf cover.

"The book was tore off the cover by Zhangsan."

b. 那本书的封面被张三撕掉了。

Nabenshu de femgnian bei Zhangsan sidiao-le.

that-CL book De cover Bei Zhangsan tear-Perf.

"The cover of the book was tore off by Zhangsan."

c. 封面被撕掉了。

Fengmian bei sidiao-le.

cover   Bei tear-off-Perf.

"The cover was tore off."

Group (b) show that there is possessive relation existing in the construction. The ungrammatical features of (77b), (78b) and (79b) are not the result of the predicate verb but the result of inalienable possessive relation. In (77), (78) (79), relational nouns bring in the possessive relation, but how about (80)-(82)? How can the construction generate possessive relation manifested in the construction?

The possessive relation contained in the construction is a kind of covert relation. It is not introduced by the verb itself.

(83) a. 我被偷了钱包。

Wo bei tou-le   qianbao.

I Bei steal-Perf wallet.

"I have had my wallet stolen"

b. 我（的东西）被偷了。

Wo bei tou-le.

I Bei steal-Perf.

* "I was stolen."

c. 钱包被偷了。

Qianbao bei tou-le.

Wallet Bei steal-Perf.

"The wallet is stolen."

(84) a. 小明被妹妹抢走了玩具汽车。

Xiaoming bei meimei qiangzou-le   wanjuqiche.

Xiaoming Bei sister   take-away-Perf toy car.

"Xiaoming had his toy car taken away by his sister."

    b. * 小明被抢走了。

      *Xiaoming bei qiangzou-le.

      Xiaoming Bei take away-Perf.

      "Xiaoming was taken away."

    c. 玩具汽车被抢走了。

      Wanju qiche bei qiangzou-le.

      toy car Bei take away-Perf

      "The toy car was taken away."

(85) a. 那本书被张三撕掉了封面。

      Naben shu bei Zhangsan sidiao-le fengmian.

      that-CL book Bei Zhangsan tear-off-Perf cover.

      "The cover of the book was tore off by Zhangsan."

    b. * 那本书被张三撕掉了。

      *nabenshu bei Zhangsan sidiao-le.

      That book Bei Zhangsan tear-off-Perf.

      "The book was tore off by Zhangsan."

    c. 封面被撕掉了。

      Fengmian bei sidiao-le.

      cover Bei tear off-Perf.

      "The cover was tore off."

    Group (b) show that the initial noun is not chosen by the verb. (83b), (84b) and (85b) can be independent sentences by themselves, but the meaning of these sentences are different from what is meant to illustrate. The initial nouns are not related with the verbs directly semantically and they are not the agents who start the action either. Group (c) show that the PM is the theme that is really related to the predicate verb. The possessor in these sentences occupies the initial position. *Xiaoming* and *naben shuare* are all definite noun phrases. What is more important is that there is possessive relation between the two elements. The eventuality of these constructions is exactly the same as the Topic Construction. Only when the initial nominal occupies the topic position can the possessive relation be generated and ensured. Therefore, we argue that the passive DPC is also a kind of Topic Construction. It is the topic possessor that triggers the possessive relation contained in the construction.

6.5.4 Eventuality analysis

From the perspective of the semantic event, passive DPC is a compound event with two sub-events. e_1 is the topic event with the possessor to be the only argument and e_2 is a event denoting a result. There is possessive relation between the topic and the theme in e_2. We take *wo bei tou-le qianbao* as the example. The logic form of *wo bei tou-le qianbao* is (86):

(86) $\exists$e [Possessor-top(e)= *wo* $\wedge$ $\exists$e'[Become-Tou(e')
　　　$\wedge$ Pm(e')= *qianbao* $\wedge$ Having (*wo, qianbao*)]
　　e_1: $\exists$e [Top(e) $\wedge$ Possessor-top(e)= *wo*]
　　e_2: $\exists$ e'[Become-beitou(e') $\wedge$ Pm(e')= *qianbao*]
　　e_3: Having (*wo, qianbao*)

We can also prove the topic status from the topicalization. *Qianbao bei toule* means that someone stole my wallet, as in (87):

(87) X　　tou-le　wo qianbao.
　　Someone steal-Perf me wallet.
　　"Someone stole the wallet from me."

In (87), there is possessive relation between *wo* and *qianbao*. It is "my wallet" that is stolen. When we move the noun forward to serve as the topic, we find the direct object and indirect object behave differently.

(88) a. wo, X tou-le qianbao.
　　b. *qianbao, Xtou-le wo.

The indirect object *wo* can be moved to the initial position to be the topic while the direct object can't.

(89) a. 我被偷了钱包。
　　Wo bei tou-le　qianbao.
　　I Bei steal-Perf wallet.
　　"I had my wallet stolen."
　　b. 钱包被偷了我。

*Qianbao Bei X tou le   wo.

wallet Bei X steal-Perf me

If (88a) is in the form of (89a), we get the passive DPC. We can see that the possessive relation between *wo* and *qianbao*.

Now we can account for the source of the possessive relation. In passive DPC, when the possessor *wo* occupies initial topic position, it triggers the possessive relation between *wo* and *qianbao*. Naturally, in (86), the wallet should be mine or at that time I am responsible for the wallet. *Wo* occupies the topic position, the subject of the sentence can be an overt lexical element like *Xiaotou*, or it can be a syntactic gap.

Xu (2004) mentions that in passive DPC, the possessor must coexist in the sentence with the PM in order to make a complete sentence. He compares (27a) and (27b). The reason why (27b) is ungrammatical and not so good semantically is that possessor nominal does not exist in the sentence. He further illustrates the conditions to assign partitive case. He maintains that when partitive case is assigned to the object, the possessor nominal should be the subject. What is more, this possessor nominal should be an overt lexical NP, rather than an empty category. We agree that there should be the possessive relation and the possessor nominal to be at the initial position. What we differ from Xu (2004) is that we think the possessor is the topic instead of being the subject. It is the initial topic that can trigger and ensure the possessive relation between two elements in the passive DPC.

(91) $\lambda e[Poss(e)=Lisi \wedge \lambda e'[Become\text{-}Tou(e') \wedge Pm(e')= qianbao$
$\wedge Having(Lisi, qianbao)]$

EventP $\lambda e[Poss(e)=Lisi \wedge \lambda e'[Become\text{-}beitou(e') \wedge Pm(e')= qianbao$
$\wedge Having (Lisi, qianbao)]$

Lisi

Event' $\lambda x[\lambda e[Poss(e)=x \wedge \lambda e'[Become\text{-}beitou (e')$
$\wedge Pm(e')=qianbao] \wedge Having (x, qianbao)]$

Event $_{Poss}$ VP $\lambda e[Become\text{-}beitou (e) \wedge Pm(e)=qianbao]$

$\lambda P[\lambda x[\lambda e[Poss(e)=x \wedge \lambda e'[P(e')$ Become-Tou   qianbao
$\wedge Pm (e') =y \wedge Having (x, y)]]]]$ $\lambda y[\lambda e[Become\text{-}Tou (e) \wedge Pm(e)= y]]$

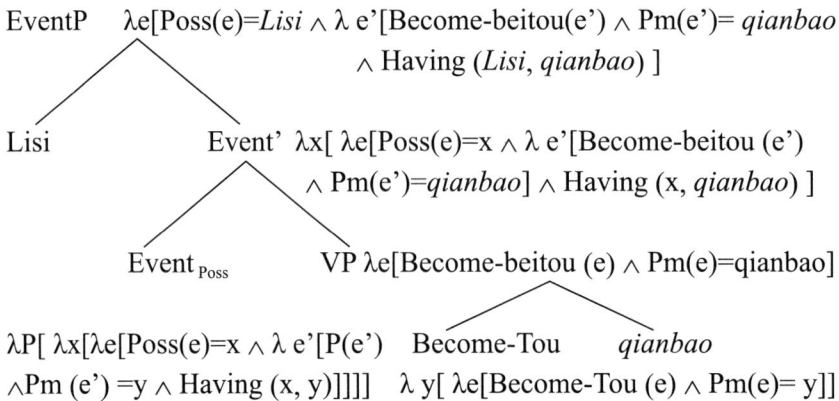

6.6 Summary

The possessive relation is reflected at different levels. It can be lexicalized as the information part of relational nouns or the verbs with depriving meaning. It is constrained within the phrase and is introduced by the lexical item by itself. In contrast, the possessive relation illustrated in this chapter is generated at clausal level. The possessive meaning is part of construction meaning of Topic Construction. The constructions discussed in this part share some similarities:

Firstly, they share the same eventuality structure. With the appearance of the extra argument, the structure of the eventuality becomes complex. These events are compound event with more than one atom event. There must be a certain connection that combines all the atom events and participants together. On the one hand, all the atom events are related in a compound event; on the other hand, all the participants in the event stand in certain relation with the events. These are the similarities underneath the surface syntactic construction.

Secondly, there is an extra argument which is not chosen by any lexical predicate verb in the construction. As far as the way we incorporate the extra element, the first constrain should be that the extra element has semantic relation with the rest part. For example, we have different kinds of clauses. The reason that we can combine two clauses into one complex one is that they have a kind of semantic relation. The relation can be overt with the help of conjunctions like *yinwei, ruguo*, and the semantic relation can be covert without any lexical items. It is the same with the constructions here. In this case, the extra element is not a clause but just a nominal denoting possessor. As the result, the semantic relation that combines the extra argument is the possessive relation rather than other kind. The extra argument has possessive relation with another entity semantically and syntacticly it occupies a position higher than the PM.

Thirdly, the event containing the PM is comparatively independent construction. The predicate verb in the atom event is either an unaccusative verb in Existential Construction, PSPO construction or Passive DPC or transitive verb in comment clause. From the perspective of the syntax, they are independent clause, which center on the theme entity.

Fourthly, functional node is employed in introducing the extra argument into the construction. The function head is the most complex part in semantic type and functions as the predicate in semantic derivation. It is of the type of $<<d,<e, t>, <d,<e, t>>>$. In the functional node, it not only takes in topic argument syntactically, but also brings in the possessive relation as well.

Despite of the similarities, there are differences in the constrains in triggering the possessive relation. First of all, they have different kinds of topics. In typical Topic Construction, the possessive relation is quite loose. The initial topic nominal is added and it must satisfy the need to build up possessive relation. It can be inalienable possession or the set-subset relation. It is the syntactic operation to bring the extra argument together with possessive relation. But for the Locative Topic Construction as *disappearing-type* Existential Construction and PSPO, the meaning of the verb plays an crucial role in triggering the possession. It is the combination of both the construction and the verb that triggers the possessive relation in the construction. As for the passive DPC, the meaning of the verb in its passive form also contributes to the formation of the construction.

Chapter Seven

Constructions with complex possession

We have employed three types of predicates to denote possessive relations, namely, Having (x, y), Belonging_to (y, x) and Included_in (y, x). The possessive relation represented by these three types predicates are entailed in the two elements in the constructions. "Belonging_to (y, x)" denotes the inalienable possession, which is brought by relational nouns from the lexicon. The inalienable possession is the prototype of possession and should be interpreted compulsorily. "Having (x, y)" is used to denote the possessive relation the possessum obtained from the verb frame. "Included_in (y, x)" is a special possession type that exists in the Topic Construction. These predicates, which are not lexical verbs in the syntactic construction, represent the semantic relation between the arguments involved in the events. It is just because this kind of covert semantic relation and the different mechanism to introduce the possessive relation that we find the "mismatch" in the construction. Possessive relation can be triggered by the lexical meaning of either the relational nouns or the *depriving-type* transitive verb frame. The relation can be part of the construction meaning and be introduced by functional node as well. No matter what kind of the mechanism is taken, there will be a singular type of possession generated in the constructions. Sometimes these two means work together and the complex type of the possession construction will come into being.

7.1 Multi-element triggered possessive relation

We propose three kinds possessive relations in the DPC and each of them has its way to enter into the construction. For the inalienable possession brought in by relational nouns, it goes all the way with the relational nouns until the possessor argument fits the variable contained in relational nouns. For the possessive relation concerned with the construction, the possession functional node makes it possible to involve in the possessive relation as well as the possessor argument. The PM in possessive relation can be either the common noun or the relational noun. When the relational noun functions as the common noun and is used in the Topic Construction or other constructions concerned in this dissertation, these two kinds of nouns share the same linear order in surface structure. For example:

(1) a. 村里丢了一条狗。

     Cun li   diu-le   yitiao gou.

     Town ins   lose-Perf one-CL dog.

     "A dog that belongs to the town is lost."

  b. 桌子断了一条腿。

     Zhuozi duanle   yitiao tui.

     Table   break-Perf one-CL leg.

     "One of the table's legs is broken."

(2) a. 王冕死了四棵桃树。

     Wangmian si-le   sike   taoshu.

     Wangmian die-Perf four-CL peach tree.

     "Four of Wangmian's peach trees died."

  b. 王冕死了父亲。

     Wangmian   si-le   fuqin.

     Wangmian die-Perf father.

     "Wangmian's father died on him."

(3) a. 张三个子很高。

     Zhangsan gezi   hen gao.

     Zhangsan   height very high.

     "Zhangsan is very high."

    b. 学生，我最喜欢张三。

    Xuesheng, wo zui xihuan Zhangsan.

    Student   I   most like   Zhangsan.

    "As for the students, I like Zhangsan the most."

(4) a. 李四被偷了两百块钱。

    Lisi beitoule   liangbai   kuai qian.

    Lisi   bei steal-Perf two hundred CL   money.

    "Lisi had his two hundred yuan stolen. "

    b. 张三被杀了父亲。

    Zhangsan beisha-le   fuqin.

    Zhangsan bei kill-Perf father.

    "Zhangsan had his father killed."

Examples (1) and (2) indicate that both the common nouns and relational nouns can appear in *disappearing-type* Existential Construction and PSPO construction. In (1a) and (1b), the possessive relation between *yitiao gou* "a dog" and *sike taoshu* "four peach trees" and *cunli* "in the village" and *Wangmian* is established by means of the interaction between the verb *diu* and *si* and the Existential Construction.

Example (3) and (4) are Topic Constructions. In (3a) and (4a), the PMs are just common nouns but in (3b) and (4b) relational nouns appear at the same syntactic position. The following questions may arise: What kind of possessive relation we may have for such constructions and how the possessive relation gets its final interpretation.

7.2 Relational nouns in *disappearing-type* Existential Construction

The possessive relation between *yitiaogou* "a dog" and *cunzi* "in the village" and *sike taoshu* "four peach trees" and *Wangmian* belong to the kind of "Having" possession defined in Chapter 6. It is most likely that there are more than one dog in the village and there are more than four peach trees in the possession of *Wangmian*. The possessive functional node is involved to introduce both the possessor and possessive relation. In (1b) and (2b), *yitiao tui* "one leg" and *fuqin* "father" bring along with them the inalienable possession, which is the "Belonging_to" possession.

Here comes the dilemma we are in: the combination of the construction and the verb offers "Having" type alienable possession while there is the compulsory interpretation of inalienable possession in the construction.

First, the semantic derivation of (2a) is shown in (5) and (6):

(5)   EventP $\exists e[Loc(e)=$*Wangmian* $\wedge \exists e'[Si(e') \wedge Pm(e')=$ *siketaoshu*
$\wedge$ Having (*Wangmian, siketaoshu*)]

Wangmian   Event'

Event$_{LOC}$ $\lambda e[Si(e') \wedge Pm(e')=$*siketaoshu*]
$\lambda y[\lambda P[\lambda x[\lambda e[Loc(e)=x \wedge \exists e'[P(e')$
$\wedge Pm (e') =y] \wedge$ Having (x, $\geqq$ y)]]]]]

(6)
EventP $<e, t>$

$<d>$ Event' $<d,<e, t>>$
$<d,<e, t>>$

Event$_{Top}$ VP $<e,t>$ type raising
$<<d,<e, t>>, <d,<e, t>>>$

V   NP
$<d,<e, t>>$ $<d>$

In (5), when *si* "die" combines with *sike taoshu* "four peach trees" to form the VP phrase, the verb does not take the operation of type-raising since there is no possessive relation at this level. *Si* "die" is of the semantic type: $<d,<e, t>>$ and *siketaoshu* 'four peach tree' is of the semantic type: $<d>$. Their semantic types match: the verb functions as the predicate and takes the argument of $<d>$ type. That is the reason why we may have the sentence as *sike taoshu sile* "Four peach trees died". The sentence is grammatical without the possessive interpretation and the corresponding semantic type is $<e, t>$, which is the type of a position or a state before the closure of the event. When *Wangman* is added to the construction, it functions as the locative topic. Together with *Wangmian*, the possessive relation comes into being as well. *Wangmian* changes the single event without possessive relation into the compound event with possessive relation. We need to add a possessor variable into the event and as the result, the semantic type of the VP should be raised from <e,t> to <d,<e, t>>. The possessive functional node becomes the predicate of the most complicated semantic type of< <d,<e, t>>, <d,<e, t>>>. After the type raising, the VP can function as the argument and the functional application can be applied to VP. It is the process to substitute λyλP, which takes in a variable. The possessive relation generated in this way is the alienable possession of "Having". In the logic form of the construction, we refer to it as "Having (x, ≧ y) ". From the derivation process, we find that the possessive relation enters the construction at VP level.

   The derivation of (2b) with the relational noun is shown as (7) and (8):

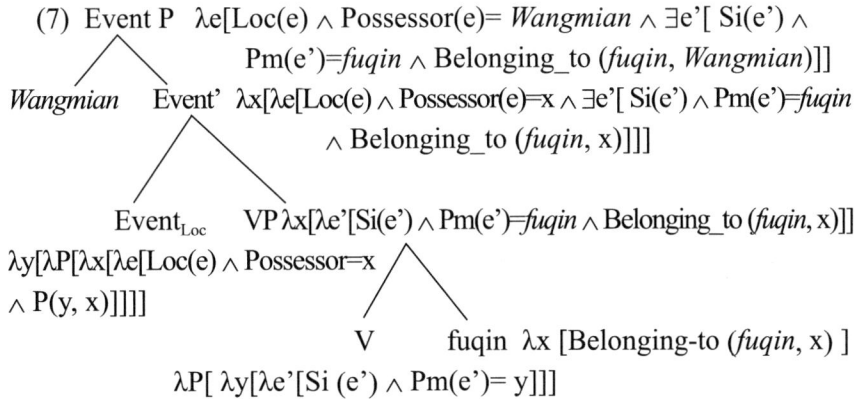

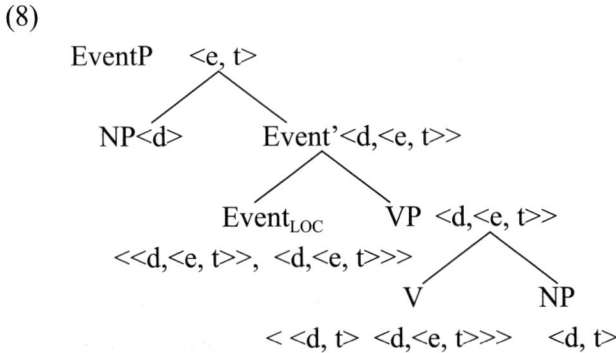

(7) Event P λe[Loc(e) ∧ Possessor(e)= *Wangmian* ∧ ∃e'[Si(e') ∧
          Pm(e')=*fuqin* ∧ Belonging_to (*fuqin*, *Wangmian*)]]

Wangmian   Event' λx[λe[Loc(e) ∧ Possessor(e)=x ∧ ∃e'[Si(e') ∧ Pm(e')=*fuqin*
          ∧ Belonging_to (*fuqin*, x)]]]

   Event$_{Loc}$ VP λx[λe'[Si(e') ∧ Pm(e')=*fuqin* ∧ Belonging_to (*fuqin*, x)]]
λy[λP[λx[λe[Loc(e) ∧ Possessor=x
∧ P(y, x)]]]]

                 V   *fuqin* λx [Belonging-to (*fuqin*, x)]
          λP[λy[λe'[Si (e') ∧ Pm(e')= y]]]

(8)

   EventP   <e, t>

      NP<d>   Event'<d,<e, t>>

         Event$_{LOC}$ VP <d,<e, t>>
      <<d,<e, t>>, <d,<e, t>>>
                        V   NP
               < <d, t> <d,<e, t>>>   <d, t>

   When the object noun is the relational noun in the construction, according to the rule we propose in Chapter 4, there will be the operation of type-raising inside the VP node. That is the type of the verb itself needs to be raised. Here in (8), *fuqin* is the relational noun and *si* needs a raising in its semantic type. The semantic type will be raised from $<d,<e, t>>$ to $<<d, t>,<d,<e, t>>>$. As the result, after functional application, we have the VP of the semantic type of $<d,<e, t>>$. Above the VP node, we find the functional node of the type $<<d,<e, t>>, <d,<e, t>>>$. The semantic types of the VP and the functional node match and the functional application is applied. The possessive relation is contained inside the VP node and it is the verb that raises its semantic type. When the calculation comes to VP, the semantic type is of the type $<d,<e, t>>$, when it is taken in by the functional node as the argument, what happens is different from the one we have in (6). Since there is the variable carried by the relational noun, when VP is incorporated, not only λy is replaced with the relational but λx is substituted for. The information of variable x covers the variable x in the function node as well as the type of the possessive relation. Therefore, when the derivation goes to the topic noun, the last argument that comes into the structure will replace variable x and becomes the topic at the syntactic structure and possessor of PM semantically. The interpretation we get at last will be the inalienable possession carried by relation noun from the lexicon.

(5) and (7) share the same surface structure but the type of the possessive relation and the way and syntactic node that generates the relation are quite different.

7.3 Relational nouns in Topic Construction

In Chapter 6, we focus mainly on the possessive relation in Chinese-style Topic Construction. The appearance of the topic nominal triggers the possessive relation in the construction. The initial topic nominal has the "aboutness" relation with the comment proposition and in Mandarin Chinese Topic Construction, possessive relation instantiates the "aboutness" relation. The generic topic triggers the set and subset possession, which is represented as Included-in relation. Besides the typical Topic Construction, there is another kind of well-accepted Topic Construction, that is, to employ subject-predicate phrase to be the comment proposition. In the comment proposition, PR usually occupies the subject position. The construction with the possessive relation between the initial topic and the subject of comment proposition is accepted to be a kind of Topic Construction, just as examples in (9) and (10):

(9) a. 大象鼻子很长。

    Daxiang   bizi   henchang.

    elephant   nose   very long.

    "Elephant's nose is very long."

  b. 这间房间门小，窗户大。

    Zhejian   fangjian men xiao chuanghu da.

    this-CL   room door small window big.

    "This room has a small door and a big window."

(10) a. 张三头发白了一大半。

    Zhangsan   toufa   baile   yidaban.

    Zhangsan   hair   white-Perf half.

    "Half of Zhangsan's hair is while."

  b. 这盆花掉了很多叶子。

    Zhepen hua   yezi   diaole   haojipian.

    this-CL flower leaf fall-Perf several-CL.

    "Several leaves of the flower fall off."

The possessive relation in (9a) and (9b) between *daxiang* "elephant" and *bizi* "nose", *fangjian* "room" and *men* "door" can be realized by inserting the possessive marker *de* as shown in (11):

(11) a. 大象的鼻子很长。

    Daxiang de bizi   henchang.

    elephant DE nose very long.

    "Elephant's nose is very long."

  b. 这间房间的门小。

    Zhejian   fangjian de menxiao.

    this-classifier room DE door small.

    "The door of this room is small."

In (11) the possessive relation is denoted by means of lexical possessive marker *de* and the possession is in the form of a possessive phrase. The possession expressed this way does not impose any influence on the combination of syntactic elements. We can illustrate it clearly from the logical form of the construction:

(12) ∃s[Chang(s) ∧ Th(s)=*daxiang de bizi*]

In the logic form, there is no particular predicate for possessive relation. The possessive relation is inside of the noun phrase.

In (9a), the possessive relation between *daxiang* "elephant" and *bizi* "nose" are not in the same constitute. *Daxiang* is just the possessor of *bizi* semantically, and as far as the syntactic status is concerned, they occupy different syntactic positions. We can insert other grammatical elements in the PR and PM nominals. For example, we can add adverb *xianran* in (13):

(13) 大象显然鼻子很长。
　　 Daxiang　xianran　 bizi　henchang.
　　 elephant　obviously　nose　very long.
　　 "The elephant's nose is obviously very long."

We can also insert *a, ne, ya*, ect or *shibushi* to test the status of the topic nominal:

(14) a. 大象是不是鼻子很长。
　　　 Daxiang shibushi　bizi　 hen　chang.
　　　 elephant is or is't　 nose　very　long
　　　 "Isn't elephant's nose long?"
　　 b. 大象啊，鼻子很长。
　　　 Daxiang a　bizi　henchang.
　　　 daxiang pause　nose　very long.
　　　 "As for the elephant, its nose is very long."

Two points can be drawn from examples in (13), (14a) and (14b). The first is that the PR and PM are in the different constituents and can be separated from each other. The second point is that the initial nominal is the topic of the construction. (9a) is different from (11a) in that (9a) is a compound event, which is composed of a topic event and a comment event. The logic form of (9a) is (15):

(15) $\exists s[\text{Top}(s)= \textit{daxiang} \wedge \exists s'[\text{Chang}(s) \wedge \text{Pm}(s)=\textit{bizi}$
$\wedge \text{Belonging\_to}(\textit{bizi}, \textit{daxiang})]$

In (9a) , the Topic Construction requires the possessive relation between the topic and the subject contained in comment proposition. In Chapter 6, we define the possessive relation in the Topic Construction as "Included_ in" relation, while in (15), we detect the "Belonging_ to" type of the possession between *daxiang* and *bizi*. If the relational noun exists in the Topic Construction, how does it realize its inalienable possession? We use the semantic derivation to illustrate the process. We choose (15) as the example:

(16) 张三个子高，脾气好。
Zhangsan gezi gao, piqi hao.

EventP $\lambda s[\text{Top}(s)= \textit{Zhangsan} \wedge \exists s'[\text{Gao}(s') \wedge \text{Pm}(s')= \textit{gezi}$
$\wedge \text{Belonging-to}(\textit{gezi}, \textit{Zhangsan})]$

Zhangsan <d>   Event'<d,<e, t>

Event$_{\text{Poss}}$ VP <d,<s, t>
$\lambda y[\lambda P[\lambda x[\lambda s[\text{Top}(s)=x \wedge \exists s'[P(y, x)]]]]]$
<<d,<s, t>> , <d,<s, t>>>   *gao*   *gezi* $\lambda x[\text{Belonging-to}(\textit{gezi}, x)$
V   NP
<d,<s, t>>   <d, t>

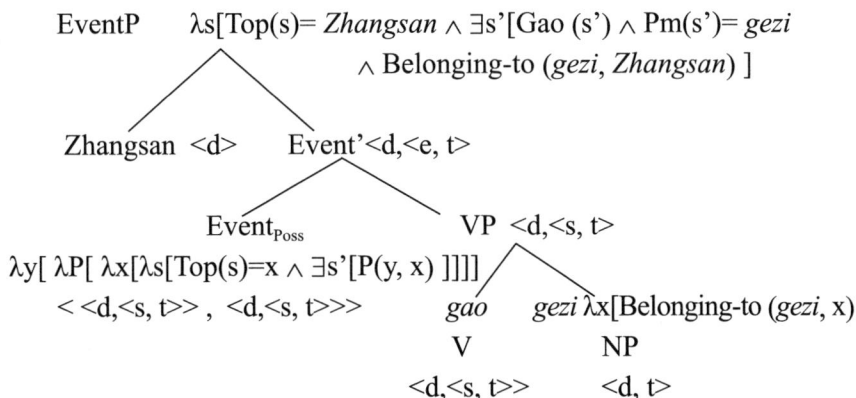

Gao 'tall' is the predicate of the semantic type of <d,<s, t> and when it goes with the argument of the type <e, t>, the semantic type of *gao* will be raised from <d,<s, t>> to <d, t>,>d,<s, t>>. When the derivation goes to the VP node, *gaogezi* has become a state clause with a possessive variable. Because the topic appears at the initial syntactic position, the possessive functional node is between the topic and the comment. The functional node is like a predicate which takes two arguments. It takes a topic entity and a comment proposition. What is more, there is "Included_ in" possession in the functional node. In (16), λP is the part that stands for the possessive relation. When the argument which contains a possessive variable is taken into the functional node, "Belonging_ to" type possessive relation covers the "Included_in" type possessive possession. When *Zhangsan* substitutes for the variable x, it becomes the syntactic topic and the argument of abstract possessive predicate. What is presented in the construction is the "Belonging_to" type possessive relation.

The functional node for the topic is used to bring in possessive relation. "Included_in" type possession and "Belonging_to" type possession are two kinds of possessive relations and are generated at different levels. "Included_in" type possession is the possessive relation for the Topic Construction, which is generated at the external layer. The node is above the VP level and it should be at the level of IP, since the comment proposition can be a complete sentence as "*wo xihuan chi pingguo*". When such kind of sentence is taken to be comment proposition, before the event Existential Closure, we can do some operation to change its semantic type. We label the proposition with possessive relation information and make the clause into an open predicate clause. The solution illustrated here can account for the fact that relational nouns can help to make Topic Construction and it can offer the account for the possessive relation in the Topic Construction with "*wo xihuan chi pingguo*" to be the comment proposition.

Usually it is not hard to interpreter the singular-type possessive relation in the constructions. We suggest three types of possession generated at different levels. When possessive relation is introduced at lexical level, the eventuality is simple, including just a single atom event. The possessive relation is represented by the abstract possession predicate "Having" or "Belonging_to" and is included into the logic form with conjunction. The eventuality becomes more complex when the possessive relation comes into the constructions with the extra argument. We will have a compound event which includes an embedded atom event. It is the possession functional node that helps to build the relation and takes in the extra argument. The most complicated eventuality is the complex-type possessive relation constructions in which both the lexical relational nouns and the Topic Construction work together. Since the possessor information carried by relational nouns is from the lexicon, in the complex type construction, it gains priority to other kind of possession type.

7.4 BA construction with possessive relation

7.4.1 *Ba* construction with retained object

We find possessive relation in *Ba* construction as the example in (17):

> (16) a. 他把橘子剥了皮。
>   Ta   ba   juzi   bo-le   pi.
>   he   ba   orange peel-Perf skin.
>   "He peeled the orange off its skin."
>   b. 大风把屋顶掀了一个角。
>   Dafeng   ba wuding xianle   yige   jiao.
>   strong wind ba roof   raise-Perf one CL corner.
>   "The strong wind raised one corner of the roof."

In (17a) and (17b), *juzi* and *pi*, *wuding* and *yijiao* are in the relation of inalienable possession, which are in part-whole relation.

As for the generation of *Ba* construction, *Ba* is usually treated as the means to prepose the object. Mandarin Chinese has a peculiar system of preverbal objects marked by controversial functional element *Ba*. Direct objects are shifted into the preverbal *Ba*-position if other complementational element is to follow the verb, if a resultative construction is involved, or if a highly transitive event is encoded. A prototypical instance of a preposed *Ba*-object is illustrated in (18):

> (18) a. 我吃完了这顿饭。
>   Wo chiwan-le   zhedun   fan.
>   I   eat-up-Perf this-CL   food.

"I have eaten up that dish."

b. 我把这顿饭吃完了。

Wo ba zhedun   fan   chiwan-le.

I   BA this-CL   food eat-up-Perf

"I have eaten up that meal."

Zhedunfan is the object of *chi* and it is proposed by *Ba* to pre-verbal position. The implication of the account is that we can put the preposed *Ba*-object back to the original syntactic position. But the examples in (17) show that in some cases, the preposed *Ba*-object can not be put back to the position after the verb, since there is another nominal object there. Therefore, *Ba*-construction instantiates extra argumentality if a pre-verbal *Ba*-object and a post-verbal object co-occur. Examples from Tsao (1987) are given in (19)-(20):

(19) a. 他把那本书撕了封面。

Ta ba naben shu si-le   fengmian.

He BA that-CL book remove-Perf cover.

"He removes the cover from the book."

b. 张三把这五个苹果吃了三个。

Zhangsan ba zhewuge   pingguo chi-le   sange.

Zhangsan BA this five-CL apple   eat-Perf three-CL.

"Zhangsan ate three of these five apples."

(20) a. 张三把门上了锁。

Zhangsan ba men shang-le suo.

Zhangsan BA door put-on-Perf lock.

"Zhangsan put a lock on the door."

b. 他把门踢了一个洞。

Ta ba men ti-le yige   dong.

he BA door kick-Perf one-CL hole.

"He kocked a hole in the door."

c. 他把壁炉生了火。

Ta ba bilu   sheng-le huo.

he BA fireplace ignite-Perf fire.

"He put on a fire in the fireplace."

(19) is a collection of examples in which the referent of the extra argument gets diminished in the course of the encoded event. The examples in (20) have it that something is added as a part to some functional whole or location. In the relevant literature, this kind of the construction is termed as the BA construction with retained object. In addition to the examples above, there is another kind of *Ba* construction with retained objects:

> (21) a. 妈妈把肉炒了青椒。
>   Mama ba rou chao-le qingjiao.
>   Mama BA meat fry-Perf green pepper.
>   "Mama fried the green pepper with the meat."
>   b. 我把水浇了花。
>   Wo ba shui jiao-le   hua.
>   I BA water water-Perf flower.
>   "I watered the flower with the water."
> (22) a. 他把池塘下了药。
>   Ta ba chitang xia-le yao.
>   he BA pond put-Perf medicine
>   "He put some medicine into the pond."
>   b. 他把钱抽了烟。
>   Ta ba qian   chou-le yan.
>   he BA money smoke-Perf cigarette.
>   "He spent the money on cigarette."

In (21), the predicate can go with either the pre-verbal object or the post-verbal object. We can have the expressions as "*chao rou*" and "*chao qingjiao*" while in (22) the verb is related just with the post-verbal object. The pre-verbal objects function as the preposition phrase denoting the tool or location. The sentences in (21) and (22) can be paraphrased as (23) and (24):

> (23) a. 妈妈用肉炒了青椒。
>   Mama yong rou chao-le qingjiao.
>   mom with meat fry-Perf green pepper.
>   "Mama fried the green pepper with the meat."

b. 我用水浇了花。

Wo yong shui jiao-le   hua.

I with water water-Perf flower.

"I watered the flower with the water."

(24) a. 他在池塘里下了毒。

Ta zai chitang-li xia-le   yao.

he zai pond in put-Perf medicine.

"He put some medicine into the pond."

b. 他用钱抽了烟。

Ta yong qian   chou-le   yan.

he with money smoke-Perf cigarette.

"He smoked the cigarette with the money."

Examples in (24) are different from the ones in (17). First of all, there is no possessive relation in the construction. *Qingjiao* and *rou*; *chitang* and *yao* do not form possessive relation. Moreover, the function of the preposition phrase is to modify the verb or the whole sentence. The *Ba* construction with retained object is the sub-type of *Ba* construction and the *Ba* construction with retained object should be considered to be base-generated construction with two objects. One is the object of the verb and the other is the object of *Ba*. What we focus here is the one in (17a), in which there is possessive relation between the two objects besides the similarities they share with other *Ba* construction with retained object. We are concerned with how the possessive relation gets triggered and what contributions it makes to the construction.

7.4.2 The possessive relation in *Ba* DPC

Since our focus is on the construction shown in (17), (19) and (20), there is possessive relation between two elements in the construction. If we concern more about the possessive relation in the construction, we will find the difference. These sentences differ in that if we put the pre-verbal object back to the object position, we have to use *de* or to form a prepositional phrase to make grammatical sentences in (17) and (19) but not the case in (20). The relation is not necessarily the possessive relation in (20). The relation in (20) is more like the location than the possession. For example:

(25) a. 他撕掉了那本书的封面。

      Ta sidiao-le   nabenshu   de fengmian.

      he tear-off-Perf that-CL book de cover.

      "He tore off the cover of that book."

   b. 张三吃了这五个苹果中的三个。

      Zhangsan chi-le zhe wuge   pingguo zhong de sange.

      Zhangsan   eat-Perf this five-CL apple of de three-CL.

      "Zhangsan ate three of these five apples."

In (25a) and (25b) , "the cover" belongs to "the book" and "the three apples" is part of "the five apples". They are in part/whole possessive relation.

(19a) is not derived from (25a) and there is no derivation relation between these two constructions. In (25a), *nabenshu de fengmian* is treated to be the patient object as an independent constituent. The structure is just a normal SVO construction. The derived *Ba* construction for (25a) and (25b) should be in the form of (26a) and (26b) respectively rather than (19a) and (19b):

(26) a. 他把那本书的封面撕掉了。

      Ta ba naben shu   de fengmian sidiao-le.

      ta BA that-CL book DE fengmian tear off-Perf.

      "He tore off the cover of the book."

   b. Wo ba zhewuge   pingguo zhong de sange chi-le.

      I   BA these five-CL apple in   DE three-CL eat-Perf.

      "I ate three of these five apples."

The possessive phrases in (26) are preposed *Ba*-object as the whole. We can not use *de* to show the possessive relation between the entities. For example, we can not have examples in (27):

(27) *a. Zhangsan shang-le meng de suo.

       Zhangsan put-Perf door De lock.

  *b. Ta ti-le yi-ge meng de dong.

      He kick-Perf one-CL door hole.

  *c. Ta sheng-le bilu de huo.

      He lit-Perf fireplace De fire.

We find the semantic confines for the *Ba* construction to definitely have possessive relation in the construction: the relational noun together with the verb denoting the diminishing or disappearing of the entity.

7.4.3 Properties of *Ba* in the construction

From the analysis of the structure of the *Ba* DPC construction, we find *Ba* plays a very important role in making the construction. From the perspective of eventuality, the construction can be treated as compound event composed of at least two atom-events. The first event is "NP$_1$+*Ba*+NP$_2$". The predicate verb is *Ba* in the eventuality. The embedded event is what follows *Ba*. The predicate in the embedded event is the V in VP.

$$(28) \ e_1 = \lambda e[Ba(e)]$$
$$e_2 = \lambda P[\ \lambda e[P(e)]]$$
$$e = \lambda P[\ \lambda e[\ \lambda e_1[\lambda e_2 \ [e=^s(e_1 \cup e_2)B \wedge A(e_1) \wedge P(e_2)]]]]$$

In (28), e_1 and e_2 refer to two atom-events before and after the *Ba*. "e" denotes the eventuality that the *Ba* DPC represents. *Ba* in the construction still has its lexical contribution in the eventuality.

What *Ba* contributes to the construction? In modern Chinese, the lexical meaning *Ba* shifted after grammaticalization to acquire its functional structure meaning. That is *Ba* represents the construction meaning. It is an abstract meaning embodied in the combination of different elements in the construction. Therefore, *Ba* not only decides the property of e_1 directly, but also extends its influence on the whole eventuality. The task of atom event e_2 is to further explain or give more specific information about the former atom event.

Whether *Ba* in e_1 denotes "CAUSE" or "DISPOSE" depends largely on the relationship between the *Ba* and the arguments before and after it. The relationship includes two kinds: one is that *Ba* and the subject NP reflect volition. The other kind is that *Ba* and the subject NP reflect causer relationship. The typical argument at subject position is agent and the object NP is the theme in volition situation. The subject argument can be causer in cause relationship. Predicate *Ba* is treated as the predicate with two arguments. Therefore, *Ba* denoting "DISPOSE" and *Ba* denoting "CAUSE" have the eventuality shown in (29a) and (29b) respectively.

(29) a. $BA_D = \lambda y[\lambda x[\lambda e[Ba(e) \wedge Agent(e)=x \wedge Theme(e)=y]]]$
b. $BA_C = \lambda y[\lambda x[\lambda e[Ba(e) \wedge Causer(e)=x \wedge Theme(e)=y]]]$

Both volition and causing reflect the relationship between the subject NP and *Ba*. Wu (2009) treats "causer" and "agent" as "force without volition" and "force with volition", so it is feasible to give a unified account for these two types of *Ba* construction. As for the relationship between the object and *Ba*, the most distinguishing feature is that the object undergoes the change. The change can be about the state or quality of the object. It can also be the change of the position or the change of the mood.

Based on the above analysis, we can get the eventuality of the *Ba* construction:

(30)   a. $e_1 = \lambda y[\lambda x[\lambda e[Ba(e) \wedge Agt/Causer(e)=x \wedge Th(e)=y]]]$
b. $e_2 = \lambda y[\lambda P[\lambda e[P(e) \wedge Th(e)=y]]]$
c. $e_1 + e_2 = \lambda y[\lambda x[\lambda P[\lambda e[\exists e_1[\exists e_2[e=^s(e_1 \cup e_2) \wedge BA_{D/C} \wedge$
   Agt/Causer
   $(e_1)=x \wedge Th(e_1)= y \wedge P(e_2) \wedge Arg(e_2)=y$
   $\wedge TPCONNECT (Cul(e1), e2, y)]]]]]]$

Usually when the *Ba* construction denotes "disposing" feature, the agent will do something out of the volition to dispose the object. As the result, the object after *Ba* may have the sense of "being disposed". For example, (31a)-(31c).

(31) a. 张三把衣服洗干净了。
Zhangsan ba yifu   xi ganjing-le.
Zhangsan Ba clothes wash clean-Perf.
"Zhangsan washed the clothes clean."
b. 小明把袖子剪短了。
Xiaoming ba xiuzi   jianduan-le.
Xiaoming Ba sleeve   cut short-Perf.

"Xiaoming cut the sleeve short."

c. 李四把竹笋砍断了。

Lisi ba zhusun kanduan-le.

Lisi Ba bamboo break apart-Perf.

"Lisi broke apart the bamboo."

The atom events are (32a)-(32c). We can see that the deposing event is the accomplishment event which combines an activity event with a resultive event.

(32) a. e_1: disposal event= Zhangsan wash the clothes.

e_2: (resulted from disposal event) resultive event= the clothes is clean as the result of washing event.

b. e_1: disposal even = Xiaoming cut the sleeve.

e_2: (resulted from disposal event) resultive event= the sleeve is short as the result of cutting event.

c. e_1: disposal even = Lisi cut the bamboo.

e_2: (resulted from disposal event) resultive event = The bamboo is broken apart as the result of the breaking event.

In the process of the grammatizition of *Ba*, its lexical meaning diminishes gradually and the functional meaning increased. The functional meaning not only keeps its original "dispose" meaning, but also develops structural meaning of "CAUSE" . The semantic focus is shifted from pre-*Ba* NP to post-*Ba* NP. Wu (2009: 122) gives the process of the change: *Ba* lexical dispose meaning → *Ba* dispose functional meaning → *Ba* cause functional meaning

7.4.4 Accomplishment event in *Ba* DPC

The researches on *Ba* construction have proved that the VP can not be in the form of a bare verb, which means that e_2 in the eventuality should be an accomplishment event. As shown in (33a)-(33b).

(33) a. 他把鱼刮了鳞。

   Ta ba yu gua-le   lin.

   he Ba fish scale-Perf scale.

   "He scaled the fish."

   *Ta ba yu gua lin.

   He BA fish scale scale.

b. 敌人把他打断了腿。

   Diren bata   daduan-le tui.

   enemy BA him break-Perf leg.

   "The enemy broke his leg."

   * Diren ba ta daduan tui.

   Enemy BA him break leg.

The absence of *le* may lead to ungrammaticalty of the sentence. *le* here is to indicate perfect aspect. It is the predicate verb that decides the property of the event. The eventuality of the accomplishment verb is as the following:

(34) accomplishment verb:

$$\lambda y \, [\lambda x[\lambda e[\exists e_1[\exists e_2[e=^s(e_1 \cup e_2) \wedge \text{Activity}{<}x{>}(e_1) \wedge \text{Agt}(e_1)$$
$$=x \wedge \text{Th}(e_1)=y$$
$$\wedge \text{Become}{<}y{>}(e_2) \wedge \text{Arg}(e_2)=y \wedge \text{INCR}(e_1, e_2, C(e_2))]]]]]$$

The purpose of the *Ba* DPC is to emphasize the change occurred in the e_2, which does not exist before the event happened. The change does not happen suddenly and has been accomplished at a certain time. It has the feature of [+process] [+telic]. The accomplishment event is composed of the activity event and the BECOME event.

In (34), $\text{Activity}{<}x{>}(e_1)$ is the activity event prior to e_2, $\text{Become}{<}y{>}(e_2)$ is the Become event that follows as the result of e_1. INCR stands for the incrementental relation between the activity event and the Become event. The theme of these two events share connect them together. We can account for the sentence in (31) in (35):

(35) a. $\exists(e)[\, \exists e_1[\, \exists e_2[e=^s(e_1 \cup e_2) \wedge \text{BA}_D(e_1)= Xi \wedge \text{Agt}(e_1)=$
   Zhang san

$\wedge$ Th(e_1)= *yifu* $\wedge$[Become-Ganjing(e_2) $\wedge$ Th(e_2)= *yifu*
$\wedge$ INCR$(e_1,e_2,C(e_2))$]]]]

b. $\exists(e)[\exists e_1[\exists e_2[e=^s(e_1 \cup e_2) \wedge BA_D(e_1)=$ *Jian* $\wedge$ Agt$(e_1)=$
Xiao ming
$\wedge$ Th(e_1)= *xiuzi* $\wedge$[Become-*duan*(e_2) $\wedge$ Th(e_2)= *xiuzi*
$\wedge$I NCR $(e_1,e_2,C(e_2))$]]]]

c. $\exists(e)[\exists e_1[\exists e_2[e=^s(e_1 \cup e_2) \wedge BA_D(e_1)=$Kan $\wedge$ Agt$(e_1)=$
Lisi
$\wedge$ Th(e_1)= *zhusun*$\wedge$[Become-D*uan*(e_2) $\wedge$ Th(e_2)= *zhusun*
$\wedge$ INCR$(e_1,e_2,C(e_2))$]]]]

We can see from (35) that *Ba* construction not only puts emphasis on the specific process, but also highlights the result of the process. Since it contains Activity event and Become event, usually we find the action verb denoting the specific action. Become event is in the form of complement. Now we come to the *Ba* DPC where the the VP is in the form of "V+NP", where NP denotes relational nouns. Some of the examples are presented here in (36) again:

(36) a. 张三把这五个橘子吃了三个。
Zhangsan ba zhe wuge juzi chile sange.
Zhangsan BA these five-CL oranges eat-Perf three-CL.
"Zhangsan ate three of these five oranges."

b. 李四把苹果削了皮。
Lisi ba pingguo xiao-le pi.
Lisi Ba apple peel-Perf skin.
Lisi peeled the apple off the skin."

c. 张三把李四打断了腿。
Zhangsan ba Lisi daduan-le yitiao tui.
Zhangsan Ba Lisi break-Perf one-CL leg.
"Zhangsan has broken one of Lisi's leg."

Based on (35), (36) is analyzed in the same way as (37).

(37) a. $\exists(e)[\exists e_1[\exists e_2[e=^s(e_1 \cup e_2) \wedge BA_D(e_1)=$*Chi* $\wedge$ Agt$(e_1)=$
Zhangsan

$\wedge$ Th(e_1)= *zhewugejuzi* $\wedge$ [Become-*chi sange*(e_2)

$\wedge$ Arg (e_2)= *zhewu-ge juzi* $\wedge$ INCR(e_1, e_2,

C(e_2))]]]]

b. $\exists$(e)[$\exists e_1$[$\exists e_2$[e=^{s}(e_1 $\cup$ e_2) $\wedge$ BA $_D$(e_1)= *Xiao* $\wedge$ Agt(e_1)= *Lisi*

$\wedge$ Th(e_1)= *pingguo* $\wedge$ [Become-X*iaopi*(e_2)

$\wedge$ Arg(e_2)= *pingguo* $\wedge$ INCR(e_1, e_2, C(e_2))]]]]

c. $\exists$(e)[$\exists e_1$[$\exists e_2$[e=^{s}(e_1 $\cup$ e_2) $\wedge$ BA$_D$(e_1)= *Ti* $\wedge$ Agt(e_1)= *Zhangsan*

$\wedge$ Th(e_1)= *Lisi* $\wedge$ [Become-D*uantui*(e_2) $\wedge$ Arg(e_2)= *Lisi*

$\wedge$ INCR(e_1, e_2, C(e_2))]]]]

Comparing (35) with (37), we find that the objects of *Ba* possesses different thematic roles. In (35), the object arguments are "patients" since the subjecst are the agent in the construction. In (37), *juzi* and *Lisi* are not patients. A unified thematic role "theme" can be assigned to all the object arguments after *Ba*. Usually the "theme" has no "volition", but in *Ba* DPC, animate theme may be put here to be the object of the disposing event. The Become events in (35) and (37) are different as well.

(38) a. $\exists e_2$[Become-G*anjing*(e_2) $\wedge$ Th(e_2)= *yifu*]

b. $\exists e_2$[Become-C*hi sange*(e_2) $\wedge$ Arg(e_2) = *zhewugepingguo*]

c. $\exists$ e_2[Become-D*uantui*(e_2) $\wedge$ Arg(e_2) = *Lisi*]

(38a) by itself is an proposition, while (38c) contains relative nouns we analyze in the former parts. The BECAME event is the compound event and it contains two atom events. The eventuality of (38b) and (38c) is (39a) and (39b).

(39) a. $\exists$ e_2[$\exists e_3$[Top(e_2)=*zhewuge pingguo* $\wedge$ Become-C*hi*(e_3)

$\wedge$ Th(e_3)=*sange* $\wedge$ Belonging-to(*sange, zhewuge pingguo*)]]

b. $\exists e_2$ [$\exists e_3$[Top(e_2)= *Lisi* $\wedge$ Become-D*uan*(e_3) $\wedge$ Th(e_3) = *yitiaotui*

$\wedge$ Belonging-to(*yitiaotui, Lisi*)]]

All the events in (39) are atom events, and the possessive relation between *Ba* object and its retained object is triggered by the subtopic status of *Ba* object. It is Ba construction that makes it possible to have *Ba* DPC in MC. The possessive relation in the construction is introduced in by relational nouns. A detailed eventuality analysis can be applied to *Ba* DPC, as shown in (40):

(40) e: disposal event e= $^s(e_1 \cup e_2)$

$e_1 = BA_D(e_1)= Da \land Agt(e_1)= Zhangsan \land Th(e_1)= Lisi$

$e_2 = Top(e_2) \land Top(e_2)=Lisi$

$e_3 = Become-Duanyitiaotui(e_3) \land Arg (e_3)= Lisi$

$\land Belonging-to(yitiaotui, Lisi)$

The relationship among the events is shown in the Chart (41):

(41) the eventuality of *Ba* DPC.

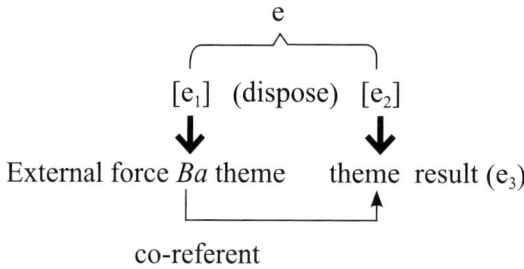

e

$[e_1]$ (dispose) $[e_2]$

↓   ↓

External force *Ba* theme   theme result (e_3)

co-referent

Zhangsan   Lisi   Lisi   Beidaduan yitiaotui

The main event in *Ba* DPC is to dispose the object by having it undergo a change. The change can be manifested as the possessor losing something or the part is added or taken away from the functional whole. In the situation, there is one more atom event embedded in Become event of *Ba* construction. The possessive relation is triggered by the relational noun. The Possessor is the focus in Become event instead of the prossessum object.

Among the three arguments, the subject and the PM are directly related with the predicate verb semantically. The PR is introduced by Ba the possessive relation is triggered by the relational noun.

7.4.5 Semantic derivation

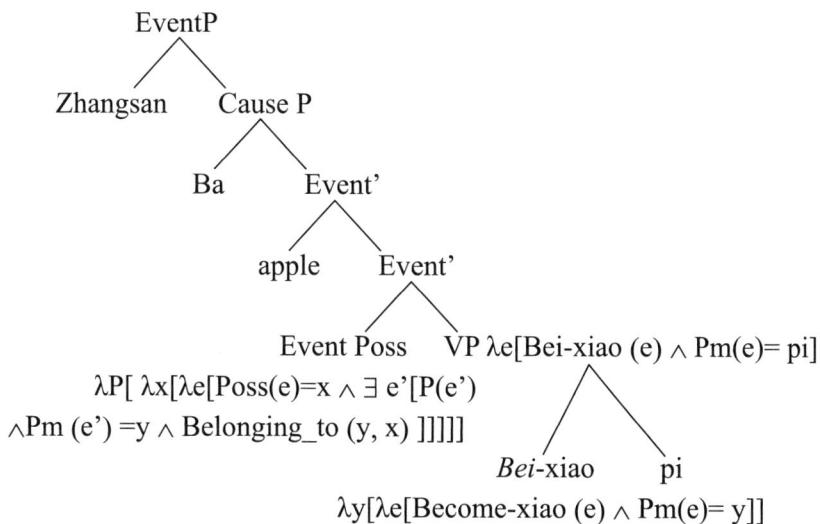

```
                    EventP
                   /     \
         Zhangsan      Cause P
                     /        \
                  Ba          Event'
                            /        \
                       apple        Event'
                                  /         \
                          Event Poss    VP λe[Bei-xiao (e) ∧ Pm(e)= pi]
                    λP[ λx[λe[Poss(e)=x ∧ ∃ e'[P(e')
              ∧Pm (e') =y ∧ Belonging_to (y, x) ]]]]]         / \
                                                    Bei-xiao      pi
                                       λy[λe[Become-xiao (e) ∧ Pm(e)= y]]
```

The possessive relation in *Ba* construction in essence has no direct relation with the *Ba* construction by itself. *Ba* has the abstract meaning to cause or to dispose the object to undergo some changes. There is one way to dispose the possessor. That is to make the possessor lose something. The possessive relation is brought in by relational nouns. The possessor information must get interpreted and the eventuality of autonomous event in *Ba* construction is the same as the *Bei* DPC. Since relational nouns bring in compulsory information, it is usually the part-whole relation found in *Ba* DPC. If there is no relational nouns in the construction, the result will be that no possessive meaning accordingly. For example :

> (42) a. 他把苹果削了皮。
>   Ta ba pingguo xiao-le   pi.
>   he Ba apple   peel-Perf skin.
>   "He peeled the apple off the skin"
>   b. 他把苹果切了块儿。
>   Ta ba pingguo qie-le   kuai.
>   he Ba apple   cut-Perf piece.
>   "He cut the apple into pieces."
>   c. 他把苹果做成了酱。

Ta ba pingguo zuocheng-le jiang.
he Ba apple   make into-Perf jam.
"He made the apple into the apple jam."

The two objects in *Ba* construction with retained object are not necessarily have possessive relation and it turns out that the *Ba* DPC is nothing special than an ordinary *Ba* construction with retained objects. It happens that the PR and PM can occupy the two object positions and form a kind of disposal for the possessor.

7.5 Summary

In DPCs, the introduction of the possessive relation is decided by the lexical information of the relational noun, the lexical information of the verb and the clause information. The three means can work individually or work together. It is most likely for relational nouns to function as the argument in another two means as the result we have complex-type possessive relation constructions. It is just the phenomenon that relational nouns and the common nouns may share the same linear surface structure. In nature, the type for the possessive relation of the common nouns and the type for relational nouns are basically different. This difference is reflected in the way they enter the construction. The possessive relation brought by relational nouns is from the lexicon. It is generated inside the VP phrase. It is the verb that should raise its semantic type to ensure the derivation. The possessor variant is carried by the verb along the derivation until it is satisfied. In contrast, the possessive relation brought by the construction has nothing to do with the VP internal part. That is, VP can be an comparatively independent constituent by itself. The possessive relation becomes the motivation for the need to involve a possessor variable in the complete VP phrase. The result is that the proposition becomes an open predicate. The operation operates above the VP. The semantic type of the VP rather than the verb should be raised to be combined with the functional node. Therefore, although the common and the relational nouns may share the same structure, the mechanism and possession type are totally different.

Once there are relational nouns in the constructions, the variable containing "Belonging_to" type possessive relation will cover other variable and the possessive relation will always be "Belonging_to"-type interpretation. This reflects that the inalienable possession is the prototype of the possession. It represents the core concept of the possession and is the most powerful. The relation between the PR and PM is the most close. The lexical information from the lexicon must get interpreted in the construction.

The possessive relation contained in relation nouns or the argument structure of the predicate verbs may enter into other constructions in Mandarin Chinese and form a special sub-type of the construction. The possessive relation found in *Ba* construction with retained objects is brought into the construction by the lexical meaning of the relational nouns or the *depriving-type* verbs. The possessive relation is not related with *Ba* construction itself and is not triggered by the construction. Therefore, we may find the possessive relation in *Ba* DPC to be "Belonging_to" type possession.

Chapter Eight

Semantic and Pragmatic Interpretation of Possession

Possessive relation is the kind of semantic relation that all the languages should come across. This kind of semantic relation can be represented at both the lexical level and syntactic level. The possessive relation at the lexical level is denoted in some particular vocabulary. It is the most common way to denote possessive relation. For example, the kinship terms and the vocabulary denoting part-whole relationship. In those languages with rich morphological markers, the possessive relation and the corresponding types can be marked with grammatical markers. Those languages do not depend too much on the syntactic device, instead, they employ the morphological markers to clearly indicate the status of the possessor, the possessum and the type of the possession.

Mandarin Chinese is one of the languages that lack morphological forms but it is rich in constructions. Mandarin Chinese possesses little inflectional or derivational morphology. Verbs are not marked for tense, number or person; nouns are not marked for number and neither nouns nor pronouns are marked for case. The possessive relation is the constrain that should be satisfied in Chinese-style Topic Construction. This particular construction requires the possessive semantic chain between the topic and its comment. Besides Chinese-style Topic Construction, PSPO construction, Existential construction, DOC and Ba DPC, *Bei* DPC can be involved in denoting possessive relation. They are ordinary constructions existing in Mandarin Chinese and a certain sub-type of these constructions is used to refer to possessive relation. Definitely possessive relation should be added in the interpretation of the constructions. These various constructions satisfy the need to describe the establishment, the existence and the transfer of the possession in different dynamic situations. At the same time, by choosing different constructions, the speakers show their own attitudes in making the decisions, since different constructions focus different aspect of the possession.

Now that both the basic possessive construction and the DPC can denote the possessive relation, what are the differences and similarities? We first illustrate some points on these two types of the possession, which may shed lights on the interpretation of the possessive relation in DPC.

8.1 DPCs & basic possessive form

8.1.1 Common properties

From the perspective of the form, the most obvious feature shared by DPCs and the basic possessive construction is that there should be two elements involved. Guo (1990) proposes that the "possession" relationship or "ownsership" is reflected in syntactic relation of "attributive" and "head". What's more, *de* is usually involved to build a constitution. *De* is considered to be a functional head to indicate possessive relation with PR as the specifier and PM as the complement. (Deng, 2006; Si, 2002). It is an overt construction in possessive relation while in DPCs there is no overt possessive marker, so the possessive relation becomes a covert semantic relation between two elements. No matter whether it is overt or covert, there must be two entities that co-exist in the construction. Or else, it is impossible to build the relationship. Since the two nominal elements co-exist in the construction, besides the semantic relationship, they must form a kind of syntactic relation. The syntactic order is that PR should always be put before the PM in the linear order. From the perspective of syntactic hierarchy, PR occupies the external layer and is higher than the PM. PM usually is inside of the internal layer and is "controlled" by possessive relation functional node. The co-existence of the PR and PM and the syntactic relation between them are the same in both these two constructions.

Secondly, the syntactic and the semantic role of the PMs in DPC and basic possession is the same. They can be direct syntactic argument and direct semantic argument of the predicate verb. PM is semantically connected with the verb and is the internal argument of the verb. It has the status of the core argument. For example:

(1) a. 小王的钱包丢了。
   Xiaowang de qianbao diu-le.
   Xiaowang De wallet   lose-Perf.
   "Xiaowang's wallet is lost."
   b. 小王丢了钱包。
   Xiaowang diu-le qianbao.
   Xiaowang diu-Perf wallet.
   "Xiaowang has the wallet lost."

In both (1a) and (1b), for the verb *diu*, the theme is both *qianbao*. The semantic relation between these two entities is the same in these two constructions. *Qianbao* is the theme and *diu* is the predicate verb. And in (1a), *qianbao* is the subject of the construction while in (1b), it is at object position. As far as *diu* is concerned, *qianbao* is the core syntactic and semantic argument.

Thirdly, from the perspective of the cognitive point, the role the PR plays in possessive relation is the same. It serves to be referential point to locate the target. Its function is like the function of the determiner, which is used to build the referential relation between the language and the outside world. Satoshi (2004) proposes the term "zooming-in" since all the instances of DPCs have in common is that the choice "narrows down" from the first case-marked NP to the second case-marked NP. In a photographic analogy, the camera zooms in the order of the NPs.

8.1.2 Difference between DPC and basic possessive construction

The distinguishing different feature between the two possessive constructions lies in the syntactic status of the PR. In DPC, both PR and PM are syntactically related with the verb. In basic possessive structure, only PM is the core argument of the verb. PR is just used to modify the PR and they are not at the same syntactic level. When PR occupies different syntactic position at different grammatical level, it has different grammatical relationship with other elements and as the result, it has different grammatical meaning. The possessive meaning the basic possession construction has is at the phrasal level while the possessive meaning in DPCs is at the clausal level.

The semantic difference lies in the possessor as well. In basic relationship construction, the possessor has no relation with the verb semantically and syntactically. In DPC, the possessor has no direct semantic relation with the predicate verb but it becomes a kind of syntactic argument, which means it has direct syntactic relation with the predicate verb. The position and the role that the possessor plays is different from that in basic possessive construction. The information structure has been rearranged to emphasize different elements in the construction. While the possessive relation remains the same, the possessor acquires a new status and the grammatical meaning. Strictly speaking, in the DPCs, the possessor is an inseparable part in the construction and develops syntactic relationship with the predicate verb.

In basic possessive construction, the possessor serves as the referential point, through which, the PM gets specific interpretation and gets located in a scope. Some possessive phrase is the definite NP, for example *Wangmian de fuqin; juzi de pi*. Some possessive phrases are of locatability, for example *ta de yige pingguo*. This kind of referential point is just an objective perspective to locate the target. The role of the PR as the referential point in DPCs is completely different, it is chosen intentionally by the speaker and show the subjectivity of the language. The speaker tries to profile the possessor by putting the possessor at the prominent position. The difference can be illustrated clearly from (2).

(2) a. 张三杀了李四的父亲。
   Zhangsan sha-le   Lisi de fuqin.
   Zhangsan kill-Perf Lisi's father.
   "Zhangsan killed Lisi's father."

　　b. 李四的父亲被张三杀了。

　　　Lisi de fuqin　bei Zhangsan　sha-le.

　　　Lisi De father Bei Zhangsan　kill-Perf.

　　　"Lisi's father was killed by Zhang san."

　　c. 李四被杀了父亲。

　　　Lisi bei sha-le　fuqin.

　　　Lisi Bei kill-Perf father.

　　　"Lisi had his father killed."

(2a) is a normal statement. The speaker just makes the state without expressing his own attitude. (2b) is in the form of passive voice with *Bei* in the construction. *Lisi de fuqin* is chosen to be the focus and the importance of the agent *Zhangsan* is weakened in passive construction. In (2c), the possessor is chosen to be the topic and other information in the sentence should all be about the possessor. It put emphasis on the influence that the unfortunate experience the possessor suffered from imposed on the possessor. In these three examples, the possessive relation between *Lisi* and *fuqin* and the killing event remains the same. possessive relation is just like other thematic relation and they are treated as the basic semantic relationship in the construction. Based on these relationships, each construction focuses on different elements and different aspects of the meaning.

In basic possessive construction, [+control] feature is the most semantic part in the meaning, which means the possessor is likely to be the agent and the possessum is likely to be the patient. Under the influence of the possessor or the external force, the possessor has the rights to dispose the PM. It reflects the information to continue the present continues [+control] relationship between the PR and PM. The DPC mainly indicate the [+lost], [-volition] or [+adversely influenced] feature. The agent of the meaning is not likely to be the possessor. In most cases, the influence is imposed on the PM by external force rather than the possessor or possessum. Under the influence of the external force, the possessor lost the control over the possessum or the rights to dispose or own PM. As the result, the possessor in DPC is usually the Malefactive. Under the influence of the external force, the original possessive relation is weakened or lost. The controlling power over the PM is reflected in the form of the language, that is, the possessor is assigned a new thematic role. It not only has semantic relationship with the PM, it also acquires a kind of relationship with the event which involved in the PR. Usually it is the M negative influence which PR suffered from the event.

8.2 Subjectivity and possessive constructions

Lyons (1977: 739) holds that "subjectivity" refers to the property of the language, that is, in the language expression, the speaker more or less tries to show his own attitude, affect towards what he has illustrated. Shen (2002) sums up the representative signs in the languages: the subjectivity in the language lies in three aspects: the speaker's affect, the speaker's perspective and the speaker's cognition.

The speaker's affect should be understood in a broad sense, which includes feelings, emotion, intention and attitude etc. The study on the affect mainly focuses on the speaker's empathy.

Here is the example proposed by Tang (1986), who tries to give the focus of the speaker's empathy and builds the corresponding empathy hierarchy.

> (3) a. 张三打了李四。
>   Zhangsan da-le Lisi.
>   Zhangsan beat-Perf Lisi.
>   "Zhangsan beated Lisi."
>   b. 张三打了他的太太。
>   Zhangsan da-le ta de taitai.
>   Zhangsan beat-Perf him de wife.
>   "Zhangsan beated his wife."
>   c. 李四的丈夫打了她。
>   Lisi de zhangfu da-le ta.
>   Lisi de husband beat-Perf her.
>   Lisi's husband beated her."
>   d. 李四被张三打了。
>   Lisi bei Zhangsan da-le.

Lisi Bei Zhangsan da-Perf.

"Lisi was beaten by Zhangsan."

e. 李四被她的丈夫打了。

Lisi bei ta de zhangfu da-le.

Lisi Bei her de husband beat-Perf.

"Lisi was beaten by her husband."

The event involves the husband *Zhangsan* and the wife *Lisi* and the event is the beating event. The speaker's empathy can be either on *Zhangsan* or on *Lisi*. (3a) is the normal objective description and in (3b) to (3e) the speaker's focus shifts from *Zhangsan* to *Lisi*.

Speaker's perspective is how the speaker observes the objective situation and it is the starting point for the illustration of the objective situation. The subjectivity of the "perspective" is usually in quite obscure way in the sentence. The typical example is the "aspect" of the verb. If the speaker uses the perfect aspect in the sentence, it shows that the speaker describes the action and the corresponding results from the present time and subjectively expects it to be connected with the present time. The speaker's recognition is closely related with the modal verb and modal adverb.

These three aspects sometimes are combined together to indicate the subjectivity in the sentence. For example, The sentences in (4) are to describe the same event.

(4) a. 张三打断了李四一条腿。

Zhangsan daduan-le Lisi yitiao tui.

Zhangsan break-Perf Lisi one-CL leg.

"Zhangsan broke one of Lisi's leg."

b. 张三把李四一条腿打断了。

Zhangsan ba Lisi yitiao tui daduan-le.

Zhangsa Ba Lisi one-CL leg break-Perf.

"Zhangsan dispose Lisi by breaking one of his legs."

c. 李四被打断了一条腿。

Lisi bei daduan-le yitiao tui.

Lisi Bei break-Perf one-CL leg.

"Lisi was beaten as the result one of his legs is broken."

d. 李四断了一条腿。

Lisi duan-le yitiao tui.

Lisi broken-le one-CL leg.

"Lisi had one of his legs broken."

The event is that *Zhangsan* broke one of *Lisi*'s leg. (4a) is the normal statement about what has happened. It fits the objective situation to the most degree. *Le* here indicates the speaker focuses on the present instead of the time when the event took place. (4b) is the *Ba* DPC, with the *Ba* construction, the agent *Zhangsan* becomes prominent and the construction emphasizes how the agent disposed the patient. (4c) is the passive construction and the emphasis is on what happened to Lisi's leg. The importance of the agent is greatly reduced. When the possessor of the leg, *Lisi,* is chosen to be put at the initial to function as the topic, the speaker wants to emphasize the loss of the possessor and the result of the event. From (4a) to (4d) we see the subjectivity is gradually increased and the speaker's empathy is on different elements in each construction.

The relatively subjective perspective gives the speaker many options to start with. The construction can be agent-oriented or speaker-oriented. The shift of the perspective is due to the fact that the speaker's personal attitude is involved in the construction. As the result, the language gets its subjectivity property. The speaker can show his attitude, emotion and acknowledgment by choosing the different constructions and employ pragmatic strategies to achieve his goal.

8.2.1 Pragmatic meaning: the affectedness of the possessor

In relevant grammatical literature, when the scholars sum up the features of the *Ba* construction or *Bei* construction, they always include the complex form of the predicate verbs. That is, the predicate verb should not be in its bare form. In essence, the form of the verb reflects the need of the semantic feature: the affected object in the construction. The bare verb represents the action without boundary, it is hard to tell any change in an event without boundary; when there is the word which indicates the result or gives the telic ending, the change of the state resulted from the event can be denoted. The affectedness can be represented at two levels: the first is the degree to which the object participates in the event; the second is the affectedness the event imposed on the participants judged by the speaker. The first effect mainly involves the PM, which is closely related with the predicate verb. The second effect refers to the PR, how the PR is affected by the event. There can be two kinds of effects: positive effect with the PR as the benefactive; negative or even adverse effect with PR as the malefactive.

The affectedness in possessive relation is hard to define, but in the study of the External Possession, whether the possessor is affected plays vital importance in judging the construction. Yoon (1989) gives an influential definition:

(5) The Affectedness Condition:
The referent of the possessor is "affected" by the action denoted by the possessee and the verb in IAP constructions.

In Yoon (1989), the notion of affectedness is strictly limited to cases of being physically affected while other language interpret the concept more liberally so that it can include emotional affectedness or adversity (ef. Shibatani 1994).

In M.C's opinion, The EPC's contribution to interpretation has been described as implying that the possessor is especially affected by whatever transpires as a result of the predication involving the possessum. We might first think of physical affectedness, Verbs of physical impact with body-part possessum are prototypical. There are cases of emotional impact as in (6a);

(6) a. 王冕七岁上死了父亲。
  Wangmian qisui shang si-le fuqin.
  Wangmian seven age at die-Perf father.
  "Wangmian's father died on him when he was seven years old."
 b * 王冕五十岁上死了父亲。
  *Wangmian wushi sui shang si-le fuqin.
  Wangmian fifty age at die-Perf father.

"Wangmian's father died on him when he was fifty
years old."

c * 王冕七十岁上死了父亲。

*Wangmian qishi sui shang si-le   fuqin.

Wangmian   seventy age at   die-Perf father.

"Wangmian's father died on him when he was seventy
years old."

As the age was altered when *Wangmian* experienced his father's death, we find the acceptability also changes. (6a) is a grammatical sentence and (6b) and (6c) are not so good. Since in speaker's opinion, when *Wangmian* lost his father at young age, it must impose great influence on him while when *Wangmian* is 70 years old, the influence will not be so great. The degree of the affectedness depends on speaker's perspective and judge. To sum up, the role of the possessor in DPC is neither the agent who initiates the event nor the patient that undergoes the event. It is an indirect affectee which is made more prominent in the construction by the speaker.

There is another feature mentioned about the affectedness of the construction, which is the so-called "possessor death" problem. In (6a), when the speaker makes such statement, *Wangmian*, as the possessor and the affectee of the event, should be an animate human being who is alive in the world. Sentence in (7) does not make sense in the situation.

(7) Situation: Wangmian died first (王冕已经去世了)

　　* 后来王冕又死了父亲。

　　*Houlai, Wamgmian you   si-le   fuqin.

　　Later, Wangmian   as well die-Perf father.

　　"Later, Wangmian's father died on him as well."

The confined restriction in meaning has nothing to do with the possessive relation, instead, it is the pragmatic constrains at practical level.

It is the PM which is closely related with the predicate semantically and the nature of the unaccusative verbs ensures the theme role of the PM. There is no agent in the construction. The semantic feature of the predicate verb, which denotes "depriving of sth" or "disappearing" of the entity, is about the diminishing of the PM. The indirect affectedness of the possessor composes great threat to the disposal rights the PR has on PM. The right is greatly harmed. The adverse effect is not directly done to the PR but it is the indirect effect generated by disposing the PM. The idea is that the effect which is done to the PM will definitely affect the PR, which has controlling power on the PM. Although the effect is in an indirect way, the speaker intends to highlight the effect the possessor suffered from the event.

8.2.2 Empathy on the possessor

As for the empathy, Kuno (1976, 2004) holds that speaker empathy can be described intuitively as an interpretive overlay in which one senses that the speaker is somehow taking on the perspective of one of the participants in the event being described. In describing an event involving two roommates, John and Bill, for example, Kuno points out that we understand speaker empathy to be with John in (8a):

(8) a. Then, John$_i$ hit his$_i$ roommate.
    b. Then, Bill$_j$'s roommate hit him$_j$.

In contrast, the empathy to be with Bill is in a different description of the same event in (8b) (Kuno 2004: 315). In the description of the possessive relation, it is natural that people all hope to obtain something and possess more and are unwilling to lose. Once someone loses something, people would feel sympathetic towards the looser. People have developed a kind of expectation in daily life. What people expect is to be good, healthy, more and gaining while what they try to avoid is to be bad, unhealthy, less and loss. Usually, people will not do the thing that will do harm to themselves intentionally and have to accept the adverse result against their own will. In the event of loss, all the elements rather than the verb may become the object of the empathy. According to Kuno (1987)'s hierarchy of the empathy, the relationship between the empathy and syntactic elements is as follows: the first is that the independent element is more likely to be empathy object than the dependent element.

For example, *Wangmian* as the topic is more likely to be empathy object than *Wangmian* as the attributive modifier. The second rule is that the initial position and the final position in the structures are more likely to raise attention and empathy. What is more, human being, individual entity and specific items are more likely to get empathy than objective item, group entity and abstract idea.

In DPCs, the rights or the interests of the PR is harmed or affected. What happens to the PM is usually out of the volition of the possessor and out of sudden. In DPCs, we may find that the grammatical meaning of unexpected and adverse construction meaning.

The DPCs show that the possessor is adversely affected by the event. It is the loss of the PM or the loss of the interests that arouses the empathy of the speaker. Suffering from the loss arouses speaker's sympathy. In communication, the speaker does not view the "loss" event in an objective way, instead, the speaker treats himself to be one of the participants and describes the event from a subjective perspective.

The affectedness and empathy will align in many cases. The contribution the possessive relation made to the interpretation requires two important dimensions. The first concern is the event depicted by the clause and the possible outcomes or results stemming from it that might be expected to affect the possessor, whether subjectively experienced by the possessor or attributed by the speaker to an oblivious possessor. The other concerns the speaker's commitment to judge, comment on, or empathically frame that event with respect to the relevant outcome. It is apparent that the speaker's stance or judgment with respect to the outcome of the event for the possessor is more relevant than any actual effect on the possessor.

8.3 Subjectivity and preference over possessive constructions

Mandarin Chinese is the topic-prominent language. Topic Construction by itself has the subjectivity, which is a common construction in Chinese. In Mandarin Chinese, the subjective expressions are quite common. There is possessive relation in the Chinese-style Topic Construction. The possessive relation and the subjectivity have a very close relationship. The way to choose the possessor to be the topic indicates the speakers' attitudes. When the possessor is chosen to be the topic, the comment must be related to the possessor and the choice of the topic is made by the speaker at his own will. The possessive relation is introduced at the level of the pragmatics, which reflects the speaker's subjectivity.

The subjectivity of the possessive relation is mainly reflected in all kinds of Topic Constructions. In communication, the conversation usually starts with the known information and then comes down to the unknown information. The establishment of the possessive relation in Topic Construction is out of the need to compose the construction. For example, *200 yuan diu le* and *zixingche huaile* are good sentences in the language and there is no possessive relation in the construction. In *Zhangsan liangbai kuaiqian diule* or *zhangsan diule liang bai kuai qian,* with the appearance of the possessive relation, the possessor becomes the initial topic of the construction.

The possessive relation can be found at different levels. In DPCs, there are constructions in which the semantic argument structure of the verb and the construction meaning work together. The possessive relation generated at semantic-pragmatic interface still entails subjectivity. The possessive relation exists in some particular constructions, such as PSPO, *Ba* DPC and *Bei* DPC. These constructions by themselves are constructions with strong subjectivity. It is just because of the subjectivity that the possessive relation has that it can go with the constructions.

The DPCs permits a new perspective for the speaker to describe the possessive relations. How can the construction represent the change of the perspective? Two examples in (9) concerned with the same event will demonstrate the representation:

    (9) a. 我吃了苹果。
          Wo chi-le   pingguo.
          I   eat-Perf apple.
          "I ate the apple."
       b. 我把苹果吃了。
          Wo ba pingguo chi-le.
          I Ba apple   eat-Perf.

"It is I who ate the apple."

c. 苹果，我吃了。

Pingguo, wo chi-le.

apple, I   eat-Perf.

"As for the apple, I ate it."

d. 苹果被我吃了。

Pingguo bei wo chi-le.

apple Bei wo chi-le.

"The apple was eaten by me."

(9a) is the objective statement of the event with the normal construction of SVO. In fact, in the real communication, people tend to avoid overusing the statement, since the purpose of the communication is to discuss about the topic which both the speaker and listener are interested in rather than the simple statement of a certain entity. Both sides in the communication need a topic to carry on the conversation and during the process, there will be a focus, which is where the new information lies. If the speaker wants to draw listener's attention to the apple, he has two options: the phonetic means and syntactic means. The speaker can put stress on *wo*, *pingguo* or *chi* to attract the focus or he can employ different constructions as (9b) to (9d). When the speaker chooses from different constructions rather than the SVO construction to describe the same event, the choice by itself reflects speaker's opinion, attitude or other subjective affect.

The constructions which are related with possessive relation in DPCs involve subjectivity. We will just take PSPO construction and *Bei* DPC as the examples. Guo (1990) illustrates the difference between the PSPO and the normal "NP_1+*de*+NP_2+verb" construction. The essential difference lies in the topic. PSPO centers on the possessor, all the information is about the possessor. What is the focus is about "someone". While "NP_1+*de*+NP_2+verb" construction takes the PM as the topic, the focus is about "something". PSPO construction usually has the sense of being unexpected and the possessor usually bears a malefactive relation to the event described by the verb. Shen (2006, 2009) thinks the construction is the expression of subjective gain or loss. He defines the construction meaning: the speaker considers the event to be about the interest and cares the gain or loss. The more the speaker cares, the larger the chance is to use the construction. From the perspective of possessive relation, it is the existence of the semantic possessive relation that makes it possible for the speaker to put the empathy on the possessor. The change of the possessive relation leads to the loss and the loss results in the subjective perspective. In PSPO, the possessor suffers the loss unintentionally or just being an experiencer.

Compared with the PSPO construction, the *Bei* construction has strong sense of suffering great negative affectedness. *Bei* construction denotes the meaning of "being suffered from a kind of misfortune". It is the typical construction which centers on the patient. The degree for the theme or the patient to be affected is quite high. Li (1980) points out that the adversity is not for the subject or for any other element in the construction. The adversity is up to the speaker's own opinion. Ma (2013) holds that the semantic constrains on predicate verb in the *Bei* DPC is that it can be done to the theme directly and cause the damage, at the same time, it imposes a certain damage to the possessor of the theme. The central construction meaning is the possessive relation between the affectee subject and the damaged object. As for the possessor, the affectedness is negative and has subjective feature. As for the Ba construction, Shen (2002) also treats it as the construction with subjectivity. The construction denotes the subjective dispose of the theme. Since the subjectivity originates mainly from the construction itself and not from the possessive relation, we do not come to details in our study.

There are possessive relations generated at lexical layer from the lexicon. It can go with either relational nouns or the *depriving-type* Double Object predicate verbs. As for the possessive relation brought by relational nouns, it is the relation generated at lexical level and there is no pragmatic element that may interfere in the interpretation of the possessive meaning. For example, when the relational nouns as *baba* and *yitiao tui* are in the normal constructions, they involve no speaker's subjectivity in the process of the identification of the possessive relation.

Therefore, we try to give a hierarchy of the subjectivity of the possessive relations in DPC:

(10) Topic Construction > Locative Construction > Double
    Object Construction > Construction containing relational
    nouns

Topic Construction is the subjective expression of the possessive relation and pragmatic element plays vital role in triggering the possessive relation. The locative in Existent Construction has the subjectivity to some degree as well, but the possessive relation is closely related with the semantic meaning of the verb. In locative construction, the possessive relation is triggered by *disappearing-type* verbs. The subjectivity at semantic-pragmatic interface is not as much as that at pure pragmatic level. The *depriving-type* Double Object Construction is a basic structure in Mandarin Chinese and the possessive relation between indirect object and direct object is in the form of the source role, which is either overt or covert in the construction. The possessive relation has not much pragmatical meaning but the possessive relation still lies in the lexical meaning of verb and not compulsorily fulfilled. When the possessive relation is part of the lexical meaning of relational nouns, there is no subjectivity and pragmatical meaning at all. It is just the semantic meaning denoting the possessive relation. The higher the position is in the hierarchy, the less it is represented in the lexical item. The possessive relation in the form of lexical items is the semantic means to denote the possessive relation between two entities. When the pragmatical element is involved, the speaker's subjectivity is greatly increased and the DPC is endowed with more information and pragmatical meaning.

In all these constructions, the possessive relation between two elements contained in the constructions remains the same. It is up to the speaker to choose from differentconstructionss and to fulfill the communicative task. The possessive relation is not just a static semantic relation between two entities, in specific language structures, it is reflected in dispersive multiple-triggered relation mechanism. The choice of the sentence constructions is out of speaker's subjective will and it is beyond the description of the eventuality of the constructions.

8.4 Summary

The speaker's role can not be neglected in the communication. The subjectivity of the speaker is reflected in two dimensions (Adamson, 2000: 40): the first is that the role of the participants who participate in the event is weakened or is omitted completely. That is, the typical objective description of the event is the subject-predication construction about the event participants. In Mandarin Chinese, it is the task of the SVO construction. With the speaker's subjectivity, the predication nature is reduced. The second dimension is that the syntactic position the subjective element occupies changes, which usually is fronted or put at the initial position to acquire some function in the discourse as the result, it gains wider scope. The Topic Construction fits these two features in that the Chinese construction describes the state or characteristic, less commonly an event, about the main subject. That is to say, the function of Topic Construction is to describe a state or characteristics of something. Describing a state or a characteristics is typically the discourse-pragmatic job of an unaccusative intransitive clause, which has only a subject, and not of a transitive clause, which allows an object. The difference in the interpretation of the possessive relation semantically and pragmatically in DPCs roots in the way it enters into the constructions.

Chapter Nine

Conclusive Remarks

9.1 Important and innovative features of the research

This book focuses on the possessive relation by presenting a formal analysis of eventuality of the possessive constructions in Mandarin Chinese under the framework of the formal semantic theories, especially the event semantic theory. The possessive constructions in Mandarin Chinese in fact includes three types:

(i) attributive possession in the form of "NP$_1$+*de* +NP$_2$" constituent;
(ii) predicative possession with the verb "*you*", "*yongyou*";
(iii) the discontinuous possession constructions.

Possessive relations are the core ideas that are concerned with in these constructions. Since the possessive marker *de* is of a primary means to express possession, the interpretation of this type of possession tends to be clear and forms the base for the further interpretation of other possessive constructions.

The discontinuous possession constructions we find in Mandarin Chinese fall into six types: (i) *disappearing-type* Existential Construction; (ii) "possessor as subject and possessum as object" construction (PSPO construction); (iii) passive construction with retained object (passive DPC); (iv) *depriving-type* Double Object Construction (*depriving-type* DOC); (v) Topic Construction and (vi) *Ba* construction involving discontinuous possession. Although all these constructions have properties of their own, we find at least they are common in the following aspects.

First, the nominal semantically interpreted as the possessor splits or separates from another nominal semantically understood as the possessum. In other words, the PR and PM fail to form a single noun phrase constituent and they are in discontinuous positions. That is the striking feature shared by DPCs in Mandarin Chinese, since there is no particular grammatical case to denote the status of the possessor.

Second, it can be observed that there is a nominal element that is not selected by the predicate verb if we consider the canonical valency properties of each verb typically related. In these constructions, the PR remains to be a core grammatical argument of the verb both syntactically and semantically. In a sense, the possessor argument becomes extra or non-core argument.

Although the possessive relation is the common feature shared by these constructions, we find that the way for the possessive relation to enter the construction is quite different. When we come to *de* construction, *de* can function as the syntactic head which introduces both the nominals and build the syntactic structure as well. Usually, it is the PR which occupies a higher position than the PM. For the DPC, which demonstrates mismatch, we propose three kinds of possessive relation generated at different layers.

First, possession gets introduced at lexical level. Relational nouns as kinship terms denoting the kinship relation like *baba, mama*; and Part-whole relation (including body-parts) like *shou, zhitiao* will bring in possession and the possessor information is carried by relational nouns from lexicon. "Belonging_to" as the logic predicate is used to denote the type of possession in its logic form. This kind of possession should be interpreted compulsorily.

Just as relational nouns carry the possessor information, the argument structure of verbs may have possessive relation information as well. It is a kind of possession information at the lexical level in that it is related with the *depriving-type* verbs. The lexical meaning of *depriving-type* verbs is to have the referents of the indirect objects lose something, or that exempt them from something. The *depriving-type* Double Object

Construction entails that the direct object in some sense belongs to the indirect object or the indirect object is responsible for it when the event happens. In the argument structure, the possessor gets source thematic role and can be covert element.

Second, possessive relation can be generated at syntactic level. Possessive relation exists in Topic Constructions and it is triggered by the topic nominal. Possessive relation is of vital importance in connecting the topic with comment proposition. The type of Topic Constructions we are concerned with is the canonical position Topic Construction. Topics can be derived via a syntactic operation so that topics are usually the arguments of the verb and are related to syntactic positions. This syntactic position may be occupied by either a resumptive pronoun referring to the topic nominal or a syntactic gap, which means that we can put the topic back to the original syntactic position. As a topic-prominent language, Chinese differs from other languages in that it not only has English-style topics related to a syntactic position inside the comment, it also has Chinese-style Topic Construction. The key idea is that the topic can not be put back to the comment directly. The semantic constrains for the topic is the definiteness of the initial noun.

With the appearance of the topic nominal, the type of the event changes from a singular event to a compound event. Besides the inalienable possession, there is a set-subset relation between initial topic nominal and the nominal contained in comment. The function of the topic is to set up a frame for the following information. Possessive relation is the semantic tie that holds the extra element to an independent part. The comment proposition is self-independent syntactically and semantically and the topic argument can not be selected by the predicate verb of comment. We assume possessive functional node is the employed to introduce topic possessor nominal. There are constrains for possessive functional node: (i) possessive function node is of predicate property, which is the most complicated in semantic type; (ii) it takes an entity and a event as its argument so as to incorporate the entity argument into the construction; (iii) with the introduction of the possessor argument, possessive relation is triggered between two entities.

Third, possessive relation can be generated at semantic-syntactic interface. Both the lexical item and the construction contribute to generation of possessive relation. When *disappearing-type* verbs enter Existential Construction, possessive relation between initial locative nominal and disappearing entity is triggered. It is the same with the *depriving-type* transitive in its passive form. The eventualities of these constructions are the same as the eventuality of Topic Construction.

After we do the detailed empirical description of the relevant constructions, there seems to be few studies that investigate these constructions within a unified framework. Since the common feature is the possessive relation, in this dissertation, possessive relations have been studied from the perspective of formal semantics. A natural language like Chinese can be considered as an abstract system analogous to formal language of logic or mathematics. Both natural and formal languages are compositional in the sense that the meaning of any syntactically well-formed expression is uniquely determined by the meaning of its constituent parts, and the pattern used to combine these constituents. With the model we constructed in this paper, the semantic properties of possession elucidated in this study are clearly represented in a compositional pattern.

Based on the features of possessive constructions in Mandarin, we have adapted Parsons' subatomic event semantics, Rothstein's predicate theory, Pylkkänen's functional node device to make it suitable for the analysis of possessive constructions. The event e' denoted by predicate verb containing PM is analyzed as an embedded event in Parsons' style. With this newly-constructed model, possessors are analyzed in a dynamic and incremental process. We analyze the eventuality of the construction following the neo-Davidsonian approach. Including Topic Construction in Mandarin as the targets of event semantic research greatly enlarges the application of this theory.

Possession is in nature a semantic relation which is manifested in syntactic construction. With the help of formal device, we try to describe and illustrate the semantic of the possessive constructions in the frame of formal semantics so that the meaning can be clearly shown and explained. The connection between elements can be illustrated from the perspective of event semantic theory. The perspective and the theory we adopt is greatly different from traditional study of possession. We focus on the mechanism to generate possessive relation, source of possession and the way to combine PR with PM. The account fits our intuition about how possessive relation is generated and interpreted. The generation of possessive relation in Mandarin Chinese is quite dispersive, which can be conducted at different levels. Our purpose is to sort out the source of possession, find out constrains and describe them in a clear formal way.

What we have found is in the support of the idea that Mandarin Chinese is typical topic-orientated language. Great importance has been attached to the topic. The concept of topic does not limit only to so-called Topic Construction. In Mandarin Chinese, there are more topics than we expect and we are not aware of the fact that they serve the function of the topic. We may further our knowledge of the role of the topic plays in triggering possessive relation. The number of the topic sentences may be quite large, but the type of the construction is quite limited from the perspective of possession. All these Topic Constructions can be classified into two types according to the possessive relation types of PR and PM have: one is the part-whole relation and the other is the generic and type relation. It is feasible for us to apply the analysis to possessive constructions.

The topic is what speakers choose to start the communication, which involve in pragmatic elements. Pragmatics plays a very important role in expressing possessive relation. All possessive constructions in Mandarin Chinese are closely connected. It is the speaker who decides how to arrange the information and how to present possessive relation. Possession is closely related with subjectivity in language. All of possessive expressions in Mandarin Chinese are related with each other, which is approved by the fact that the underlined eventuality is the same in Locative Constructions, PSPO construction and Topic Construction. They demonstrate different features in syntactic structure, but they share the common semantic properties.

The possessive relations we analyze in this dissertation are represented in normal constructions in Mandarin Chinese, which serves as the base for us to study them from a new perspective. Although they have different forms, the possessive relation contained in possessive constructions remains the same. The possessive relations exist at different layers of the constructions.

9.2 Further questions

This study lays the groundwork for a further investigation into the semantics of possession in Mandarin Chinese. Although three kinds of possessive constructions have been studied, more remains to be done for a complete account of possessive relation in Mandarin.

Firstly, the eventuality analysis we adopt does not include in the time features. That is we do not consider the role of verb aspect plays in the construction. In most of the constructions, we find time and aspect of the verb make a difference. Verbs usually should be in its compound form with *le* or other means denoting result. The nature of the atom event is decided by verb type. With the help of these means, the eventuality can change as well. The relation is not just reflected in participants in the event but also reflected in the abstract relation between atom events.

Secondly, the research of possessive relation in this paper is mainly in comparison with English and other languages occasionally. In order to understand possession well, we must study possessive relation from a typological perspective. The study on discontinuous possession constructions and predicative possession arouse more interests and is within the scope of possession.

The study in this paper is just a beginning of research on possession in the framework of formal semantics. My hope is that the model proposed in this paper can be applied to the analysis of a diverse collection of constructions with common semantic properties.

References

Amy Rose Deal. 2013. External Possession and Possessor Raising University of California, Santa Cruz To appear in M. Everaert & H. van Riemsdijk (eds.), *The Companion to Syntax*, 2nd edition,Wiley-Blackwell.

Asher, Nicholas. 2000. Events, facts, propositions, and evolutive anaphora. In *Speaking of Events*. J. Higginbotham, F. Pianesi & A. Varzi (eds.), Cambridge, MA: MIT Press, 123-150.

Alexiladou, A. 2003. *Some notes on the structure of Alienable and Inalienable Possessors [M]//COENE,M.,D'HULST,Y. From NP to DP Volume 2: The Expression of Possession in Noun Phrases*. Amsterdam: John Benjamins Publishing Company, 167-188.

Baker,Mark. 1988. *Incorporation: A Theory of Grammatical Function Changing*. Chicago: University of Chicago Press.

Barshi, Immanuel & Doris Payne. 1996. The Interpretation of "Possessor Raising" in a Maasai Dialect. In *Afrikanistische Arbeitspapiere*. Lionel Bender & Thomas Hinnebusch (eds.) 45. 207-226. Köln: Universität zu Köln.

Barshi, Immanuel & Doris Payne. 1998. Argument Structure and Maasai Possessive Interpretation: Implications for Language Learning. In Alice Healy and Lyle Bourne, Jr. (eds.), *Foreign Language Learning: Psycholinguistic Experiments on Training and Retention*. Mahwah, NJ: Erlbaum, 213-229.

Beck & Johnson. 2004. Double objects again [J]. *Linguistic Inquiry, 35(1)*: 97-124.

Bierwisch, Manfred. 2005. The event structure of CAUSE and BECOME. In C. Maienborn & A.

Brennan, Jonathan & Liina Pylkkänen. 2008. Processing events: Behavioral and neuromagnetic correlates of aspectual coercion. *Brain and Language* 106(2), 132-143.

Belletti, A. 1988. The case of unaccusatives [J]. *Linguistic Inquiry* 1: 1-14.

Chappell, Hilary. & William McGregor. 1995. Prolegomena to a Theory of Inalienability. In *The Grammar of Inalienability: A Typological*

Perspective on Body Part Terms and the Part-Whole Relation, Hilary Chappell & William McGregor (eds.), 3-30. Berlin: Mouton de Gruyter,

Chappell, H. 1995. Inalienability and the Personal Domain in Mandarin Chinese Discourse. In *The Grammar of Inalienability: A Typological Perspective on the Part-Whole Relation and Terms for Body Parts.*

Hilary Chappell and William McGregor (eds.), 465-527. Berlin: Mouton de Gruyter,

Chappell, H. & McGregor, W. 1996. *The Grammar of Inalienability. A Typological Perspective on Body Part Terms and the Part-Whole Relation*. Berlin/New York.

Cheng,Lisa L-S.& Elizabeth Ritter. 1987. A small clause analysis of inalienable possession in Mandarin and French. In *Proceedings of NELS 18*, James Blevins and Carter (ed.), 65-78. Amherst, Mass: GLSA.

Croft, William. 1994. Voice: Beyond Control and Affectedness. In *Voice: Form and Function,* Barbara Fox & Paul Hopper (eds.), 89-117. Amsterdam: John Benjamins.

Croft, William. 1990. *Typology and Universals*. Cambridge: Cambridge University.

Dowty, D. 1979. *Word Meaning and Montague Grammar.* Dordrecht: Reidel.

Dowty, D. 1991. Thematic proto-roles and argument selection. *Language* 67: 547-619.

Davidson Donald. 1967. The logical form of action sentences. In Nicholas Rescher, (ed.), *The logic of decision and action*, 81-95. Pittsburgh, Pa.: University of Pittsburgh Press.

Gavruseva, E. On the Syntax of Possessor Extraction. *Lingua*, 2000, 110: 743-772.

Guéron, Jacqueline. 2006. Inalienable possession. In *The Blackwell companion to syntax*, Martin Everaert and Henk van Riemsdijk, (ed.), chapter 35, 589-638. Malden, Mass: Blackwell.

Harley, H. 1995. *Subjects, Events and Licensing*. Ph,D. Dissertation, Massachusetts Institute of Technology.

Harley, H. 1996. If you have, you can give. In *Proceeding of the 15th West Coast Conference on Formal Linguistics*.

Harley, H. 2003. Possession and the double object construction [A].

Yearbook of Linguistic Variation, 2, 31-70

Heine, Bernd. 1997. *Possession: Cognitive Sources, Forces, and Grammaticalization.* New York: Cambridge University Press.

Hsu, Y.Y. 2009. Possessor Extraction in Mandarin Chinese. *University of Pennsylvania Working papers in Linguistics* 15: 95-104.

Hole, Daniel. 2004. Extra argumentality-a binding account of "possessor raising"in German, English and Mandarin. In *Possessives and Beyond: Semantics and Syntax,* Ji-Yung Kim, Yury Lander, & Babara H. Partee (ed.), 365-383. Amherst, MA: GLSA.

Hole,Daniel. 2005. Reconciling "possessor" datives and "beneficiary" datives-towards a unified voice account of dative binding in German. In *Event arguments: foundations and applications*, C. Maienborn and A. Wollstein, (ed.) 213-242. Tubingen: Niemeyer.

Hole, Daniel. 2006: "Extra argumentality – affectees, landmarks, and voice." – In: Hole, Daniel & Peter Siemund (eds.). Operations on Argument Structure, *Linguistics* 44(2), 383-424.

Huang, C.T. James. 2001. Chinese passives in comparative perspective. In *Tsing Hua Journal of Chinese Studies* 29, 423-509.

Higginbotham, James. 2005. Event positions: Suppression and emergence. *Theoretical Linguistics* 31(3), 349-358.

Higginbotham, James, Fabio Pianesi & Achille Varzi (eds.), 2000. *Speaking of Events.* New York, Oxford: Oxford University Press.

Hamm, Fritz & Michiel van Lambalgen. 2005. *The Proper Treatment of Events.* Oxford: Blackwell.

Higginbotham, James. 2000. On events in linguistic semantics. In *Speaking of Events.* J. Higginbotham, F. Pianesi & A. Varzi (eds.), 49-79. New York, Oxford: Oxford University Press,

Katz, Graham. 2003. Event arguments, adverb selection, and stative adverb gap. In Ewald Lang, Claudis Maienborn & Cathrine Fabricius-Hansen (eds.), *Modifying Adjuncts, Interface Explorations*, vol.4, 455-474. Mouton de Gruter, Berlin.

Katz, Graham. 2008. Manner modification of state verbs. In Louise McNally & Christopher Kennedy (eds.), *Adjectives and Adverbs: Syntax, Semantics, and Discourse, Studies in Theoretical Linguistics.* Oxford University Press, Oxford.

Kim, K. 2012. Argument Structure Licensing and English Have.

Journal of Linguistics, 48: 71-105.

Krifka, Manfred 1992. Thematic relations as links between nominal reference and temporal constitution. In *Lexical Matters*. I. Sag & A. Szabolcsi (eds.). 29-53. Stanford, CA: CSLI.

Krifka, Manfred 1998. The origins of telicity. In *Events and Grammar*. S. Rothstein (ed.). 197-235. Dordrecht: Kluwer.

Kratzer, Angelika (1995): "Stage-level and individual-level predicates as inherent generics." – In: Gregory N. Carlson, Francis Jeffry Pelletier (eds.). *The Generic Book*, 125-175. Chicago: Chicago University Press.

Kratzer, Angelika.1996. Severing the external argument from its verb. – In: Johan Rooryck, Lauri Zaring (eds.): *Phrase Structure and the Lexicon*, 109-137. Dordrecht: Kluwer.

Kratzer, Angelika. 2003. The event argument and the semantics of verbs. Ms. University of Massachusetts at Amherst. [http://semanticsarchive.net/Archive/GU1 NWM 4Z/]

Kuno, Susumu. 1976, Subject, theme, and the speaker's empathy. In *Subject and Topic*, Charles Li (ed.), 315-343. Malden, MA: Blackwell.

Landau, Idan.1999. Possessor Raising and the Structure of VP. Lingua 107: 1-37.

Langacker, R. W. 1995. Possession and possessive constructions. In J. R. Taylor and R. E. Macauley (eds.), *Language and the Cognitive Construal of the World*. 51-79. Berlin: Mouton De Gruyter,

Langacker, R.W. 1997. Constituency, dependency, and conceptual grouping. *Cognitive Linguistics* 8: 1-32.

Li-Thompson. 1976. Subject and topic: a new typology of lauguage in : Charles N. Li (ed.), 163-195.

Li-Thompson. 1981. Mandarin Chinese A functional reference grammar. Berkeley: University of California Press.

Landman, Fred. 2000. Event and Plurality: The Jerusalem Lectures. Dordrecht: Kluwer.

Li, Yen-hui Audrey. 2001. *The Ba Construction*. Ms. University of Southern Cali-fornia, Los Angeles. studies in Natured Language and Linguistics Theiry (SNLT, volume 44).P131–181 Rint Sybesma. The Mandarin Vp springer.

Lyons, J. 1967. A note on possessive, existential and locative sentences. *Foundations of Language* 3: 390-6.

Maienborn, Claudia & Angelika Wöllstein (eds.), 2005. *Event Arguments: Foundations and Applications*. Tübingen: Niemeyer.

Maslova and Bernini. 2006. Sentence topics in the languages of Europe and beyond in Gailiano Bernini & Marcia Schwartz (eds). *Pragmatic arganization of discourse in the language of Europe*, 20-28. Berlin: Mouton de Gruyter.

Nichols, J. 1988. On alienable and inalienable possession. In W. Shipley (ed.), *In Honor of Mary Haas: From the Haas Festival°on Native American Linguistics*, 557-609. Berlin: Mouton De Gruyter.

O'Connor, Mary Catherine. 1992. *Topics in Northern Pomo Grammar.* New York: Garland.

O'Connor, Mary Catherine. 1994. The marking of possession in Northern Pomo: privative opposition and pragmatic inference. In *Proceedings of the Twentieth Annual Meeting of the Berkeley Linguistics Society,* 387-400S. Gahl, A. Dolbey, and C. Johnson (eds.). Berkeley, CA: Berkeley Linguistics Society.

O'Connor, Mary Catherine. 1996. The situated interpretation of possessor raising. In *Grammatical Constructions: Their Form and Meaning*, S. Thompson and M. Shibatani (eds.), 125-156. Oxford: Oxford University Press.

Partee, Barbara H. and Vladimir Borschev. 1998. Integrating lexical and formal   semantics: Genitives, relational nouns, and type-shifting. In R. Cooper and Th. Gamkrelidze (eds) Proceedings of the second Tbilist Symposium on Language, Logic, and Computation. Center on Language, Logic, Speech, Tbilisi State University: Tbilisi: 229-241.

Partee, Barbara H. and Vladimir Borschev. 2003. Genitives, relational nouns, and argument-modifier ambiguity. In Modifying Adjuncts, eds. E. Lang, C. Maienborn and C. Fabricius-Hansen, 67-112. Berlin: Mouton de Gruyter.

Patee, Barbara H. 2009. Formal semantics, lexical semantics, and compositionality: The puzzle of private adjectives. *Philologia* 7: 7-19.

Parsons, T. 1980. Modifiers and quantifiers in natural language *Canadian Journal of Philosophy, Suppl. vol.* 6, 29-60.

Parsons, T. 1985. Underlying events in the analysis of English In LePore & McLaughlin (eds.), 235-267.

Parsons, T. 1990. *Events in the Semantics of English: A Study in Subatomic Semantics*. Cambridge, MA: Massachusetts: The MIT Press.

Pylkkänen. Liina. 2008. *Introducing Arguments*. The MIT Press.

Pylkkänen, Liina & Brian McElree. 2006. The syntax-semantics interface: On-line composition of meaning. In: M. A. Gernsbacher & M. Traxler (eds.). *Handbook of Psycholinguistics*. 2ndedition. New York: Elsevier, 537-577. 1st edition 1994.

Payne, Doris L. 1997a. The Maasai External Possessor Construction. In Joan Bybee, John Haiman and Sandra Thompson (eds.), 395-422. *Essays on Language Function and Language Type*. Amsterdam: John Benjamins,

Payne, Doris L. 1997b. Argument Structure and Locus of A ffect in the Maasai External Possession Construction. Berkeley Linguistics Society, 23. *Special Sessionon African Languages*, 98-115.

Payne, Doris. & Immanuel Barshi. 1995a. A Sentence-Processing Account of Possessor Raising in Maasai. Paper presented at *the Eighth CUNY Conference on Sentence Processing*, Tucson, Arizona.

Perhnutter, D, M. 1978 Impersonal passives and unaccusative hypothesis [J]. Berkeley Linguistic Society 4: 157-189

Rappaport Hovav, M.& B. Levin. 2001. An event structure account of English resultatives. Language 77: 776-797.

Rothstein, S. 1999. Fine-grained structure in the eventuality domain: the semantics of predicative adjective phrase and *be. Natural Language Semantics* 7: 347-420.

Rothstein, S. 2001. *Predicates and Their Subjects*. Dordrecht: Kluwer.

Rothstein, S. 2004. *Structuring Events*. Blackwell, Oxford.

Shibatani, Masayoshi. 1994. An integrational approach to possessor raising, ethical datives, and adversative passives. *Proceedings of Berkeley Linguistics Society* 20: 461-486.

Tomioka, Satoshi, and Chang-Yong Sim. 2007. *The event semantic root of inalienable possession*. Ms, university of Delaware.

Taylor, J. R. 1996. *Possessives in English: An Exploration in Cognitive Grammar*. Oxford:

Taylor, J. R. 1989. Possessive genitives in English. *Linguistics* 27: 663-86. Clarendon Press.

Tsao, Feng-fu. 1987. A topic-comment approach to the ba construction. *Journal of Chinese Linguistics* 15.1: 1-53.

Vergnaud, Jean-Roger and Marie-Louise Zubizarreta. 1992. The definite determiner and the inalienable constructions in French and English. *Linguistic Inquiry* 23: 595-652.

Vendler, Z. 1967. *Linguistics in Philosophy.* Ithaca: Cornell University Press.

Yoon, James Hye Suk. 1990. Theta theory and the grammar of inalienable possession constructions. In *Proceedings of NELS 20*, (ed.) J. Carter et al., volume 2, 502-516. Amherst, MA: GLSA.

Williams, E. Argument structure and morphology [J]. 1981. The Linguistic Review 1: 81-114.

Zhang, Ning. 1998a. The interactions between construction meaning and lexical meaning. *Linguistics* 36.5: 957-980.

Zhang, Ning. 1998b. Argument interpretations in the ditransitive construction. *Nordic Journal of Linguistics* 21: 179-209.

安丰存. 题元角色理论与领有名词提升移位. 解放军外国语学院学报. 2007年5期.

程琪龙. 领属框架及其语法体现. 外语与外语教学. 2003年第4期.

陈宗利 肖德法. "领主属宾句"的生成句法分析. 外语与外语教学. 2007年第8期.

陈昌来. 现代汉语动词的句法语义属性研究. 上海：学林出版社. 2002年.

陈昌来. 论语义结构中的与事. 语文研究. 1998年第2期.

陈平. 汉语双项名词句与话题–陈述结构. 中国语文. 2004年第6期.

崔建新. 隐现句的谓语动词. 语言教学与研究. 1987年第2期.

程杰. 论分离式领有名词与隶属名词之间的句法和语义关系. 现代外语. 2007年第1期：19-29

程杰. 虚介词假设与论元增容—论不及物动词后非核心论元的句法属性. 现代外语. 2009年 第1期：23-32

邓思颖. 作格化和汉语被动句. 中国语文. 2004年第4期.

丁声树. 现代汉语语法讲话. 北京：商务印书馆. 1961年

邓昊熙. 基于MP的现代汉语非连续性领属结构研究. 天津：南开大学博士学位论文2015年.

范晓，张豫峰等．语法理论纲要．上海：上海译文出版社．2003年．

范晓．领属成分在汉语句子中的配置情况考察．汉语现状与历史的研究.中国社会科学出版社1999年版，第28-46页

方勇，王优．两种领有名词移位句式中动词的语法和语义分析．辽宁科技大学学报．2008年第6期．

冯志伟．基于短语结构语法的自动句法分析方法．当代语言学．2000年第2期．

郭继懋．领主属宾句．中国语文．1990年第1期．

郭锐．表述功能的转化和"的"字的作用．当代语言学．2000年第1期．

郭锐．语法的动态性和动态语法观．在"商务印书馆语言学出版基金发布会暨青年语言学者论坛-21世纪的中国语言学"（2002，1，17-18）.北京．

顾阳．生成语法及词库中动词的一些特性．国外语言学．1996年第3期．

顾阳．关于存现结构的理论探讨．现代外语．1997年第3期．

顾阳．双宾语结构．载徐烈炯（主编），共性与个性：汉语语言学中的争议[C]．北京：北京语言文化大学出版社，60-69.1998

韩景泉．领有名词提升移位与格理论．现代外语．2002年第3期：261-272

胡建华．现代汉语不及物动词的论元和宾语—从抽象动词"有"到句法–信息结构接口．中国语文．2008年第5期：396-409

黄洁．事件语义学理论与汉英句式的表征—从"王冕死了父亲"说起．西安外国语大学学报．2009年第4期．

黄正德．题元理论与汉语动词题元结构研究，载当代语言学理论研究．北京：商务印书馆．2008年．

黄正德．汉语动词的题元结构及其句法表现．语言科学．2007年第4期．

何晓炜．双宾结构和与格的关系分析．外国语．2003年第2期．

胡旭辉．汉语话题结构制约的认知语义与语用分析．外国语．2009年第3期．

李洁．被动式领主属宾句．云南师范大学学报．2007年第1期．

刘丹青．汉语给予类双及物结构的类型考察．中国语文．2001年第5期．

李晋霞．现代汉语"V双+N"双定中结构研究．北京：中国社

会科学院博士学位论文. 2002年.

李临定. 现代汉语句型. 北京：商务印书馆，1986

吕叔湘. 现代汉语八百词. 商务印书馆. 1999年版.

吕叔湘. 中国文法要略（1942）. 吕叔湘文集第1卷. 商务印书馆. 1990年版.

刘探宙. 一元非作格动词带宾语现象. 中国语文. 2009年第6期.

陆俭明. 再谈"吃了他三个苹果"一类结构的性质. 中国语文. 2002 年第4期.

陆俭明. 确定领属关系之我见. 南大语言学（第2辑）. 商务印书馆. 2004年.

陆俭明. 关于句处理中要考虑的语义问题. 语言研究. 2001年第1期.

陆俭明. 对"NP+的+VP"结构的重新认识. 中国语文. 2003年第5期.

陆俭明，沈阳. 汉语与汉语研究十五讲. 北京大学出版社. 2003年.

李宇明. 领属关系与双宾句分析. 语言教学与研究. 1996年第3期.

刘洋. 汉语领有名词提升的最简方案研究. 外国语言文学. 2007年第4期.

刘宇. 双宾构造和两种特殊句式. 汉语学报. 2008年第1期.

刘晓林. 也谈"王冕死了父亲"的生成方式. 中国语文. 2007年第5期.

李杰. 试论发生句—对隐现句和领主属宾句的句式意义的重新审视. 世界汉语教学. 2009年第1期.

李钻娘. 出现式与消失式动词的存在句. 语文研究. 1987年第8期.

林宗宏. 论汉语的处所突现性质. 现代中国语研究. 2008年第10期.

梅德明，韩巍峰. 显性非宾格结构的主体化分析. 外语教学与研究. 2010年第5期

满在江. 与双宾结构同形质异的两类结构. 语言科学. 2004第3期.

马志刚. 移位性特征、句法操作限制与句首名词的话题和/或主语属性—以汉领主属宾句及及物句为例. 外国语. 2011第5期.

马志刚. 局域非对称成分统治结构，题元角色和领主属宾句的

跨语言差异. 语言科学. 2008年第5期.

马志刚. 基于狭义领属关系论领主句、保留宾语被动句与抢夺类双宾句的关联性. 华文教学与研究. 2013 年第3期.

潘海华. 词汇映射理论在汉语句法研究中的应用. 现代外语. 1997（4）：1-16

潘海华，韩景泉. 显性非宾格动词结构的句法研究. 语言研究. 2005 年第3期：1-13.

潘海华，韩景全. 汉语保留宾语结构的句法生成机制. 中国语文. 2008年（6）期.

任鹰. "领属"与"存现"：从概念的关联到构式的关联—也从"王冕死了父亲"的生成方式说起. 世界汉语教学. 2009 年第3期.

施春宏. 试析名词的语义结构. 世界汉语教学. 2002年第 4期.

宋玉柱. 定心谓语存在句. 语文教学与研究. 1982年第3期.

司富珍. 赵本山的爷爷和赵本山的帽子 —漫谈汉语中的两种领属结构. 语言教学与研究 . 2014 年第2期.

司富珍. 双宾语中的领属关系. 外国语文研究 . 2015 第3期.

沈阳. 领属范畴及领属性名词短语的句法作用.北京大学学报（哲社版）. 1995年第5期.

沈阳. 汉语句法结构中隐含成分的语义所指关系. 语言研究. 1994年（2）期.

沈阳. 现代汉语句法结构中名词短语部分成分移位现象初探. 语言教学与研究. 1996年第1期.

沈阳. 名词短语分裂移位与非直接论元句首成分. 语言研究. 2001年（3）期.

沈阳. 再议领属性名词短语的定义与分类，载汉语语法研究的新拓展.

徐烈炯，邵敬敏 主编. 杭州：浙江教育出版社，2002.

寿永明，朱少秦. 领属关系主谓谓语句分析. 浙江大学学报（人文社会科学版）. 2002年第3期.

税昌锡. 领属性"NP1的NP2"结构的组合理据—附论领事话题句及其谓语动的语义型. 云南师范大学学报. 2008年第2期.

沈家煊. "王冕死了父亲"的生成方式—兼说汉语糅合造句. 中国语文. 2006 年第4期: 291-300

沈家煊. "计量得失"和"计较得失"—再论"王冕死了父亲"的句式意义和生. 成方式. 语言教学与研究. 2009 年第5期：15-22.

沈家煊. 说"偷"和"抢". 语言教学与研究. 2000年第1期.

沈家煊. 语言的"主观性"和"主观化". 外语教学与研究. 2001年 第4期.

沈家煊. 如何处置处置式—论"把"字句的主观性. 中国语文. 2002年 第5期.

孙晋文, 伍雅清. 再论"领有名词提升移位". 语言科学. 2003年第6期.

孙天琪, 李亚非. 汉语非核心论元允准结构初探. 中国语文, 2010（1）：21-33

孙天琦, 潘海华. 也谈汉语不及物动词带"宾语"现象—兼论信息结构对汉语语序的影响. 当代语言学. 2012年第4期.

隋娜、王广成. 汉语存现句中动词的非宾格性. 现代外语. 2009年第3期.

王奇. "领主属宾句"的语义特点与句法结构. 现代外语. 2006年第 8期.

王奇. 领属关系与英汉双宾构式的句法结构. 现代外语. 2005年第2期.

文贞惠. 表属性范畴的"N1（的）N2"结构的语义分析. 世界汉语教学. 1998年第1期.

文贞惠. "N1（的）N2"偏正结构中N1与N2之间的语义关系的鉴定. 语文研究. 1999年第3期.

温宾利, 陈宗利. 领有名词移位：基于MP的分析. 现代汉语. 2001年（4）期.

吴平. 句式语义的形式分析与计算, 北京：北京语言大学出版社. 2009年.

吴平. 评Parsons 的亚原子语义学. 河北大学学报（哲学社会科学版）. 2008年第4期.

吴平. 汉语特殊句式的事件语义分析与计算. 北京：中国社会科学出版社. 2009年.

吴平. 广义存现句的事件语义学分析. 东方学术论坛. 2014年第2 期.

吴早生. 领属关系研究的方法与视野. 北京：中国社会科学出版社. 2011年.

徐阳春, 钱书新. "N1+的+N2"结构歧义考察. 汉语学习. 2004 年第5期.

徐杰. 两种保留宾语句式及相关句法理论问题. 当代语言学. 1999年第1期.16-29

徐杰．普遍语法原则与汉语语法现象．北京：北京大学出版社．2004年．

徐杰．被动句式与非宾格句式的一致与差异．Contemporary Research in Modern Chinese．2005 年第7期．

徐烈炯 汉语是话语概念结构化语言吗？中国语文．2002年 第5期．

徐烈炯，沈阳．题元理论与汉语配价问题．当代语言学．1998年第3期．

徐烈炯，刘丹青．话题的结构与功能．上海：上海教育出版社．1998.44-58

熊仲儒．领属性致使句的句法分析．安徽师范大学学报（人文社会科学版）2012年 第2期

熊仲儒．论元结构与汉语构式．芜湖：安徽师范大学出版社．2014年．

宣恒大．现代汉语隐现句研究．安徽大学博士论文．2011年．

杨大然．领有名词短语分裂与汉语话题结构．解放军外国语学院学报．2008年第3期．

俞理明，吕建军．"王冕死了父亲"句的历史考察．中国语文．2011 年第1期．

杨成凯．汉语语法理论研究．辽宁教育出版社．1996年版

袁毓林．谓词隐含及其句法后果．中国语文．1995年第4期．

袁毓林．从焦点理论看句尾"的"的句法语义功能.中国语文．2003年（1）期．

袁毓林．一价名词的认知研究．中国语文．1994第4期．

袁毓林．话题的结构与功能评述．当代语言学．2003年第1期．

袁毓林．话题化及相关的语法过程．中国语文．1996年第4期．

袁毓林．论元结构和句式结构互动的动因、机制和条件—表达精细化对动词配价和句式构造的影响．语言研究．2004年第4期．

袁毓林．一套汉语动词论元角色的语法指标．世界汉语教学．2003年第3期．

杨素英．从非宾格动词现象看语义与句法之间的关系．当代语言学．1999年第1期．

杨安红．NP$_1$有NP$_2$句式新探．东方论坛．2004年第4期．

赵元任．中国话的文法．中国现代学术经典：赵元任卷．石家庄：河北教育出版社，1996年．

张伯江．领属结构的语义构成．语言教学与研究．1994年第2期．

张伯江. 从施受关系到句式语义. 北京：商务印书馆. 2009年.

张伯江，方梅. 汉语功能语法研究. 江西教育出版社. 1996年版.

张国宪. 制约夺事成句位实现的语义因素. 中国语文. 2001年第6期.

朱德熙. 汉语句法里的歧义现象. 中国语文. 1980 年第2期.

朱德熙. 语法讲义. 北京：商务印书馆. 1982年.

朱德熙. 语法答问. 北京：商务印书馆. 1985年.

张翼. 动词延伸义和双重范畴化关系：对领主属宾句和存现句的统一解释. 外语研究. 2012年第 2期.

张宁. 汉语双宾语句结构分析. 陆俭明主编 面临新世纪挑战的现代汉语语研究. 山东教育出版社. 2000年版.

朱德熙. 说"的". 中国语文. 1961年第12期.

朱行帆. 轻动词和汉语不及物动词带宾语现象. 现代外语. 2005年第3期.

Epilogue

The contents of the book are based on my doctoral dissertation and there exists differences between these two kinds. The doubts and puzzles left during the process of writing inspired me to further explore in this field and kept correcting some ideas and enriching parts of the book in the following few years. In order to make it easier for the readers, some examples are revised and all the logical expressions and syntactic derivations are carefully checked and illustrated. The latest development of event semantic is included as well in the book.

The possessive structures discussed here belong to marked structure, which can be explained and derived by means of formal linguistic devices at the layer of grammar, semantic and pragmatic interface while the typical possessive structure is "DE" structure. Whether event semantic can be applied to analyze "DE" structure and whether it can be formalized in the same way are my next concern. It is hoped that "DE" structure will be further studied and depicted systematically and explicitly .

Upon the completion of the book, my thanks first go to my tutor, Professor Wu Ping, who helped with my dissertation by framing the structure and focusing on the details. After my graduation, he keeps offering suggestions and inspirations, which contribute a lot to the book as well. Secondly, I want to thank all the leaders and colleagues in Guangdong Ocean University for their courage and financial support. Last but not the least, all the editors of the book gave great efforts to proofread the full text with great patience and attentiveness.

It is a tentative study to describe the abstract semantic relationship of possession by means of formal devices and all mistakes and errors in this book are entirely mine.